Super, Natural Christians

Super, Natural Christians

How we should love nature

Sallie McFague

Fortress Press
Minneapolis

SUPER, NATURAL CHRISTIANS
How we should love nature

Unless otherwise noted, biblical quotations are from the New Revised Standard Version Bible, copyright © 1989 by the National Council of the Churches of Christ in the United States of America. Used with permission.

Cover design by Ellen Maly
Book design by Joseph Bonyata
Author photo by Harry Redl, courtesy of *The Chronicle of Higher Education*
Cover photo: Karl Blossfeldt, "*Adiantum pedatuntum,* American Maidenhair Fern," copyright © 1997 Karl Blossfeldt Archiv/Ann & Jurgen Wilde, Cologne / ARS, New York.

Library of Congress Cataloging-in-Publication Data

McFague, Sallie.
    Super, natural Christians : how we should love nature / Sallie McFague.
       p. cm.
    Includes bibliographical references.
    ISBN 0-8006-3076-9 (alk. paper)
    1. Nature—Religious aspects—Christianity. I. Title.
BR115.N3M34 1997
231.7—dc21   96-50992
                                                                              CIP

The paper used in this publication meets the minimum requirements of American National Standard for Information Sciences—Permanence of Paper for Printed Library Materials, ANSI Z329.48.1984.

Manufactured in the U.S.A.   AF 1-3076

01   00   99   98   97   1   2   3   4   5   6   7   8   9   10

Dedicated to
my mother, Jessie McFague
and
my sister, Maurine McFague Upton

Contents

Acknowledgments

I AM GRATEFUL TO MANY PEOPLE FOR HELPING ME write this book. First of all, I want to thank the students at Vanderbilt Divinity School and Vancouver School of Theology who worked with me in class on these materials. I owe an enormous debt of gratitude to the people who read the manuscript while it was in process: Janet Cawley, Elizabeth Johnson, Catherine Keller, Harry Maier, Joan McMurtry, and John TeSelle. I benefited greatly from their careful readings and perceptive suggestions for revisions.

I also want to thank the Vancouver School of Theology for inviting me to give the G. Peter Kaye Lectures for 1996, which allowed me to try out some of the ideas in this book. I am grateful to Principal William Phillips of the School as well as its faculty and staff for making my sabbatical a productive and interesting one as I wrote *Super, Natural Christians.*

Without the support of Vanderbilt Divinity School and Dean Joseph Hough, I would not have had the sabbatical, so I thank them as well. Finally, I appreciate once again the fine editorial work of Michael West and the staff at Fortress Press.

Introduction

THE THESIS OF THIS BOOK CAN BE STATED SIMPLY: Christian practice, loving God and neighbor *as subjects*, as worthy of our love in and for themselves, should be extended to nature. We are to love God with our whole heart, mind, and soul and our neighbor as ourselves, but nature usually comes up blank. How *are* Christians to love nature? Most Christians either do not know how to relate to nature or they relate to it as Western culture does, as an object for our use. Even notions of stewardship are often couched in the language of conserving resources for future generations—an implicit acknowledgment of its usefulness to human beings. Most Christians draw a line at nature: while God and other people are subjects, nature is not. My suggestion is that we should relate to the entities in nature *in the same basic way* that we are supposed to relate to God and other people—as ends, not means, as subjects valuable in themselves, for themselves. We read in Genesis that God looked at creation and said: "It is good"—not good for people or even for God, but just good. We should say the same thing. If we did so, we would simply be extending Christianity's *own* most basic model, the subject-subjects one, to nature.

This is just one small change that Christians need to make in our relationship with nature—this change in sensibility, in how we view nature. We Christians in the first world also need to lower our energy consumption, work for environmental protection, and vote in governments that will strive for greater justice between the world's haves and have-nots. In this book, however, we will be concerned with one

1

basic thing: a change in attitude, of sensibility, toward nature—thinking differently about it. It is just one element in the global agenda of making our planet a good place to live for all its inhabitants. It is what a theologian might offer. A theologian's job is to help Christians think about God, other people—and nature—so that we can, will, act differently toward them. It is this neglected third—nature—that is the subject of this volume.

Super, Natural Christians is the last in a series of four books on religious language. *Metaphorical Theology* laid the groundwork with the claim that since all religious language is metaphorical, alternatives to traditional metaphors are possible. *Models of God* experimented with several alternative models: God as mother, lover, and friend and the world as God's body. *The Body of God* attempted a systematic theology through the lens of one of these models. The present book suggests that a Christian nature spirituality should be based on a subject-subjects model of being, knowing, and doing in place of the subject-object model of Western culture.

This change in sensibility, small as it may seem, can have large consequences. It would mean, for instance, that Christians could feel integrated, whole: we would have *one way* of being, knowing, and doing in relation to God, other people, and nature. We would have a "functional cosmology," an understanding of who we are in the natural world and a practice toward these earth others that was on a continuum with our understanding of and action toward God and other people. Things would hold together, be of one piece, as they have not been for Christians for several centuries. Being, knowing, and doing fit together: who we believe we are in the scheme of things influences what we think about others and how we act toward them. If, in *all* our relations, including with nature, we believe we are subjects relating to other subjects, then we might treat them that way.

That is my thesis in a nutshell. Two of the greatest influences on my thinking while developing it have been process philosophy and feminist epistemology. One could say that the ecological model of the self and world that figures centrally in the book is an attempt to combine process and feminist thought with ecological science in a way that will be readily available to ordinary readers. The ecological model says that the self only exists in radical interrelationship and interdependence with others and that *all* living and nonliving entities exist somewhere on this continuum. In other words, everything is in some sense a "subject"—an entity that has a center, a focus, an intention in itself, for itself (often an unconscious one), but is also at the same time in radical relationship with others. Everything influences others and is influenced by others. I find this understanding of who we are, who earth others are, and who God is, relevant to humane living on our planet as well as a persuasive way to model Christian faith in our time. Unfortunately, process thought is often presented in highly technical language, as is ecological science, making them unavailable to most readers. Likewise, feminist thought has often not included nature, limiting its reflections to relations between women and men. This book attempts, in a modest way, to use some of the central insights from process thought, feminist epistemology, and ecology to experiment with one model—the subject-subjects or ecological one. The book claims that nature is central to the model and tries to communicate the model in nontechnical language.

Super, Natural Christians begins with a chapter suggesting how Christians should love nature by defining three central terms: "Christian," "nature," and "spirituality." What would a Christian nature spirituality *be?* The second chapter presents an overview of the entire book: it is the book in miniature. Most of the themes of the book are touched on here, albeit in an often poetic and sometimes autobiographical fashion. This chapter will tell readers whether they want to bother to read more. In chapter 3 we look at a successful functional cosmology—the medieval one—which for its time was what we are suggesting the subject-subjects model might be for our time: a way to think and act that integrates God, nature, and human beings. Chapter 4 illustrates the breakdown of the medieval synthesis and the rise of post-Enlightenment predominance of the "arrogant eye," knowledge of the world based on subject-object dualism. The chapter details the distancing, objectifying, controlling knowledge that issues from the arrogant eye in such media as camera, film, television, and advertising. The effects of the subject-object model, of the predatory stare, on nature, women, and subjugated people, are elaborated. In chapter 5 we turn to the subject-subjects model as an alternative, a model based on the sense of touch and issuing in the "loving eye," knowledge of others that recognizes them as subjects in their own worlds demanding our respect and calling for our care. This model rests upon insights from process philosophy, feminist epistemology, and ecological science, all of which, in different ways, stress both radical individuality and radical unity—an individuality that does not hyperseparate from others and a unity that does not fuse with them. The subject-subjects model is not the reverse of the subject-object model, but a different one for our understanding of who we are, what we know, and how we act. Chapter 6 makes some suggestions on how we might develop the sensibility that emerges from this model as it relates to nature. Two ways are investigated: direct encounters with nature, especially experiences available to city dwellers and children, as well as indirect or mediated encounters through the works of nature writers. The last chapter focuses on the practical implications of a subject-subjects relationship with nature. Should a nature ethic guard the rights of nature or focus on the care of the natural world? What are some hopeful, local efforts on behalf of nature and people sharing space? What is the special contribution of Christian faith to an ethic for nature? We will suggest that within an overarching care ethic the rights of nature are important and that Christianity's special contribution is to press a care ethic in the direction of the neediest—care for both the most oppressed people and the most vulnerable parts of the natural world. This implies, I believe, that Christians' special focus might be on the shared earth of our cities, where people, often poor ones, and nature, often deteriorating land, meet. The book ends with some comments on Christianity's oldest and perhaps most noble nature tradition: nature as sacrament of God. We suggest that Francis of Assisi was on the right track: he saw the wind and sun and water as subjects, as brothers and sisters, who were valuable in themselves, but at the same time he saw them as manifestations of God, as images of divine glory. Our conclusion, then, is that we should love nature by relating to it in the same basic way we relate to other people; that is, with respect and care. We see these earth others as we see the human others—as made in the *imago dei*—and therefore as both subjects in themselves and as intimations of God. All of this is what it means, I believe, to be super, natural Christians.

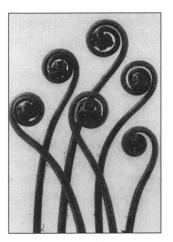

1

Super, Natural Christians

Supernatural vs. Super, Natural Christians

YEARS AGO, WHEN I FIRST CAME TO BRITISH COLUMBIA TO HIKE, I was startled and delighted by the province's tourist advertising slogan. It read: "Super, Natural British Columbia." I remember thinking, "*That* is the proper use of the word 'supernatural.' It should always have a comma." In the intervening years I have wondered if we Christians would be willing to accept that comma. Should Christians be "natural," perhaps even "super, natural"? Are we willing to give up our long allegiance to being "supernatural" and live *in* the earth and *for* the earth? We should pause before answering, because this tiny addition, this little comma, is deeply subversive and cannot be inserted lightly. It suggests a mind-change, a heart-change, a total-change from some common views of Christianity, such as that of Ludwig Feuerbach: "Nature, the world, has no value, no interest for Christians. The Christian thinks only of himself, and the salvation of his soul."[1] Though written in the nineteenth century, Feuerbach's comment accurately describes a large number of Christians, both on the right (the evangelical movement) and the left (those influenced by New Age thinking). Neither group would, I suspect, accept that small mark of punctuation; neither would identify themselves as natural, and surely not as super, natural, Christians.

And why should *we?* Thomas Aquinas put us on the right track when he said that any error about creation leads to an error about

5

God. In the eighteenth century Alexander Pope gave us an example of how a *false* view of creation results in a *false* view of God with his dictum, "The proper study of mankind is man." Pope got it wrong on creation (our proper study is not "man" but *men and women in the world)* and, therefore, the eighteenth century got it wrong on God (they ended up with a distant but controlling maker/master type of God, not unlike the "man" they studied). So why should we identify ourselves as natural, let alone as super, natural Christians? Because, apparently, a proper or improper view of ourselves, of who we are in the world, in nature, has wide ramifications. Our view of where we fit in the scheme of things affects what we think of the world (nature) and what we think of God. Humans, world (nature), and God form a unity called a "worldview." Everyone and every culture has one or more, usually implicit rather than explicit. It is this often-unspoken belief about how the three basics (humans, world, God) fit together that fuels the engines of a society.

It is the thesis of this book that Christians should not only be natural, understanding ourselves as *in* and *of* the earth, but also super, natural, understanding ourselves as excessively, superlatively concerned with nature and its well-being. Christians are those who should love the oppressed, the most vulnerable of God's creation, for these are the ones according to the Gospel who deserve priority. Christians, then, should be super, natural, for in our time, nature can be seen as the "new poor," not the poor that crowds out the human poor, but the "also" poor; and as such it demands our attention and care.[2] Nature demands our love, as do the human oppressed. It is my proposal, then, that we will begin to get things right about the humans–world–God complex when we see ourselves as natural, as belonging to the earth utterly and completely, as well as super, natural, by responding to this earth, our beleaguered home, with special attention and care—that is, with love.

This book is mainly about *how* that change in sensibility might occur. How can we begin to think about ourselves as both natural creatures and as caretakers of the natural world? And how can we do this *as Christians?* This change in Christian sensibility is only one of the many things that needs to be done if our planet and its creatures are to prosper. The "planetary agenda" presents many tasks: an economic revolution for global equity and sustainability, profound lifestyle changes by first-world consumers, educational and status reforms for women throughout the world, environmental restoration and pollution control legislation, etc.[3] The list is long and there is

l piece of the agenda we will be
nsibility, the mind-and-heart-set
ong had a reputation for being
. It is a sensibility that has often
rld and, at best, has seen it as
that should be preserved. At its
d to the destruction of nature
ominion" over nature has served

d? Attitudes toward nature *do*
no such thing as a natural view
not natural. The ways we think
are hundreds of different ways to
stance, a tree is not just a tree: it
eet, shade for a weary traveler, a
eauty, the cross of Christ, the
famous pear tree, the icon of the
n and on. All of this should give
ve think of nature and ourselves
convention, a way of seeing that
olute, not eternal, and not "nat-
possible. Change of this sort, a
changing metaphors. We think
nodels that implicitly structure
lf, world, and God.[4]
understanding self, world, and
bject." Whatever we know, we
the subject knowing the world
objects. It is such a deep struc-
at we are not usually aware that
the way things are. But it is a
it is implicitly dualistic, hierar-
n. It is a model that has been
ince the scientific revolution in
the seventeenth century, when nature was first seen as a dead
machine rather than as the living body it was imagined to be during
the Middle Ages, nature has become *the object* par excellence. It is
nothing but object; it is never subject.

But what if we changed the model for knowledge from subject-
object to subject-subjects? This suggestion is a radical one and it is at
the heart of my proposal: we need a different *basic model* for all our

knowing—our knowledge of other people, the natural world, and God. We may believe that we think of other people and of God as subjects, but the model of Western knowing scarcely allows us to do so. It encourages utilitarian, dualistic, individualistic, hierarchical thinking. For instance, it lies behind the common notion of God as a heavenly, lordly super-person whose function is to save the good and punish the bad. It also lies behind our tendency to deal with differences among human beings in terms of hierarchical dualisms—male/female, straight/gay, whites/people of color, Westerners/Easterners. The first named is the subject, the second the object. In a similar way and to an extreme degree, the natural world is objectified in this knowledge model; in fact, the suggestion that nature (and its billions of lifeforms as well as material entities, such as mountains, rocks, and oceans) might be seen as "subjects" is ridiculous to many people. It seems romantic, sentimental—perhaps even a bit soft-headed.

It is none of these things. It is, I believe, a no-nonsense, hard-headed suggestion that emerges from serious attention to who we are in the scheme of things and how, therefore, we should relate to others—others in the natural world, other human beings, and God. The reason why the subject-subjects model makes better sense than the subject-object one is that, according to the evolutionary, ecological picture of reality current in our time, we are, at base, *relational creatures.* But so is everything else. Every lifeform and entity is relational in the primary sense of being in active interrelationship and interdependence with the others. All of us, in different ways, are "ecological subjects," centered beings/entities that affect others and are in turn influenced by them. We are all, men and mountains, children and caterpillars, women and wheat, intrinsically, internally, and thoroughly relational to the core. We humans are not solitary individuals who have occasional relations (when we feel like it) with other people, the natural world, and God. We are through and through relational beings who not only affect these others but are affected by them. And so also are microbes, oceans, and plants. This is what it means to be a subject in the subject-subjects model. For instance, a tree is not an object whose parts we can destroy at will with no effect on the rest of the tree; nor is it a solitary entity whose well-being or destruction has no effect on the others in its environment, including us. Objects are "things" that others can change as they please with no consequences, while subjects both affect others and are affected by them. So, if we are subjects, so are "they" (all the other earth entities). We are all in the network of life together, and while the analogy of subject will apply differently to human beings, a tree, a tiger, a mountain—or to God—it is a better way of thinking of the human/world/God complex than the subject-object model. It is better for several reasons. The model is closer to the view of reality current in our time—the ecological, evolutionary picture coming to us from postmodern science.[5] Moreover, this model results in a more humane and healthy practice: treating the other, whether human being or the natural world, as subject rather than as object can make for immense changes at both personal and public levels. Finally, the model dovetails with the biblical view of God and the world, which is one of appreciation for the others in creation—from God's "It is good!" in Genesis to Jesus' love for sinners and outcasts.

We will have much more to say on these matters, but for now, the main point is that we have a *choice* in the world we inhabit. Unlike other animals, who occupy their worlds through instinct, we construct ours—not absolutely, for a falsely constructed world will eventually show tell-tale stains and strains, but we are not passive bystanders. This book is about experimenting with the subject-subjects world *model*. This understanding of the self and world is not a description, nor is the subject-object view. Neither is a realist account; both are interpretations, models, discourses, "texts."[6] Our task will be to unravel some of the central parts and pieces of the subject-subjects model: its contrast with the subject-object model as well as the history of both models; the present dire consequences of the subject-object model; the re-emergence in our time from many quarters (from ecologists, feminists, process philosophers, and phenomenologists) of the subjects model. This book, then, is meant to be a laboratory to experiment with, try on, a new sensibility, one that sees everything, *all others*, as subjects. As much as a book of this sort can do, it is meant to be an experience, a test case, of whether a proposal for seeing everything through the lens of subjecthood is helpful and perhaps even necessary for Christians in our time. In the remainder of this chapter, we will suggest some working definitions of spirituality, Christian, and nature. By doing so, we will specify more clearly the character of this experiment—what we might call a Christian nature spirituality.

Christian Nature Spirituality

Most simply, a Christian nature spirituality is Christian praxis (reflective practice) extended to the natural world. The simplicity of this statement hides a host of questions: What is meant by "spirituality" (a word that in current popular culture is applied to anything uplifting or vaguely religious)? What is meant by the adjective "Christian" (a word that characterizes hundreds of very different sorts of beliefs and practices)? And what is meant by "nature" (a deceptively obvious term that is actually fiendishly complex and steeped in old, deep power struggles). So our first task will be to define these central words.

Spirituality

Spirituality is a risky word to introduce because it is everywhere in contemporary culture: it includes near-death experiences, being embraced by angels, New Age practices, what one does with one's solitude, and direct experiences of God. It is also seen as the opposite of religion (especially what goes on in churches) as well as any uplifting, generally positive philosophy of self-help. But spirituality is an old and honorable Christian term, and we will take our cues on what it means from a 1977 definition by the Scottish Churches Council that is startlingly contemporary and relevant. It defines spirituality as "an exploration into what is involved in becoming human," and describes "becoming human" as "an attempt to grow in sensitivity to self, to others, to the non-human creation, and to God who is within and beyond this totality."[7] The stress in this definition is on becoming human through *relationships*, with nature included as a central one. The *way* we become human is "to grow in sensitivity," to develop awareness of, feeling for, sympathy with, these others. Christian spirituality is not, then, principally a "religious" relationship. It is not mainly or only about a relationship with God: the individual alone with God, as some popular views of it would suggest. In these views, spirituality is the opposite of ethics, whereas it should actually be seen as the preparation or grounding for action. Spirituality is developing the attention to, awareness of, knowledge about, the other (whether another person, a lifeform or entity in nature, God, or even the self) so that one can respond to that other appropriately. Leonardo Boff speaks of Christian spirituality as solidarity with the poor and of people who practice this solidarity as "contemplatives in liberation."[8] Prayer is not one thing (practiced by contemplatives) and Christian praxis something else (practiced by activists). Prayer and action must go together: "a synthesis of prayer in acting, prayer within activity, prayer with the deed."[9] Or as Jon Sobrino says, Christian prayer is "nothing more than life in the Spirit of Jesus."[10]

Piety and praxis go together. This certainly appears to be the case with the saints of the Christian tradition. For over twenty years I have taught a course on religious autobiographies. Two things have stood out for me in the lives of these extraordinary Christians: first, a profound relationship with God as the basis for their works of justice and mercy and, second, the growth of their love in ever-widening circles. Three shining examples are John Woolman, the eighteenth-century Quaker and abolitionist; Dietrich Bonhoeffer, the German theologian who, as a participant in a plot to assassinate Adolf Hitler, was imprisoned and executed; and Dorothy Day, the Roman Catholic journalist and founder of urban hospitality houses for the most destitute. They are "contemplatives in liberation" who were moved to extraordinary acts on behalf of others out of the depths of their own spiritual lives. It would not have been possible to sustain the kind of lives they lived, lives of great endurance and sacrifice, if they had not been grounded in God. At age eighty, Day was still writing for *The Catholic Worker* and feeding the homeless in her soup kitchens. Great praxis demands great piety. Their love for others was not only deep; it was also wide. It often began with family and friends but grew into a universal love. Bonhoeffer developed a relationship with his jailers, and Woolman saw the connections between greed and the destruction of life, both the lives of slaves and the well-being of nature. The Christian practice of radical love knows no bounds: it does not stop at any border, even the human one.

The lives of these modern saints are instructive as we try to define what a Christian nature spirituality might be. We have suggested that it is Christian praxis extended to the natural world. Like the action of Christian saints toward oppressed human beings, it must come out of and be sustained by deep piety. Such piety is a growing sensitivity to others; this occurs gradually as prayer and action develop an awareness of the real needs of others. There is no reason, however, why these "others" should not include other lifeforms. For our Christian saints, radical love was never tribal: it was not "for me and my kind." While only Woolman hints at the extension of God's radical love to nature, the pattern is evident in the others. For Bonhoeffer, whatever is human is on the side of Christ; and for Day, no person, however degraded, is beyond God's grace. I believe that Woolman, Bonhoeffer, and Day would find a Christian nature spirituality thoroughly in keeping with Christian piety and praxis. They would, I imagine, see the deterioration and destruction of the natural world in continuity with human oppression. Oppressed human beings and degraded nature are both victims of selfishness, greed, and domination. They are both victims of objectification, seeing others as objects rather than subjects. The universal love of the saints would not, I believe, find the extension of Christian praxis to the natural world as odd. On the contrary, the saints would see it as very "natural," as in fact what Christians should naturally do.

Hence, spirituality in regard to the natural world means attempting to grow in sensitivity to it *in the same way* we are to grow in sensitivity to God and other people. Christian spirituality is defined by radical love—as we see in the piety and praxis of the saints. A Christian nature spirituality, then, is beginning to take form: it means loving nature in a Christian way. We turn now to defining "Christian" in order to see what loving nature as Christians might mean specifically and concretely.

Christian

Christian nature spirituality as Christian practice in relation to the natural world means caring for nature. It means applying "the liberation of the oppressed" to nature. It is recognition of and response to the fact that in our time the natural world is vulnerable, needy, sick, and deteriorating. It is an affirmation that the redeemer God is also the creator God, that God loves *all* of creation, especially the neediest and most vulnerable. In our time the Gospel of destabilizing, inclusive love must be extended to nature and not stop at our own species. To those who say, "But Jesus did not extend this love to nature," we reply, "But neither did he extend it explicitly to slaves, women, or people of color."[11] Christians in subsequent generations have done so, however, because "the oppressed" change over time. If God the redeemer is concerned for the well-being of all of creation, then we have to extend the line we have drawn which puts us *within* the circle of divine concern and the rest of creation *outside*. And we must do this, first of all, for theological reasons. It is what Christian praxis demands. We do not do it because unless we care for nature, humans cannot survive or because Christianity had better get on the environmental bandwagon, but because commitment to the God of Jesus Christ demands it. A Christian nature spirituality is the logical next step away from a tribal God toward the universal God, away from a God concerned with "me and my kind," toward the One concerned with the entire creation.

But such Christian praxis should not be a creation theology or a nature spirituality, neither a theology that revels in the wonders of creation nor a spirituality that merges with nature.[12] Not, that is, if it claims to be Christian. Christian action is concerned with liberation of and care for the oppressed, not with creation eulogies or nature worship. As the circle of *who* is oppressed widens to include the natural world, Christian practice becomes very complex, very challenging. While most of us have accepted that charity toward the poor is false Christian praxis and must be replaced by the empowerment of oppressed people, we are less certain about what a Christian nature spirituality, a Christian praxis toward the natural world, might mean.

At base it must be grounded in what the Latin American liberation theologian Leonardo Boff calls "social ecology, the ways that human social and economic systems interact with the natural ecosystem."[13] Just as charity to needy human individuals will not even begin to address the deep systemic changes needed in economic, political, educational, familial, and cultural institutions if poverty and discrimination are to be alleviated, so also minor lifestyle changes such as recycling and car-pooling are little more than band-aids on nature.[14] We now know that human systems, especially economic ones, are inextricably interlocked with natural ones. A "social ecology" defines the human/nature relationship in such profound ways that justice and liberation for the one are intrinsically bound up with justice and liberation for the other. Unless the natural world is healthy, it cannot provide the basics of life for the poor; and unless all of us, especially the privileged of the first world, limit our energy use, the natural world cannot be healthy.[15] Hence, justice and ecology—the liberation of the poor and the well-being of nature—are not separate issues, but two sides of the same coin.

This is now becoming painfully obvious, and yet the economic system that rules the globe, the gospel of unlimited growth, refuses to acknowledge "social ecology." It refuses to acknowledge the limitations of our finite planet and the radical, inexorable interconnections between our well-being and nature's. John Cobb calls our devotion to this economic system the religion of "Economism": its god is endless economic growth; its priests are economists; its evangelists are advertisers; its laity are consumers.[16] The cathedral of this religion is the shopping mall; virtue is the competitive spirit and sin is inefficiency. The way to salvation is to "shop till you drop." The religion of Economism is not just an amusing metaphor for how we spend our leisure time but a serious analysis of a deep and deadly sickness in the soul of Western (and increasingly, global) culture. In such a religion nature *and* people are objectified, seen as either "raw materials" or "human resources" for the production of consumer needs and desires.[17] Nothing has intrinsic value; no one and no thing is a subject; all are objects in the economic machine, serving the insatiable appetite called the Gross National Product.

But Christians cannot take on revamping the global economic system (though, like all citizens, we can and should work through political channels to change it), nor is it enough just to join the recyclers and car-poolers (though these are minimal expectations demanded of all of us). Rather, there is something else, something more, that we Christians must face: doing something about our basic attitude and practice toward the natural world. We alone cannot save nature, but we might be able to stop contributing, as we have done for centuries, to its objectification and degradation and begin to see it as God's beloved—as we claim people are—as having intrinsic worth in God's eyes and in ours. This shift in perspective and hopefully, also, in practice should be distinctively *Christian*. If we have anything to contribute, it ought not to be what the economists or ecologists or some other religious tradition can do better, but what is special about a *Christian* voice. Admitting that there are many Christian voices, the liberation Christian paradigm is, nonetheless, a strong candidate for contributing to the global ecological conversation, for it links human and natural well-being. Unlike evangelical Christianity, which focuses on human and especially individual redemption, and unlike creation spirituality, which focuses on nature's well-being, Christian liberation reflection extended to the natural world sees human and natural salvation as inextricably linked. A *Christian* nature spirituality, then, is not Christian praxis *for* nature apart from or opposed to the well-being of the human oppressed. It is not a nature religion, a nature mysticism, or a nature ethic. It extends the paradigm of the destabilizing radical love we see in Jesus' parables, healing stories, and eating practices *to nature*. This kind of radical love for the vulnerable and oppressed is counter-cultural; it is at sharp odds with the religion of Economism; it places the Christian in a prophetic and uncomfortable position vis-à-vis culture; it is a *distinctive* voice in the global ecological conversation.

What are the distinctive features of a *Christian* nature spirituality? Most broadly, it will be based on the tradition's incarnationalism: on the Word made flesh, on God as embodied. The incarnate God is not a spiritualized, abstract, distant, or mental deity but a bodily, concrete, near, and physical One. The paradigmatic shape of this

God for Christians is Jesus: Christians look Godward through Jesus.[18] The ministry of Jesus tells us that God loves the poor in body, which implies that God's love can be extended to nature, the new poor. While nature is not *only* body (as we shall see), it is certainly the prime marker in our society and in most societies of the physical, the bodily. On our reading of Christianity, a distinctive characteristic of its incarnationalism is a focus on oppressed, vulnerable, suffering bodies, those who are in pain due to the indifference or greed of the powerful. Thus, in a time of the earth's deterioration, Jesus' radical, inclusive love ought to embrace the earth others who are suffering bodily oppression.

More specifically, how can we understand Jesus' ministry as extended to nature? It can be seen in three ways: a deconstructive phase in the parables, a reconstuctive phase in the healing stories, and a prospective phase in Jesus' eating practices. Jesus' praxis on behalf of nature—one that gives content and direction to a Christian nature spirituality—involves three steps. First, it means overturning the hierarchy of humans over nature, just as in the parables other hierarchies of the rich/poor, righteous/unrighteous, powerful/weak are overturned. The destabilizing of conventions central to Jesus' parables can be extended to the contemporary hegemony of human beings over the natural world. This is a first but necessary deconstructive step: the acknowledgment that nature is not just an object, not just useful to us, but is valued and loved in itself, for itself by God in Christ. The second step, a reconstructive one, is manifested in Jesus' healing acts, which underscore that salvation means the health of bodies, that the deterioration and dysfunction of the ecosystems of our earth are affronts to God, who desires the well-being not just of humans but of all creation. The healing stories, often considered an embarrassment to educated Christians, focus on bodies, undermining attempts to spiritualize Christianity. They support super, natural Christians in our goal to *love the earth as Christians*. The third step, a prospective one, is revealed in Jesus' eating practices. He ate with sinners, tax collectors, and prostitutes—the outcasts of society. His eating practices highlight solidarity with the oppressed and, as with the healing stories, focus on bodily health and justice at the level of basic needs: all bodies need to be fed. Thus, the eating practices are not only a call for justice but also a foretaste of the eschatological banquet when all creation will be satisfied and made whole.

The three phases of Jesus' ministry suggest a deeply subversive

, according to the reading just
e extended to nature. The "shape"
uily: Jesus was himself a body and his
g hierarchies in favor of the poor, of healing
eating with outcasts is concerned with physical
right. The justice ministry of Jesus is open to, in
 of, extension to nature.

A Christian spirituality insists that we work out right relations with
God and neighbor. It should include right relations with creation as
well. What right relations with nature means for Christians should be
on a continuum with love of neighbor. According to the interpretation of Christianity given here, the distinctive note of Christian faith
is divine embodiment as shaped by Jesus' practice of destabilizing,
inclusive solidarity with the poor and the oppressed. Nature is certainly among the poor and oppressed in our time. Our right relations
with nature should therefore be guided by Jesus' praxis.

How can we begin to relate to nature this way? A first, critical step
and the heart of this book is to see nature as subject. While Christian
praxis should go beyond the recognition of the intrinsic value of nature
(nature as subject) to fighting its oppression, it is unlikely to do so
until it accepts the natural world as valuable in itself. In the last chapter we will return to Christianity's special contribution to a nature
spirituality, but first we must go the slow route toward establishing
what nature is and how we should relate to it as another subject.

Nature

If "Christian" has many meanings, "nature" has more. In a sense,
nature is everything, including ourselves; hence, trying to define it is
like a fish attempting to define the ocean. Nature is "the totality of
processes and powers that make up the universe,"[19] which of course
includes human beings, but also black holes, electromagnetic fields,
dirt, DNA, gravity, death, time and space, apples, quarks, trees,
birth, microbes, tigers, and mountains. It is hard to think of anything that is *not* nature, although another definition of nature as
"that which exists independently of all human artifice" attempts to.[20]
We do speak of nature *and* culture, meaning by culture what humans
have done with and to nature, that is, transforming it through
human powers into books and paintings, universities and governments, gourmet dinners and McDonald's hamburgers, tents and
palaces, religions and magic. So, in one sense there is nothing but
nature, for none of our cultural transformations could have occurred

except through the physical evolution of the remarkable human brain. But in another sense, we construct nature: nature is never "natural," for while we and everything we think and do comes from nature, all our thoughts about it and actions in it are distinctively human, that is, both *distanced* and *particular*. As the self-conscious creature, the only one, as far as we know, who does not live in nature like a fish in the ocean but can reflect on nature, human beings interpret their surroundings, their world, that is, nature. Our relationship with nature is like our relationship with our own bodies: we can live only in and through them, we are nothing without them, we are intrinsically and entirely embodied and yet, we can distance ourselves *from* them and have many different views *of* them. We both *are* our bodies, *and* we drag them around after us like cans tied to a dog's tail. That oneness and distance create the peculiar difficulty and complexity of trying to define nature.

It means, first of all, that there will be many views of what nature is, depending on different historical, cultural, geographical, political, economic, and personal contexts. To the Hebrew tribes, nature was a harsh, spare desert that fed their dreams for another nature, one of milk and honey. For the medieval peasant, nature was an allegory for human and divine realities—the cunning fox, lustful goat, and busy bee offered lessons for human behavior, while wildflowers with names like Christ's Ladder and Solomon's Seal reminded Christians that nature belonged to God. To a child living near a landfill in an American city, nature is the stink of the garbage as she goes to school and the fear she feels in the small neighborhood park after dark. For a molecular biologist working on the genome project, nature is reducible to the graph the project will produce of all the genes in the human body. In other words, nature is not one thing, but many things: it is a child's first crayfish caught in a local ditch; it is the daily, drudging search for cooking firewood in many parts of the world; it is a wilderness experience of spectacular beauty; it is also the death that visits us all, whether from cancer or AIDS or old age.

A few examples should make the point—nature as meaning many different things—even more clear. Today most of us like nature calendars—the ones with color pictures of snow-capped mountains gleaming in bright sunlight against a clear blue sky. This is the contemporary, environmentally correct view of mountains. Mountains are beautiful. But our taste for mountain scenery is not universal. For instance, an early visitor to Pike's Peak describes it as follows: "The dreariness of the desolate Peak itself scarcely dissipates the dismal spell, for you stand in a confusion of dull stones piled upon each other in odious ugliness."[21] "Odious ugliness"!? We react with unbelief and revulsion to such a view of a splendid mountain peak. But as a commentator on our different view of mountains remarks, "We see in Nature what we have been taught to look for, we feel what we have been prepared to feel."[22] Indeed we do.

A second and very different example of nature as a highly interpreted category is from a now-famous statement by the novelist Jorge Luis Borges. We think the taxonomy developed by Linnaeus in the eighteenth century is the only system of classification for animals and plants. But Borges's amusing paragraph widens our horizons.

> A certain Chinese encyclopedia divides animals into: (a) belonging to the Emperor, (b) embalmed, (c) tame, (d) sucking pigs, (e) sirens, (f) fabulous (g) stray dogs, (h) included in the present classification, (i) frenzied, (j) innumerable, (k) drawn with a fine camel's-hair brush, (l) *et cetera*, (m) having just broken the water pitcher, (n) that from a long way off look like flies.[23]

A final example takes us into the world of the wood tick, a world very different from any of our views of nature.[24] The wood tick is blind to our world of mountain scenery and animal classifications, existing within its own world comprised of just three things: light, sweat, and heat. The fertilized female needs blood from a mammal to complete its lifecycle and can wait up to eighteen years to get it. Having climbed to the top of a bush to activate the photosensitivity of her skin, she becomes aware of the sweat of an approaching mammal, lands on its warm body (perceiving by her sensitive skin that it *is* a mammal), and sucks its blood. That bubble composed of light, sweat, and heat is the wood tick's world, and within this world, she is a subject: the world is tailored to the wood tick and the wood tick to its world. As Barry Lopez points out, every animal has its *Umwelt*, its "self-world," its experience of nature. Here he is speaking of various inhabitants of an Arctic island called Pingok:

> Because the fox is built so much closer to the ground and is overall so much smaller than a human being, the island must be "longer" in its mind than four and a half miles. And traveling as it does, trotting and then resting, trotting and then resting, and "seeing" so much with its black nose—what is Pingok like for it?. . . . What is the island to a loon, who lives on the water and in the air, stepping awkwardly ashore only at the concealed spot at the edge of the pond, where it rests? What of the bumblebee, which spends its evening deep in the corolla of a summer flower . . . ?[25]

Anyone who has taken their dog on a walk in the woods knows that the hermeneutic of smell creates a world different from ours of vision and sound. Unlike the wood tick, the fox, the bee, and our dogs, who inhabit their bubble worlds more or less instinctively, we inhabit ours with varying degrees of self-consciousness. And we each have several, often overlapping bubbles that define what nature is for us: we live *within* our personal, cultural, historical, geographical, economic, racial, class, and gender understandings of the natural world. There is no *one* view of nature. Nature is not an essentialist category.[26]

The second implication of our oneness with and distance from nature is that none of our many interpretations are innocent, natural, or absolute—though they are often claimed to be. As Simon Shama in *Landscape and Memory* reminds the backpacker who believes in the educational value and moral uplift of mountains and forests, the Nazis were nature-lovers par excellence and in fact saw profound connections between their racial theories and the Germanic forests. "It is of course painful to acknowledge how ecologically conscientious the most barbaric regime in modern history actually was. Exterminating millions of lives was not at all incompatible with passionate protection of millions of leaves."[27] Using nature as a norm is a very old business, going back at least to Aristotle, who saw slaves and women as naturally inferior to free males. The power of nature as norm is precisely in passing it off as *not* a norm (that is, as not a judgment or opinion), but as "the way things are." If, for instance, heterosexuality can be seen as the natural sexual orientation, then homosexuality must be unnatural. The goal in such statements is to collapse the "is" and the "ought": what is natural is what ought to be. What is natural is good; what is unnatural is bad. Every society has attempted to make its desired conventional behavior, especially though not exclusively in regard to sexual, bodily, and familial matters, pass as natural. To the extent that it can do so, it has won a major battle.

In no area is this more clearly seen than in the relations between women and nature. Aristotle claimed that mares and hence, by implication, human females were sexually wanton with unbridled appetites, whereas G.W.F. Hegel saw females as just the opposite, as passive like plants.[28] In each case, nature was used as a way to support the author's opinion of women's proper place. During the Enlightenment, when all people were declared to be equal, natural law was brought into the debate on the status of women to support a theory of men and women as "complementary opposites," which claimed that women naturally belonged in the private sphere and men in the public.[29]

Nature has, however, suffered the same inferior status as women, even as it has also been used as a norm to oppress women. "Naturism," the domination of nature, is a lifelong partner to sexism: "the feminization of nature and the naturalization of women have been crucial to the historically successful subordination of both."[30] One common legacy of this old partnership is our scolding of Mother Nature's fury whenever earthquakes, torrential rains, or hurricanes occur. The angry, out-of-control feminized nature gets back at her human tormentors through unleashing some solid strikes now and then. It is, sadly, one of the few times in our culture that we address nature as subject.

In summary, nature has many meanings and none of them is "natural" or absolute. Once we realize that nature is constructed by us (even as we also realize we are one of its productions), it need not be seen as a revengeful female, nor need women be reduced to their bodies. There are many different definitions of nature, and they are all interpretations, including those of the molecular biologist as well as the Pike's Peak hiker. We have a choice about how we are to interpret nature and the choice we make will be important.

As Christians, then, how should we understand nature? Let me suggest two possibilities: the big answer and a small one. The big answer is that we should think of nature in terms of the picture of the physical world coming to us from postmodern science and ecology. The natural world, according to this picture, is characterized by evolutionary change and novelty, structure as well as openness (or law and chance), relationality and interdependence, with individual entities existing only within systems, systems that can be expressed by the models of organism and community.[31] This understanding of the big picture of nature is different from the medieval view, which saw nature as fixed, teleological, hierarchical, anthropocentric, and dualistic, with substances (individual entities) more important than systems and "kingdom" as an appropriate expressive model. It is in even sharper contrast to the Newtonian view of nature, which was deterministic and atomistic, reductionistic and dualistic, with the machine as the prime analogy.[32] Unfortunately, many Christians as well as Christian doctrines still operate with either a medieval or a Newtonian view of nature, or a combination of the two. The medieval picture (as we will see in the third chapter) was in many ways a successful model integrating God, humans, and world, with nature as symbolic *of* God and hence seen as a way *to* God. It brought these three crucial elements of any worldview into a coherent unity: people lived in close proximity to other animals and plants while at the same time seeing them as emblems of God. While the picture was anthropocentric and hierarchical, with its focus on the salvation of human individuals, it can still provide us with an interesting case study in God-human-nature integration as we attempt to undo the much more devastating effects of the Newtonian worldview, the one that dominates contemporary thinking.

In the Newtonian picture, individualism rather than relationship is stressed, as well as human differences from nature. God is far removed from nature and so are human beings. In this view, humans alone have minds (patterned on *the* Creative Mind, God) while the rest of nature is mere matter, dead and inert like a machine. The Newtonian view is in clear opposition to the contemporary ecological model, in which relationship is central, not individual entities (including human ones), and where human similarities with the rest of nature are stressed, while our distinctiveness is also acknowledged.[33] As Martin Buber eloquently and simply says, "In the beginning is relationship."[34] That is what the postmodern view of nature insists. It means that in this picture neither God nor human beings are distant from the natural world; on the contrary, both are "in touch" with it. Whereas the God of the Newtonian worldview is the all-seeing One who surveys his creation from a distance, the God of the contemporary view is in touch with every creature and aspect of creation, being nearer to each than they are to themselves. All of us also are in touch with the others in nature—every second, every minute, every hour of every day. A Buddhist text puts it well: "The essence of nature is socialism; nothing can exist independently; everything exists interdependently."[35]

This is the big answer. It is the worldview, the picture of nature, that should operate implicitly and substantially in Christian thinking and speaking. It is the image of reality that needs to become commonplace, even conventional, within all aspects of Christianity—its doctrines, liturgy, hymns, preaching, and ethics. It needs to become as accepted as the medieval and Newtonian views presently are in Christian circles, because the evolutionary, ecological, relational, community model of nature is *the contemporary picture of reality*. It *is* a picture, a model (and not reality "as such"), but so are the medieval and Newtonian views; the difference is that the latter ones are outmoded, anachronistic, and incredible pictures *to us*. Christians need to internalize the new picture so that it functions at a daily level in their ordinary experiences and decisions. We need to think of this picture as "natural," as the way things are, while at the same time remembering that this picture can and will change.

This picture of reality will be central to all our reflections in this volume, for it is the context for the subject-subjects model of self and world, God and world. It is the picture of reality that says, "In the beginning is relationship"—and relationship is only possible between subjects. This view of reality is highly compatible with the spirituality of Jesus' ministry, for it sets us in a world of radical relationality at all levels and dimensions of our existence. While this worldview does not itself indicate *how* we should relate to all the others, it does insist that life is about relationships. To pose the opposite possibility: this picture is not compatible with an individualistic view of human life, morality, or religion. In the postmodern view of reality, human beings are not solitary beings who enter into contractual agreements with other human beings or who have a private, one-to-one relationship with God. The ecological, evolutionary understanding of nature is, on the contrary, open to Christians who understand themselves in radical relationality with God and other creatures. This understanding of nature is one that Christians should embrace, for they can both learn from it and contribute to it.

The small answer to the question, How should Christians understand nature? assumes the big answer as its context ("In the beginning is relationship"), but sees nature in the near neighbor, whether that be another human being, a tree, or even a goldfish. Christians understand and attempt to practice seeing the face of Christ in a suffering human sister or brother, but have little theology or practice to support caring relationships with other lifeforms, let alone such entities as mountains and oceans. Most of us feel a little embarrassed by Buber's cryptic words about a mutual relation with a tree or Annie Dillard's praise of her goldfish, Ellery, who is not only, to her, a marvel of creation but also a responsive being.[36] And yet, as with our human relationships, we do not love "people in general," but particular people; in fact, those who *do* love people in general but hate the near neighbor are suspect. The same might be true of "loving nature" while having little time for a tree or a goldfish. It might be that the environmental slogan of "think globally and act locally" should be reversed; perhaps we might act more appropriately and energetically globally if we were to think locally. In other words, we are more likely, I suspect, to love nature if we love one small bit of it, even just a tree or a goldfish.

Most people who develop a lifelong love of the natural world begin by loving particular places—Tinker Creek, the Saskatchewan prairie, a small city park—and they also have often had opportunities as children to collect bugs, explore vacant lots, spend time "doing nothing" outdoors.[37] These early as well as lifelong experiences with particular, local, available bits and pieces of nature (often, for children, ditches and creeks) are critical, both for our well-being, since most of us feel better in such settings, and for the development of a real relationship with nature. *We will not care for what we do not know, and we cannot know what we do not experience.* We can know "about nature" without experiencing it, but we cannot become acquainted with it—we cannot develop what biologist E. O. Wilson calls "biophilia."[38] Secondhand experience of nature—through television nature films, interpretive nature walks, eco-tours, shopping at the Nature Store, wearing L. L. Bean clothes, and supporting the World Wildlife Fund—is not the same as firsthand encounters. A panoramic view of the Grand Canyon, whether from a nature calendar or one's own camera, may be less rewarding and less connecting to nature than time spent observing the habits of birds in one's own backyard. Robert Pyle speaks of "the extinction of experience" for both children and adults: increasingly, many people have little direct relationship with nature, and those who do are the privileged, especially by race and class.[39] Robert Coles reports a conversation with a twelve-year-old black girl who had been bussed to a previously all-white Boston school:

> I guess I'm doin' all right. I'm studyin', and, like the teacher says, it pays off. A lot of time, though, I wish I could walk out of that school and find myself a place where there are no whites, no black folk, no people of any kind! I mean, a place where I'd be able to sit and get my head together; a place where I could walk and walk, and I'd be walking on grass, not cement, with glass and garbage around; a place where there'd be the sky and the sun, and then the moon and all those stars. At night, sometimes, when I am feeling real low, I'll climb up the stairs to our roof [she lived in a triple-decker building with a flat roof], and I'll look at the sky, and I'll say, hello there, you moon and all you babies—stars! I'm being silly, I know, but up there, I feel I can stop and think about what's happening to me—it's the only place I can, the only place.[40]

Gustavo Gutiérrez has said that even the poor have the right to think; they also have the right to have a relationship with the natural world. This relationship should not be reserved for those with the leisure and money to go trekking in the wilderness. A Christian understanding of nature cannot be the preservation of the wilderness for the elite. We certainly need to preserve wilderness areas for bio-diversity and for other species to prosper and reproduce, but a Christian view of nature is not the same as the agenda of the Sierra Club. It is, rather, extending the radical, destabilizing, inclusive love of Jesus Christ to the natural world and this praxis is best begun, I am suggesting, by developing real relations with some particular places, lifeforms, entities in nature. Caring for a small backyard garden—or even a single houseplant—is more likely to develop into fighting city hall for an inner-city pocket park than is an armchair "love of nature" gained from watching the Discovery channel. In a moving passage Buber speaks of an experience he had at eleven years of age stroking a dapple-gray horse, an experience that surely lies behind his mature insight into the power of relationship, even across the species divide. The following paragraph could not have been written, I believe, from secondhand information:

> If I am to explain it now, beginning from the still very fresh memory of my hand, I must say that what I experienced in touch with the animal was the Other, the immense otherness of the Other, which, however, did not remain strange like the otherness of the ox and the ram, but rather let me draw near and touch it. When I stroked the mighty mane . . . and felt the life beneath my hand, it was as though the element of vitality itself bordered on my skin, something that was not I, certainly not akin to me, palpably the other, not just another, really the Other itself; and yet it let me approach, confided itself to me, placed itself elementally in the relation of *Thou* and *Thou* with me.[41]

This kind of particular experience with another lifeform is at the heart of all genuine understandings of nature, for it meets the other as subject. A Christian understanding of nature must begin here, I believe, with the Thou and the Thou. Only from such a beginning, seeing nature as subject and not merely as object, will we develop a praxis, a Christian spirituality, in relation to it.

In sum, a Christian nature spirituality is Christian praxis extend-ed to nature. It is becoming sensitive to the natural world, acknowledging that we live *in* this relationship as we do also in the relationships with God and other people. It means extending the way we respond to God and other people—as subjects and not as objects—to the natural world. Christian spirituality insists that we should love God because God is God and deserves our adoration; likewise, we should love other people for themselves, as ends and not means. A Christian nature *spirituality*, then, is loving nature in the same way that we love God and other people: as valuable in itself, as a "subject." A Christian *nature* spirituality extends this subject-subjects love to nature. A *Christian* nature spirituality tells us further that in our time nature is oppressed and needs our special care. To care for it properly, we must pay attention to it, learn about its needs, become better acquainted with it.

In the next chapter we will turn to this issue—how to know nature better so that we might love and care for it more appropriately. Most of the themes of the book will be touched on in the upcoming chapter, often in a poetic and sometimes in an autobiographical way. This overview is general and on many issues brief and cursory; the rest of the book will flesh out the argument with more precision and depth.

2

Consider the Lilies
of the Field

*How Should Christians
Love Nature?*

S HOULD CHRISTIANS LOVE NATURE? Most have not over the last
2,000 years and many today still don't. In some circles, loving
nature is pagan or what Goddess worshipers do. Of course, Christians should respect nature, use it carefully, and even protect it, but
isn't loving it a bit extreme? *Should* we love nature? My answer is a
resounding Yes. Christians should because the Christian God is
embodied. That is what the incarnation claims. God does not
despise physical reality but loves it and has become one with it. The
Christian tradition is full of body language: the Word made flesh,
the bread and wine that become the body and blood of Christ, the
body of the church. Physical reality, earthly reality—bodies and
nature—are central to an incarnational theology.

Paying Attention

But *how* should we love nature? That is the more difficult and interesting question. Most people love nature in a general way and some
even in a religious way. Most of us get a high from spectacular sunsets and cute panda bears; many of us have religious feelings in a
cathedral of the pines. We all like to fuse with nature, enjoy oceanic
feelings of oneness with it. But that is, of course, just another use of
nature, a higher use than eating it or using it for recreational purposes, but a use nonetheless. Some Christians have loved nature—
loved it as a way to God. The sacramental tradition, most evident in
Roman Catholicism, Eastern Orthodoxy, and Anglicanism and
including the wonderful voices of Augustine, Hildegard of Bingen,
and Gerard Manley Hopkins, has told us, in Hopkins's words, that

26

"the world is charged with the grandeur of God." The sacramental tradition assumes that God is present with us not only in the hearing of the Word and in the Eucharist but also in each and every being in creation. This tradition has helped to preserve and develop an appreciation for nature in a religion that, for the most part, has been indifferent to the natural world as well as justly accused of contributing to its deterioration and destruction. The sacramental tradition should be acknowledged as contributing to a sense of the world as valuable—indeed, as holy—because it is a symbol of the divine and can help us reach God.

The natural world is here, then, a stepping-stone in our pilgrimage to God—a means to an end. Its value does not lie primarily in itself: other lifeforms and other natural entities do not have intrinsic value. Rather, they are valuable as pathways connecting human beings to God, as ways we can express our relationship with God. Everything in the world can become a symbol for the divine-human relationship, as Augustine so eloquently says: "But what is it I love when I love You? Not the beauty of any bodily thing. . . . Yet in a sense I do love light and melody and fragrance and food and embrace when I love my God—the light and the voice and the fragrance and the food and embrace in the soul. . . ."[1]

But I would like to suggest a different way that Christians should love nature—a way in keeping with the earthly, bodily theology suggested by the tradition's incarnationalism, a way that allows us to love the natural world for its intrinsic worth, to love it, in all its differences and detail, in itself, for itself. Francis of Assisi epitomizes this sensibility in his praise of the sun, moon, earth, and water as his brothers and sisters (we will return to Francis several times throughout our reflections, for he exemplifies a kind of Christian sacramentalism grounded in respect for earth others). Emily Dickinson suggested this way of loving nature when she wrote to a friend that the only commandment that she never broke was to "consider the lilies of the field"—not to use them to decorate her yard or pick them for her table (or even for the altar), but just *consider* them.[2] How Christians should love nature is by obeying a simple but very difficult axiom: *pay attention to it.*

But how can we learn to pay attention to something other than ourselves? What does it mean to really pay attention? Iris Murdoch, the British novelist, gives a clue when she says, "It is a *task* to come to see the world as it is." We will bracket for the moment the thorny hermeneutical issue implicit in the phrase "the world as it is" (to return to it many times), focusing now on the "me" versus "other" issue—the problem of attending to another, any other. Murdoch's suggestion is that paying attention is difficult and contrary to how we usually see the world, which is, as she says, in terms of our "fat relentless ego."[3] She gives a personal example: "I am looking out of my window in an anxious and resentful state of mind, brooding perhaps on some damage done to my prestige. Then suddenly I observe a kestrel. In a moment everything is altered. There is nothing but kestrel. And when I return to thinking of the other matter it seems less important."[4] There is a natural and proper part of us, she adds, that takes "a self-forgetful pleasure in the sheer, alien pointless independent existence of animals, birds, stones, and trees."[5] The message is that we pay attention to difference, that we really learn to see what is different from ourselves. That is not easy. We can acknowledge a thing in its difference if it is important to us or useful to us, but realizing that something other than oneself is real, in itself, for itself, is difficult. To acknowledge another being as different—perhaps even indifferent to me, as for instance a hovering kestrel—is, for most of us, a feat of the imagination.

One of the greatest contributions of contemporary feminism is its celebration of difference. To date this has been limited principally to differences among human beings—recognizing that there is no universal human being nor even any essential woman. As a recent book on liberation theologies comments, "People only look alike when you cannot be bothered to look at them closely."[6] But how does one learn to celebrate difference, differences among people and differences among lifeforms? How can we know and accept real differences? The first step, we have suggested, is by paying attention. Art often helps us to do so. Art stops, freezes, and frames bits of reality and, by so doing, helps us to pay attention, as for instance in this haiku by a Japanese poet:

> An old silent pond
> Into the pond a frog jumps.
> Splash! Silence again.

The poet has put a frame around this moment. As novelist Frederick Buechner comments on this haiku, "What the frame does is enable us to see not just something about the moment but the moment itself in all its ineffable ordinariness and particularity. The chances are that if we had been passing when the frog jumped, we wouldn't have noticed a thing or, noticing it, wouldn't have given it a second thought."[7] Art frames fragments of our world: paintings, poetry, novels, sculpture, dance, music help us to look at colors, sounds, bodies, events, characters—whatever—with full attention. Something is lifted out of the world and put into a frame so that we can, perhaps for the first time, *see* it. Most of the time we do not see: we pass a tree, an early spring crocus, the face of another human being, and we do not marvel at these wonders, because we do not see their specialness, their individuality, their difference. As Joseph Wood Krutch reminds us: "It is not easy to live in that continuous awareness of things which alone is true living . . . the faculty of wonder tires easily. . . ."[8]

Simone Weil deepens the meaning of paying attention with her comment that "absolute attention is prayer." She does not say that prayer is absolute attention, but that absolute attention is prayer. By paying attention to something she says, we are, in fact praying. May Sarton, poet and essayist, comments on this phrase from Weil: "When you think about it, we almost never pay absolute attention. The minute we do, something happens. We see whatever we're looking at with such attention, and something else is given—a sort of revelation. I looked at the heart of a daffodil in this way the other day—deep down. It was a pale yellow one, but deep down, at the center, it was emerald green—like a green light. It was amazing."[9] By paying attention to some fragment, some piece of matter in the world, we are in fact praying. Is this what Alice Walker means when she writes in *The Color Purple*, "I think it pisses God off if you walk by the color purple in a field somewhere and don't notice it"?[10] Is this what an incarnational theology, an earthly, bodily theology, implies? Perhaps it is.

We are asking the question, how should a Christian love nature? The answer emerging is that we must pay attention—detailed, careful, concrete attention—to the world that lies around us but is not us. We must do this *because we cannot love what we do not know.*[11] This profound truism is contained in the phrase we have all uttered at sometime: "If they really knew me, they wouldn't love me," implying that only love based on real knowledge is valuable. We must, as Murdoch says, try to see "the world as it is" in order to love it. To *really* love nature (and not just ourselves in nature or nature as useful to us—even its use as a pathway to God), we must pay attention *to it.* Love and knowledge go together; we can't have the one without the other.

Two Ways of Seeing the World

I would like to suggest that a branch of science, nature writing, can help us learn to pay attention. The kind of paying attention that one sees in good nature writing suggests a paradigm for us. Nature writing is not scientific writing that hides behind pseudo-objectivity; rather, it combines acute, careful observation with a kind of loving empathy for and delight in its object. In fact, as we shall see, it is more like the interaction of two subjects than the usual dualism of a subject observing an object. Nature writer Edward Abbey describes it as "sympathy for the object under study, and more than sympathy, love. A love based on prolonged contact and interaction. . . . Observation informed by sympathy, love, intuition."[12] The best nature writing has this sense of personal testimony and detail, what Murdoch calls engagement with the "unutterable particularity" of the natural world.[13] In the writings of Annie Dillard, Gretel Ehrlich, Barry Lopez, Aldo Leopold, and Alice Walker, we see this sense of personal call opening the self to the surprise and delight of deeper and deeper engagement with concrete detail, the particularities and differences that comprise the natural world. It is a way of seeing, a kind of paying attention, that thrives on differences and detail. It is also an interactive kind of knowing—the knower must be open to the known, be sympathetic to, and engaged by the known. It is a knowing that is infused with loving, a love that wants to know more.

Let me illustrate this kind of nature writing by contrasting two very different ways of seeing the world. The first example is Annie Dillard's description of a goldfish named Ellery. The detail in this passage—Dillard's paying attention to the particularities of Ellery—calls forth in her, and in me, a sense of wonder and affection.

> This Ellery cost me twenty-five cents. He is a deep red-orange, darker than most goldfish. He steers short distances mainly with his slender red lateral fins; they seem to provide impetus for going backward, up, or down. It took me a few days to discover his ventral fins; they are completely transparent and all but invisible—dream fins. He also has a short anal fin, and a tail that is deeply notched and perfectly transparent at the two tapered tips. He can extend his mouth, so it looks like a length of pipe; he can shift the angle of his eyes in his head so he can look before and behind himself, instead of simply out to his side. His belly, what there is of it, is white ventrally, and a patch of this white extends up his sides—the variegated Ellery. When he opens his gill slits he shows a thin crescent of silver where the flap overlapped—as though all his brightness were sunburn.

For this creature, as I said, I paid twenty-five cents. I had never bought an animal before. It was very simple; I went to a store in Roanoke called "Wet Pets"; I handed the man a quarter, and he handed me a knotted plastic bag bouncing with water in which a green plant floated and the goldfish swam. This fish, two bits' worth, has a coiled gut, a spine radiating fine bones, and a brain. Just before I sprinkle his food flakes into his bowl, I rap three times on the bowl's edge; now he is conditioned, and swims to the surface when I rap. And, he has a heart.[14]

Every time I read this passage I am unnerved by the juxtaposition of twenty-five cents with the elaborateness, cleverness, and sheer glory of this tiny bit of matter named Ellery. I am learning both by reading nature writing like this as well as from my own experience that the closer attention I pay to whatever piece of the world is before me the more amazed I am by it. It is not that I "see God in it" in any direct or even general way; rather, it is the specialness, the difference, the intricacy, the "unutterable particularity" of each creature, event, or aspect of nature that calls forth wonder and delight—a knowing that calls forth love and a love that wants to know more. "Amazing revelations" come through the earth, not above it or in spite of it. An incarnational theology encourages us to dare to love nature—all the different bodies, both human and those of other lifeforms, on our earth—to find them valuable and wonderful in themselves, for themselves. That is what an incarnational view assures us: it is all right to love nature; in fact, we should. We pray to God through knowing and thereby being able to love all the wild and wonderful diversity of creatures. The prayer is simple: "*Vive les différences.* Long live the differences."

A very different way of seeing the world is epitomized in the now-famous whole earth picture of our planet from the NASA files—the photograph of the earth as a blue and white marble floating in black empty space, lonely and vulnerable. Unlike the subject-subjects kind of knowing in nature writing, it can be seen as an example of subject-object knowing. As one commentator notes, "This distancing, disengaged, abstract, and literalizing epistemology is quintessentially embodied in the whole Earth image. . . . From a distance of tens of thousands of miles away, transcendent, serene, and unaffected, we survey the whole Earth at once."[15] Since the whole earth image is for many people *the* ecological icon, this comment may seem strange. And it did initially to me as well, for I use it in my book *The Body of God* to raise consciousness about the fragility of our planet. But there is a somber underside to this bright, aesthetically pleasing image: it eliminates all detail, not only the smells and sounds and tastes of earth (the blood, sex, feces, sweat, and decay that make up the life of the planet) but also all the signs of deterioration, rape, and pillage that have resulted in holes in the ozone, topsoil erosion, and clear-cut forests. The view from space is of a clean, sterile, beautiful—and manageable—planet, rather than the going-to-pieces one we actually inhabit. The whole-earth view simplifies and objectifies the earth: it is the outsider's view, the spectator view, as in astronaut Russell Schweichert's description of it as "a blue and white Christmas ornament." The earth is a plaything, a beach ball, a yo-yo, a lollipop. This objectifying view underlies computer games in which the earth is destroyed on the screen but instantly restored by the reset button. We can do what we want with this earth, for in the astronaut's view, there are other possibilities, other planets, as we read on the *Star Trek* bumper sticker: "Beam me up, Scotty, this planet sucks." This view from space is also, ironically, claimed to be the "God's eye view": as we are, so God is also distant and disengaged from the earth, finding it pleasing only if all the mud and guts, all the blood and sweat, all the billions of creatures, from creepy-crawly ones to two-legged ones, are invisible. "The whole Earth poster decorating the wall of a Manhattan apartment is no substitute for a true belonging to place."[16] Indeed, it is not.

The Arrogant Eye vs. the Loving Eye

Seeing Ellery and seeing the earth from space: behind these two very different ways of seeing, of paying attention, lie two different ways of knowing: what one commentator calls "the loving eye" versus "the arrogant eye."[17] We want now to reflect in some depth on the differences between these two ways of seeing. We are suggesting that a certain kind of paying attention, a certain kind of knowing, is how Christians ought to love nature. Let us now analyze this claim.

But we are immediately drawn up short: we are trying, as Murdoch says, to see the world as it is so that we can love it rightly. But how, what, *is* it? How can we "see the world as it is"? There is no "natural" view of nature. We know there is no innocent eye, that what we see is determined in large measure by where we stand. The importance of social location for interpreting the world is by now a platitude, but that does not make it any less true. We see from our *Umwelten*, our self-worlds, which are personal, cultural, even genetic.

As two-legged creatures of a certain height, formed by specific personal histories as well as by different gender, racial, economic, national, and cultural realities, we each see the world differently.

Hence, when we turn now to an investigation of paying attention, of a certain kind of seeing and knowing, we must remind ourselves that all seeing, all knowing, is perspectival. The specific issue with which we are concerned—how should we love nature?—will necessarily be based on perspectival knowing. The question is, which perspective, which kind of seeing, is better for nature?

There are many kinds of seeing, many kinds of knowing, but the contrast suggested between the arrogant eye and the loving eye epitomized by the whole-earth image and the description of Ellery is a fruitful one for our purposes. The terms are from feminist philosopher Marilyn Frye, who describes the arrogant eye as acquisitive, seeing everything in relation to the self—as either "for me" or "against me." It organizes everything in reference to oneself and cannot imagine "the possibility that the Other is independent, indifferent."[18] The arrogant eye simplifies in order to control, denying complexity and mystery, since it cannot control what it cannot understand. Frye illustrates the arrogant eye with the example of how it has functioned to exploit and enslave women, "breaking" and "training" them so as to serve male interests. This breaking and training can be so subtle that the oppressed eventually willingly conforms to the wishes of the oppressor—as in the pimp-prostitute relationship—or, more commonly, the way the standardized visual images of women's bodies in the media induce women into extreme diets and even anorexia in order to conform to the arrogant male gaze. The arrogant eye is also the patriarchal eye, which, of course, is not limited to the male perceptual standpoint. All of us in the Western world share this gaze, especially as we move the object of the eye's focus from women to nature. Like women, the natural world has been the object of the arrogant eye: we have broken and trained other lifeforms—domestic, farm, and zoo animals—to do our will and have perceived the forests, air and water, plants and oceans as existing solely for our benefit. The natural world with its lifeforms has not been seen as having its health and integrity in itself, for itself, but rather in and for us. We can scarcely imagine what it would mean for nature to be considered Other in the sense of being independent of and indifferent to human interests and desires. We Westerners all perceive with the arrogant eye. If you doubt this, answer the following question: How important would creation be if we were not part of it? Can we honestly say, "It is good!" and mean it? Don't we always implicitly believe that it would be considerably less good without us, in fact, perhaps not much good? We never ask of another human being, "What are you good for?" but we often ask that question of other lifeforms and entities in nature. The assumed answer is, in one form or another, "good for me and other human beings."

The loving eye, on the other hand, acknowledges complexity, mystery, and difference. It recognizes that boundaries exist between the self and the other, that the interests of other persons (and the natural world) are not identical with one's own, that knowing another takes time and attention. In Frye's words, "It is the eye of one who knows that to know the seen, one must consult something other than one's own interests and fears and imagination. One must look at the thing. One must look and listen and check and question. . . . It knows the complexity of the other as something which will forever present new things to be known. The science of the loving eye would favor The Complexity Theory of Truth and presuppose The Endless Interestingness of the Universe."[19]

The loving eye is not the opposite of the arrogant eye: it does not substitute self-denial, romantic fusion, and subservience for distance, objectification, and exploitation. Rather it suggests something novel in Western ways of knowing: acknowledgment of and respect for the other as *subject*.

Rather than the classic relationship between knower and known as subject versus object, the model here is two subjects: what I see is another subject (like me in some ways). What I know is another being with its own integrity and interests—and this model is extended to the natural world and its lifeforms. In other words, rather than the standard paradigm for knowledge being subject-object (with myself as subject and all others, including other human beings, as objects), we are suggesting two subjects. Feminist philosopher Lorraine Code puts it this way: "It is surely no more preposterous to argue that people should try to know physical objects in the nuanced way that they know their friends than it is to argue that they should try to know people in the unsubtle way that they claim to know physical objects."[20] This seemingly slight perceptual shift can have enormous implications. It means that the route to knowledge is slow, open, full of surprises, interactive and reciprocal, as well as attentive to detail and difference. And it will be embodied. The disembodied, distant, transcendent, simplifying, objectifying, quick and easy arrogant eye becomes the embodied, lowly, immanent, complexifying, subjectifying, proximate, and "make-do" loving eye. The pure mind's eye becomes the messy body's eye, and those lowly senses (the so-called female ones of taste, touch, and smell) are allowed back into the knowledge game.

In the West, however, knowledge has been associated almost exclusively with sight and since Plato sight has been associated with the mind (as in "the eye of the mind").[21] This kind of vision discovers truth by recognizing likenesses—universals—and by dissociating itself from the messiness, complexity, and teeming differences of the body and the earth. This view of sight connects truth with what transcends the earth: we can see the more universal and hence "truer" truth the further we are from the bodily. For this kind of truth, we need the God's eye view, the angelic view: we must objectify in order to simplify, we must distance ourselves in order to see the big picture. Recall the whole-earth image: we can see the whole object only from a great distance; and it is then easy to say high-sounding things about the earth, for instance, that it is a beautiful Christmas ornament. Of course, such statements have little to do with the actual mind-boggling unknown or little-known mud-and-guts complexity of the planet's lifesystems, let alone the baffling mystery of even one of its lifeforms, from an earthworm to a human being.

A very different kind of vision from the so-called God's eye view is suggested by the phrase "locking eyes." Imagine shifting your vision from the picture of the whole earth to the eyes of another person—not to look at him or her, but into their eyes. Sight is not necessarily the eye of the mind; it can also be the eye of the body—in fact, it rightly and properly is. When we lock eyes something happens: we become two subjects, not subject and object. Locking eyes is perhaps the ultimate subject-subject experience: it is what lovers do and what nursing mothers do with their babies. A version of it can happen with other animals, especially the eerie experience of locking eyes with a lowland gorilla or chimpanzee at a zoo. It is possible even with a tree or plant. It all depends on whether we can "see without staring."[22] The loving eye, paying attention to another (another person, animal, tree, plant, whatever) is not staring; it is, in Martin Buber's suggestive phrase, relating to the other more like a Thou than an It. There is nothing sentimental or weak-minded about this: it is simply a refusal to assume that subjectivity is my sole prerogative. Iris Murdoch puts it bluntly, "Love is the extremely difficult realization that something other than oneself is real. Love . . . is the discovery of reality."[23] The loving eye is not the sentimental, mushy, soft eye; rather, it is the realistic, tough, no-nonsense eye, acknowledging what is so difficult for us to recognize: that reality is made up of *others*. Love, then, is no big deal or a specific virtue reserved for Christians; it is simply facing facts. It is, in a nice twist, being "objective."

But as we all know, this is not what objectivity usually means. In fact, just the opposite. It has been reserved for the mind's eye, the distant eye, the arrogant eye, the eye that can objectify the world. This eye lies behind the Western scientific understanding of objectivity. From the time of René Descartes on, science has advanced on the assumption that what is known is passive and inert, laid out before the subject so it can be reduced to its smallest parts, studied exhaustively, and thereby known. As Hans Jonas puts it, "I see without the object's doing anything . . . I have nothing to do but to look and the object is not affected by that . . . and I am not affected. . . . The gain is the concept of objectivity."[24] Feminists and others have criticized this view of objectivity, seeing it as a mask for Western male privilege as well as for technological exploitation of women and nature.[25]

The Subject-Subjects Model

What is the alternative? There may well be more than one, but an intriguing possibility is the suggestion from feminists, ecologists, process philosophers, phenomenologists, and others that we pattern our knowledge, all knowledge, on a subject-to-subjects model, and more specifically, on friendship. This will involve the eye—the loving eye—but also the other senses, for it moves the eye from the mind (and the heavens) to the body (and the earth). It will result in an embodied kind of knowledge of other subjects who, like ourselves, occupy specific bodies in specific locations on this messy, muddy, wonderful, complex, mysterious earth.

But appreciation for the particular and concrete is not the way I began my acquaintance with the natural world. I am going to become autobiographical now, using my own experience with nature to illustrate how I've come to believe a Christian should love nature: as subject to subject, on the analogy of friendship. My love for nature began when I was fourteen years old, hiking in the White Mountains in Vermont. I was not captive to the Western Platonic-Cartesian-scientific subject-object dualism (of which I was blissfully unaware) that I and other feminists have criticized. Just the opposite: I wallowed in oceanic feelings of oneness-with-it-all. I fused with nature: lying on mountaintops covered with billowing clouds, I sank into Wagnerian religious raptures. The New England transcendental poets were my favorites—I could sense Ralph Waldo Emerson's "oversoul" enveloping me as I relaxed into the arms of Mother Nature. I was one with nature. As a critic of deep ecology (a sensibility close to mine at that time) writes: "The correct metaphor for such fusion is of a lonely but megalomaniacal pond sucking up all the water of the world and becoming itself the ocean."[26] Indeed. I was not relating to nature as subject to subject but as the one and only Subject: I was the whole, the only one.

Gradually, over the years, I changed. I became "Elleryfied," interested in detail, in difference. I learned the names of some birds and wildflowers—a study that encourages paying attention to what is other than oneself. In fact, you can't identify a bird or a flower unless you pay close attention to detail. Such a simple desire as wanting to know the names of things is an opening to other attitudes toward the natural world. One day while hiking, I recall coming across a bi-footed, tri-colored violet, a rare and extraordinarily beautiful, tiny flower. It was all alone by the side of the trail. I had never seen one before. I squatted down to look at it closely and for a few minutes it was my whole world. I was transfixed by its beauty, its specialness, its fragility, and by the sense of privilege I felt to be looking at it. I was, I believe, seeing it as a subject; that is, I was relating to it with a recognition of its own intrinsic value quite apart from me. I was surprised and delighted by it and felt respect for it as well as a desire to care for it (in fact, I thought of putting some rocks around it to protect it from a careless hiker's boot, but decided this was too controlling). The violet was not a subject in the way you or I or one of the higher mammals is, but I could recognize its otherness and yet at the same time feel a connection with it. It was not simply an object to me. Rather, it had its own very special being, which surprised and delighted me even as I appreciated and felt empathy and concern for it. Which analogy is more appropriate for describing this experience—a subject viewing an object or a subject trying to know another subject?

Lorraine Code calls the subject-subjects analogy an ecological model of knowing because it assumes that we always know *in* relationships: we are not solitary individuals who choose to be in relationship with others, but we *are* in relationships, from before our birth until after our death.[27] Hence, the language of relationship—respect, reciprocity, interest in the particular, listening, openness, paying attention, care, concern—all this sort of language becomes relevant to how we know others. The way we come to know another, for instance a friend, becomes a model for ecological knowledge: it is a practical knowledge with the goal of responding to the other in terms of their own well-being. We want to know them better so we can empathize with and care for them more appropriately. It is a more-or-less knowledge, based on hints and nuances, open to surprises and changes, and infinitely more complex than knowing an object. Feminists have come to realize that knowing other women, especially across racial lines, involves this sort of thing—recognizing that the other must be taken as a subject in all her own irreducible particularity and difference. Knowledge of an African-American woman by a white woman, for instance, is proximate and always open to revision, because it is a practical knowledge, concerned first of all not with a theory about the other but with her concrete well-being.

To sum up: we have been asking how a Christian should love nature and have suggested that practicing the loving eye, that is, recognizing the reality of things apart from the self and appreciating them in their specialness and distinctiveness, is a critical first step. It is opposed to the arrogant eye, the objectifying, manipulative, and disengaged kind of knowledge that supposes that I am the only subject and the rest of reality merely an object for me or against me. We have suggested further that a helpful way to think about knowledge with the loving eye is in terms of a subject knowing another subject, especially on the analogy of friendship.

There are several things to note about this model. First of all, it is not the reverse of the subject-object model, but a *different* model. The subject-object model assumes a hierarchical dualism of one over another. It is the basic pattern for a number of other common hierarchical dualisms: male/female, whites/people of color, rich/poor, heterosexual/homosexual, West/East, North/South—and humans/nature. One solution proposed for this problematic pattern is to reverse it (female/male or nature/humans), but the difficulty here is that the domination intrinsic to this way of thinking continues. The arrogant eye remains; it simply becomes someone else's. The model we are suggesting is a different one, not the old one reversed. It is a relational model derived from the evolutionary, ecological picture of reality, a picture that underscores both radical unity *and* radical individuality. It suggests a different basic sensibility for *all* our knowing and doing and a different *kind* of knowing and doing, whether with other people or other lifeforms. It is a different posture and presence in the world, in all aspects of the world. It says: "I am a subject and live in a world of many other different subjects."

The second thing to note about this model is that what I know is *many* subjects. The model is not subject-subject, replacing the singular object with a singular subject, but subject-subject*s*. The other is a multitude, a myriad of subjects. If the other were one subject, we could know all subjects by knowing just one—all others would be forms or reflections of the one basic or universal subject. Presumably this would be the human subject with all other subjects simply variations of it. But just as feminists have insisted that there is no essential human being, no one type which can stand for all, so also we must insist that there is no one, essential subject that I know. In the subject-subjects model, I know a *world* of subjects, different subjects.

The third thing to note, then, is the *differences* among subjects. We have praised difference as our planet's glory (the heart of the daffodil, the color purple, the uniqueness of each human face), but difference also means that we will not respond to all subjects in the same way. The AIDS virus, just like a wood tick, is a subject in its own world. This does not mean, however, that when it attacks my body I should honor it or allow it to have its way. I should fight it (if "natural" can ever be used literally, it would be of such a response). The subject-subjects model could, however, in this case, help me see that the virus is not against me; as a subject, it is simply "doing its thing" in its own world. The model would help me to avoid seeing it as punishment: the world is not organized around me, for my benefit *or* my punishment. In an unbelievably complex world of billions of subjects, the sole criterion cannot be what is "good for me." In this instance, then, the model would operate to neutralize demonizing fantasies.

Chickens being raised for human consumption in inhumane conditions present a different level of subject, and my response would be different. In the subject-subjects model I might decide that the cruelty involved in commercial chicken farming is such that I will not eat chicken. Another possible response is to eat only free-range chickens or to work for legislation to improve the conditions under which chickens are raised. Vegetarianism is also an option, but not the only one (Native American traditions that have related to animals as subjects have also condoned hunting and meat eating).

Care or Rights?

What is beginning to emerge from the subject-subjects model is a clue for an environmental ethic of care. At the present time, a lively debate among environmentalists concerns a "rights" versus a "care"

ethic. A rights ethic seeks to extend the rights accorded to human
beings since the Enlightenment—the right to "life, liberty, and the
pursuit of happiness"—to all animals and even forests, oceans, and
other elements of the ecosystem. A rights ethic functions on the
model of the solitary human individual (originally the landed,
white, Western male); it details what one such person owes to another similar one. This ethic is beset with a number of problems when
applied to the natural world (although as we will see in chapter 7, it
has a place within a care ethic). Does the lamb or the wolf have the
right to survive—does the wolf have the right to eat the lamb for dinner, or does the lamb have the right to protection against the wolf's
needs? Can such an ethic address the complex issue of biodiversity
or only the more simple one of individual animal rights? Is it an
appropriate and helpful one for the natural world, given its human,
individualistic base?

A care ethic, on the other hand, is based on the model of subjects
in relationship, although the subjects are not necessarily all human
ones and the burden of ethical responsibility can fall unequally. The
language of care—interest, concern, respect, nurture, paying attention, empathy, relationality—seems more appropriate for human
interaction with the natural world, for engendering helpful attitudes
toward the environment, than does the rights language. As with
friends, we come to know and love the natural world with an open
and inquiring mind, trying to discern what will be best for its health
and well-being. Often there is no easy answer, for it is seldom so
clean a matter as one creature's rights over against another's.

A case in point: logging companies engaged in clear-cutting old-
growth forests replant the areas with a monoculture—a single
species of fast-growing tree—claiming they are restoring what they
have removed. Thus, they have presumably respected the right of the
forest to survive. However, these monoculture forests are not only
vulnerable to fire and blight, but they lack the rich, complex diverse
insect, bird, and mammal life as well as underbrush and underground root systems of a natural forest with its many different kinds
of trees. In fact, they are not forests at all, but plantations of single-
species trees. The appropriate ethic in this instance is not one of
rights but of care—paying attention to what truly constitutes forests
and then providing the conditions to maintain and restore them; for
instance, selective tree cutting for intact forests and reseeding for
biodiversity in clear-cut areas.

But is all of this *Christian*? What makes the subject-subjects model a Christian option? Is it commensurate with the radical, destabilizing, inclusive love of Jesus? It appears to be, for Jesus is reputed to have made the classic subject-subjects statement when he said, "Love your enemies." Treat the person who is against you, perhaps even out to kill you, as a subject, as someone deserving respect and care, as the Good Samaritan treated his enemy in need. The subject-subjects model is counter-cultural: it is opposed to the religion of Economism, to utilitarian thinking, to seeing the world as for me or against me. So is Christianity. Christianity is distinctly opposed to the subject-object way of thinking, to the arrogant eye. If Jesus could say, "Love your enemies," surely he would find the much milder statement, "Love nature," perfectly acceptable. If enemies are to be shown respect and care, should not other lifeforms also, as well as the habitats that support them? Loving nature this way, not with mushy feeling or charity, but with respect for its otherness, its Thouness, and with a desire to care for it, will not be easy. But loving other humans, especially enemies, is not either. Christianity is not an easy religion. As counter-cultural, it will make outrageous demands, like "Love your enemies" and "Love nature."

Map or Hike?

So what does all this come to? How should we relate to the natural world? More like to another subject than to an object, and to a subject, many subjects, who are very different from ourselves. This is extremely difficult. We can learn how difficult by looking at the analogy of how feminists came to realize that there is no such thing as wom*an*, but only wom*en*. Early in the feminist movement, white, North American, middle-class women glibly used the phrase "as a woman"; later, they came to recognize that "as a woman" was a mask for their own particular, racial, sexual orientation, or class version of what it means to be a woman. To understand what very different women in various other social locations experience, white North American, middle-class women would have to become, as Maria Lugones puts it, "world-travelers," or as Elizabeth Spelman suggests, "apprentices."[28] In other words, they would have to give up the center, admit ignorance, pack their bags, and go on a journey, a journey that would require them to listen and pay attention to others. It is not enough to imagine how women in very different circumstances might experience their lives; rather, one must learn about the lives of these different subjects much as a traveler learns her way around in a

foreign country or as an apprentice studies with an expert crafts-
person. Might we need to do something similar with nature—that
is, to consider ourselves travelers in the world of nature we do not
know, apprentices who need to listen to the others in that world?

An example might help. Anne Sellar, a British feminist who spent
six months teaching at an Indian university, hoped to instill feminist
theory into the minds of her women students.[29] Instead, she learned
from them about their lives, for their notions of family, feminism,
and patriarchy were radically different from hers—not to mention
the importance of dowries and of instructing village women about
infant diarrhea. Nothing was more important to these women than
family; and feminism was a bad word, symbolizing all they disliked
about Western civilization—individualism, sexual promiscuity, and
loss of femininity. Sellar became a world-traveler and an apprentice:
she said she went to India with a map—a theory of how to teach the
women about feminism—but ended up taking a hike, learning by
paying attention to the lay of the land, ready for discoveries around
the next bend in the trail, realizing that she was in an unknown place
without a map, one that would require the full engagement of all her
senses and skills.

Map or hike? Which metaphor is the better one for our relationship with the natural world? We have depended heavily on the map
metaphor, for we believe we *know* what nature is. As Thomas Berry
says, nature has become resource, recreation, or retreat for human
beings: it supplies our needs, gives us a place to play, and refreshes us
spiritually. But what if we saw it more like a different subject, one vast-
ly different from ourselves with infinite particular entities and
strange, wonderful lifeforms? What if we saw nature as "a world of difference"?[30] Then we might realize that we have to take a hike (without a map), become world-travelers, become apprentices to nature.

In other words, imagination is thin compared to the perception of
other persons and real things. What we imagine a person or entity in
nature to be cannot begin to compare with the depth, richness, detail,
and complexity of the simplest object—even the heart of a daffodil,
let alone another person. Looking at the world with full attention—
any bit of it—should stun us, leaving us amazed and wanting to know
more. We come to value the world and want it to prosper through
local, particular knowledge, for the world as it is is more amazing,
more interesting, than any theory or image about it. If we practiced
this sort of attention we might come to say with Annie Dillard, "My
God what a world. There is no accounting for one second of it."[31]

To return to the autobiographical and to conclude: I have found that the route to some of these insights is through paying attention to the particular, to what is, as it were, in one's own path—as, for instance, a bi-footed, tri-colored violet. Anything will do, as Ellery, the twenty-five cent goldfish, illustrates. In fact, the smaller the better in some respects. A little city park is probably a better place for one's lessons than the Grand Canyon. I took my last sabbatical in Vancouver, British Columbia, and every morning walked in a small city park—Jericho Park, an area of a few acres beside the bay. I came to know it very well. It has a duck pond and small wooded section. It also has lots of rabbits (probably unwanted released Easter bunnies), several kinds of ducks, many species of birds (including red-winged blackbirds), blue and purple lupines in the summer as well as blackberries, and even an occasional Great Blue Heron, raccoon, and red-necked pheasant. I always felt interest and even some excitement when I started out, because the sky and clouds varied every day, and I never knew what animals I might see. I came to love this small plot of land: its familiarity and its daily concrete, particular delights combined to make me feel at home there. My knowledge of the park was certainly not a mind's eye experience; rather, it was a body's eye one—my eyes reveled in the scurrying of a rabbit only a few feet away, the glory of a field of fuchsia sweetpeas, the sight of a heron resting on one leg. And knowledge of this park involved my other senses as well—the smell of the salt water, the sound of bird calls, the touch of a flower's petal. These are the embodied senses, the ones that remind us that we are involved and open in our knowing: we cannot touch without being touched, or hear without listening to what comes to us. The initiative is not just ours. As I walked in this little park, soaking up its sounds and smells and sights, I came to know it—and love it—more or less as I would a friend.

But why bother with such unimportant, autobiographical, personal stories? What possible relevance can such idiosyncratic and seemingly minor incidents have for the well-being of a planet that is falling to pieces? Isn't this sort of caring for a small bit of the earth just sentimentality? Shouldn't Christians love nature in terms of the global picture—be concerned about the ozone layer, the rainforests, the greenhouse effect? Shouldn't we love the "whole earth" rather than Jericho Park? Yes, surely, but there is a connection here; in fact, a critical one. No one, I believe, loves the whole earth except as she or he loves a particular bit of it. It is more likely, I suspect, that loving Ellery or Jericho Park—appreciating, respecting, and caring for them—will move one to care for the whole earth, than admiring the NASA image will generate the energy and concern to save Ellery and Jericho Park.

Here are a few thoughts along these lines from some wise people. From Alice Walker:

> Helped are those who find the courage to do at least one small thing each day to help the existence of another—plant, animal, river, human being. They shall be joined by a multitude of the timid.[32]

From the Veda:

> O God, scatterer of ignorance and darkness,
>   grant me your strength.
> May all beings regard me with the eye of a friend,
>   and I all beings!
> With the eye of a friend may each single being regard
>   all others.[33]

And from Rabbi Abraham Heschel:

> Just to be is a blessing.
> Just to live is holy.[34]

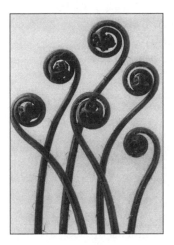

3

Christians and
Nature

Past and Present

WITH A SKETCH IN HAND OF HOW CHRISTIANS should love nature, we now turn to a historical overview of Christians and nature in order to situate our model in relation to other options. In our search for a way to be super, natural Christians in our time, three kinds of relationships between Christians and nature are especially relevant: the medieval, the Enlightenment, and the ecological. While these relationships emerged in particular historical times, they are also types that will help us see various basic patterns for human-nature relationships. The *medieval* model is important because it illustrates a successful subject-subjects relation between Christians and nature in the past; the *Enlightenment* because it shows the deterioration of the medieval view and the consequences of that loss; the *ecological* because it suggests the renewal of a subject-subjects relation but one significantly different from the medieval pattern. In the following reflections we will weave in and out of these three models, noting the values and the problems with each in an attempt to deepen our awareness of what a super, natural Christian might look like at the turn of the millennium. We will begin with some general reflections on the human-nature relationship during the past few hundred years, a relationship that began in the Enlightenment and is new in history. We will then, in broad strokes, compare and contrast the medieval and ecological worldviews, before moving on in the next section to a case study of the medieval picture of reality that will help us develop a functional cosmology for our own time. Finally, we will reflect on how difficult this task will be, given the many ways in which we have lost deep, daily connections with the natural world. Throughout these reflections on the medieval, Enlightenment, and ecological models, we must remain aware that all typologies are partial and limited.

Is Nature like Us?

Strange as it may seem, it is only during the last few hundred years that human beings have considered nature more like an object than like another subject. For most of human history we have believed that nature is more like us than we are like it. In other words, we have anthropomorphized nature, seen it as alive, changing, intentional, and influencing us as we in turn influence it. We have seen nature, both as a whole (Mother Nature) and in particular (individual animals and plants) more like us than unlike us. This does not mean that people in other times always or usually treated the natural world with respect and care as they would another subject. Sometimes they did (as Native cultures testify), but often they saw the natural world as fearful, dangerous, and full of evil intent toward human beings. But whether they saw it as friend or foe, they considered it alive: it was a subject with a being and purposes independent of human usefulness. Nature was not merely a natural resource for human gain. A radical shift in Western perception, a shift that included how we see other people as well as the natural world, began during the scientific revolution of the seventeenth century and continues to our day. This shift is one of objectification of everything, including human beings. For instance, it allows present-day multinational corporations to speak of workers as "human resources" and to hunt for the lowest-salaried human resources worldwide. The common expressions "natural resources" and "human resources" reveal the objectifying sensibility that characterizes our time. What matters is the bottom line. Capitalism of the 1990s, freed from the "soft-headedness" of liberalism (as well as the "gross errors" of socialism), has made no pretensions toward providing workers with a living wage, medical insurance, or pensions. People, like trees, cattle, wheat, or minerals, are, from a business point of view, merely means of increasing production. Hence part-time jobs with no benefits and no assurance of continuation are seen as acceptable and appropriate by business. The fact that people cannot live on such wages (or even on full-time employment at minimum wage) is not at issue.

But it would be an issue if our economy considered people to be subjects and not merely objects. In fact, the shift to seeing workers as subjects would be revolutionary—a revolution exceeded only by seeing nature (i.e., "natural resources") in terms of subjecthood. One can scarcely imagine such a revolution: Economism and the consumer society would die overnight. An entirely different set of values would emerge; for instance, quality of life would be primary, not the quantity of consumer goods. The criteria for the good life would be gauged in terms of happiness, health, and well-being—for *all* subjects. Such a society has never existed and never will; but a utopian vision is useful as a prophetic critique of what is the case (for us, an increasingly cruel capitalism) as well as a vision of what might be (a society that saw all others, people and the natural world, more like subjects than objects).[1]

The metaphors and models through which we view the world are critical: if we see human beings and nature as resources, we gain permission to treat them that way. If we see them as subjects, stretching the model to cover even plants and trees and oceans, we are more likely to treat all others, whether human or nonhuman, in a manner that respects their integrity and differences. This does not mean that we treat an ant as we do a human being, for the subject-subjects model underscores that we are related to many subjects; hence, we must relate to each differently. More on this later: the point here is simply to avoid premature scrapping of the model because it does not fit everything in the same way. The objectifying model does not either. Remember that this model reduces people to objects. Is it not preferable to elevate trees and mushrooms, the sun and the moon, ticks and tigers, to subjects? Which model will have better consequences for the lives of all? Both ways of seeing the world are just that—ways of seeing. The reduction of everything, including people, to objects is a metaphor; in other words, we make a decision to see people this way. It is not a description of "the way things are." Neither, of course, is the subject way of seeing and thinking. It, also, is a model. But why, then, is the one praised as factual, hard-headed, and objective, while the other is rejected as primitive, sentimental, and romantic? Could it be that the objectification of people and nature is convenient from an economic perspective? In terms of contemporary postmodern science, where no firm lines can be drawn between the living and the nonliving, between matter and mind, between humans and other living things, the subjects model makes as much if not more sense than its alternative. It can certainly claim to be in keeping with the picture of reality in our time. For, if we humans and the natural world are intrinsically interrelated and interdependent, if everything that we are came from our roots in nature and if we cannot live a day without the plants and the microorganisms in the sea, then "we are like it" and "it is like us." Shall we identify that intimacy by objectifying ourselves or by subjectifying nature?

Most cultures have chosen the second alternative for the simple reason that it is the commonsense choice: the assumption that human beings are *unrelated* to nature would never have occurred to most people. But it did occur to seventeenth-century philosopher René Descartes, whose famous dictum, "I think, therefore I am," located human existence in the mind. The only connection of the lofty human mind with the human body (and thus with the rest of nature) was, for Descartes, through the narrow channel of the pineal gland![2] This quaint and absurd suggestion, which a medieval peasant, a Native person, or a contemporary ecologist, would receive with hearty guffaws, was calmly accepted by the Enlightenment and became received opinion as human beings were increasingly removed from all contamination by nature.

So our culture is an anomaly. Our refusal to embrace our rootedness in nature, our refusal to work out, in terms of metaphors and models of our own time, an understanding of how we are related to nature—and to act on that understanding—makes us strange beings indeed. It is as if we saw ourselves as aliens, tourists, or strangers on our own planet. The reigning philosophy of life, the religion of Economism, takes no account of how we should fit in here on planet Earth as permanent residents, as creatures who embrace this place as home. Every successful culture, however, must do this work of developing a functional cosmology—an overall picture of the relations of humans and nature—so that people will know *how* to live appropriately with all the others who inhabit the planet.[3]

Many of the cultures that have developed functional cosmologies have been Native or so-called primitive ones. But has there been a Western, and particularly, a Christian one? Medieval culture provides an interesting case study for us because it saw human life as intricately and profoundly interrelated with all other forms of life, from the wildflowers and busy bees to the celestial bodies and the source of all life, the Divine. Everything on earth and in the heavens was a sign of something else. Everything was connected to other things through a network of correspondences that painted the world as a cryptogram to be interpreted. Everything had meaning; everything, from the lowliest weed to the most distant planet, was alive with significance. Everything was a way to God or a moral on how to live the good life.[4] The modern mentality dismisses this as superstition, as the basis for astrology and alchemy, as pre-scientific naiveté, but it functioned to situate human beings *in a world, in nature,* in a historical and natural realm created and governed by God, that provided guidelines for daily praxis. Can we say as much for our reigning philosophy?

We turn now to a comparison of the medieval and ecological worldviews in order to lay the groundwork for a more detailed case study of the medieval picture.

Medieval vs. Ecological Relationality

The medieval picture was a sacred world order uniting God, human beings, and nature into a coherent whole through a complex network of interconnections. Things held together—*all* things. Human beings lived in an orderly universe created and controlled by God in which each creature had its place—even if that place was less than desirable. Each entity, living and nonliving, was connected to the others through an intricate system of signs, symbols, allegories, myths, and analogies. Nothing was just itself: everything signified one or more things beyond itself, either God or other creatures. The human being was the privileged place where all analogies met—the link between heaven and earth—as Michel Foucault vividly describes:

> This point is man: he stands in proportion to the heavens, just as he does to animals and plants, and as he does also to the earth, to metals, to stalactites or storms. Upright between the surfaces of the universe, he stands in relation to the firmament (his face is to his body what the face of heaven is to the ether; his pulse beats in his veins as the stars circle the sky according to their own fixed paths; the seven orifices in his head are to his face what the planets are to the sky); but he is also the fulcrum upon which all the relations turn, so that we find them again, their similarity unimpaired, in the analogy of the human animal to the earth it inhabits: his flesh is a glebe, his bones are rocks, his veins great rivers, his bladder is the sea, and his seven principal organs are the metals hidden in the shafts of mines. Man's body is always the possible half of a universal atlas.[5]

The medieval picture of the world was structured on a vertical grid of decreasing value: God was at the top (in heaven), followed by the angels who inhabited the range between heaven and earth, with human beings (men first, women second) the dominant creatures on earth, for whom the rest, other animals and plants, had been created. The underworld, the realm of the devil, awaited the damned. Each creature was supposed to keep in its place, an ordering that extended to all facets of life: ecclesiastical (the pope and clergy over the laity, the church over the secular realm); governmental (kings and lords over commoners); familial (fathers over mothers and children).

This crude sketch of a hierarchical, patriarchal, and dualistic picture does not begin to suggest the many, subtle forms of connection between and among the divine, human, and natural realms that were current in medieval life. It is those connections—which we will investigate in the next section—that are the heart of the matter for they provide the rich, lived-in character to the medieval world that makes it so attractive. The significant point for our concerns—how the Middle Ages might be a case study in subject-subjects thinking—is that this world, whatever its faults (and they were many), *held together*. It offered a home, an ordered and inclusive reality, to its inhabitants. One could say that it offered a "homey" universe, as woodcuts and paintings of the period suggest: an enclosed, dome-like heaven or roof, a solid ground for the main floor—earth—and a basement, the nether regions of hell. Human beings, plants, and animals fitted cozily into this house, a house that was solid and simple while at the same time fascinatingly diverse, rich with myths and stories, allegories and symbols, meanings and associations, correspondences and interdependencies, attachments and relationships. The glue between and among all its parts, from the tiniest to the greatest, *held*. That is, it did until the seventeenth century. The agony felt at the break-up of this worldview was profound. The Copernican revolution was not simply a scientific issue; it was a deeply personal and religious one. If the earth was not the center of the universe, then human beings might not be the crown of creation and the fulcrum of all the signs and correspondences that linked heaven and earth. John Donne, seventeenth-century poet and cleric, expresses this agony, this loss of a world that worked, with his lament,

> 'Tis all in pieces, all cohaerence gone;
> All just supply, and all Relations.

"The world's whole frame" Donne finds to be "quite out of joynt."[6]

The harmony, proportion, and stability that characterized the medieval picture was breaking up, never to be regained.

While this unified world order is not credible to most of us today, there is another kind of radical relationality and interconnection among all things that is possible for us: ecological interdependence. It has many of the benefits of the medieval sacred order, for it is, as that was, a functional cosmology. But it is a more appropriate one for our time, because it is in keeping with the contemporary scientific picture of reality. Moreover, and of great importance, it is a kind of relationality that underscores not only unity, as the medieval pictures does, but also individuality and difference. The six million leaves on a big elm tree are each toothed, and these toothed leaves are also toothed—all differently—*and* the six million individual leaves survive only through being united by means of an intricate network of ducts, veins, capillaries, and roots as well as an extended underground set of connections with other life forms. It is hard to imagine individuality and unity in a more radical way. The medieval understanding of unity did not preserve individuality as well. It was based on a symbolic ontology: the assumption that all things participate in the ground of being and hence symbolize one another due to ontological similarities.[7] While this worldview brought everything together into an ordered whole, it tended to subsume the lesser under the greater: the things of this world were either symbols of divine presence or created to benefit human beings, as in the case of the plants and other animals. While there were tendencies to the contrary as we shall see, medieval sacramentalism did not, for the most part, underscore *the intrinsic value of things.*

Ecological interdependence, however, does not rest on a symbolic ontology. Rather, it is closer to a metaphorical understanding of connection: things are and are *not* similar, with the emphasis on the latter, on the surprise and delight in the ways things are nonetheless connected when they seem so disparate. Symbol underscores unity; metaphor, difference. The "ecological shock of recognition" is for many of us today, including myself, the astonishment of realizing that I am, at some remote time in the past, related to a deer, an oak leaf, and to the stars, while I am nevertheless and decidedly also myself, in all my ineradicable difference from everything else. The medieval sensibility, based on a participative, hierarchical ontology (everything is related to everything else by participation in Being-itself), felt the immediacy and power of *connection,* the oneness among all things, making for a sense of harmony and proportion among all parts of the order. The postmodern sensibility, however, wary of any ontology and conscious of alienation, disjunction, and difference, nonetheless may be able to respond with interest and hope to intimations of deep connectedness when these are made taking into account the No, the fang and the claw, the accidental and outrageous, the Holocaust and Hiroshima. Ecological interdependence, built upon evolutionary theory, takes full account of the negativities of existence; in fact, some see it as nothing but an advertisement for the survival of the fittest and the accidental, arbitrary character of existence. It also proclaims, however, a view of kinship, interdependence, and relationality so radical that we can speak, metaphorically, of the earth as the common mother of all that exists on our planet.

Our sacred world order cannot be the medieval one. It must protest the sense of continuity and connection, optimism and harmony, the subservience of the many to the one, the gradations of being and power, implicit in the medieval sacramental order. It must, in a sense, be more "Protestant" while at the same time remaining "Catholic." "Protestant" here stands for the disjunctive, divided, skeptical, postmodern mind-set that sees difference and difficulties wherever it turns. "Catholic" here stands for the wish, nonetheless, for connection, continuity, and coherence, that sees possibilities and prospects wherever it looks.[8] Needless to say, either of these mind-sets can exist in actual Catholics and Protestants; and both can exist in the same person or culture—and I believe they should. Our thesis is that the Catholic sensibility is greatly to be desired; that its insistence on a sacred world order is right and needed but that such an order must be one that satisfies the steely-eyed Protestant head-shaking at how bad things really are and how different things are. The Catholic sensibility celebrates creation; the Protestant sensibility is astonished that, in spite of differences, decay, and death, there is *nonetheless* creation—and we all belong within it. The Catholic sensibility is symbolic, seeing connections, similarities, and unity among all parts of the whole; the Protestant sensibility is metaphorical, seeing differences, divergencies, and deterioration but *also* surprising and profound relations. The Catholic sensibility recognizes another as subject because it is like me; the Protestant sensibility accepts another as subject in spite of being different from me.

So, is nature like us? Yes and no. It is like us in being a subject (actually, billions of subjects), but unlike us in innumerable particular ways. The so-called primitive urge to anthropomorphize nature is a correct one—nature has its own forms of subjecthood—but that urge must not lose sight of the real differences among subjects. If human beings are different in their concrete, embodied contexts and circumstances, nature's billions are much more so. The celebration of difference—*Vive la différence!*—is the corrective that an ecological interdependence will suggest to the medieval sacred order.

The Medieval Picture

Let us now look more closely at the medieval world as a case study: what might we learn from its version of the subject-subjects model? As we begin this study, we need to recall the dualistic, hierarchical, static, and deterministic character of the medieval view: we are by no means suggesting it as a picture to which we can return. The Great Chain of Being at the heart of the medieval picture, with God at the top as the transcendent Determiner of Destiny and all creatures arranged in descending order—angels, men, women, children, animals, plants, matter—is antithetical to an ecological and feminist perspective. The medieval solution cannot be ours; rather, what it suggests is that we must do *for our time* what that picture did for its time—namely, to work out a functional cosmology. But it has much to teach us.

The culture of the Middle Ages was extroverted, not introverted; people looked outward to find signs of God in nature, rather than inward to find the divine within themselves.[9] Whereas Augustine says in his *Confessions* that his world consists of just his own soul and God, the medievals saw a rich, incredibly complex world outside of themselves, every fragment of which was a significant symbol or allegory of God. Hildegard of Bingen, writing in the twelfth century and recently resurrected by feminists and ecologists for her creation spirituality, was in her own time a noted systematic theologian. Her work is typical of the medieval extroverted sensibility, which saw correspondences among all aspects of human, natural, and divine reality.[10] Her vision of the creation of the universe as an egg surrounded by fire, whirlwinds, thunder, and ether becomes the occasion for an exhaustive exegesis of the many ways that "the visible and temporal is a manifestation of the invisible and eternal."[11] Hildegard goes through her vision phrase by phrase, telling the reader how each visible aspect of it stands for an invisible divine reality. The brilliant sun signifies divine justice that illuminates all creatures; the three torches that hold up the globe are the Trinity; the ascent of the sun each day suggests the uplifting of the human race through the incarnation; the descent of the sun signifies the great miseries that the Son of God suffered on our behalf; the whirlwinds surrounding the universe egg show that the truth of the Almighty God rushes into and fills up the whole world. And so on through visions covering every conceivable aspect of the world and its divine significance. At the heart of the entire cosmology is the human being. Hildegard sees the "sandy globe" of the earth as the center of the universe, placed there in order to signify the centrality of human beings, the focus of all the signs and meanings of creation. "This openly shows that, of all the strengths of God's creation, Man's is most profound, made in a wondrous way with great glory from the dust of the earth and so entangled with the strengths of the rest of creation that he can never be separated from them; for the elements of the world, created for Man's service, wait on him, and Man, enthroned as it were in their midst, by divine disposition presides over them. . . ."[12]

We can scarcely imagine living in such a world, living with nature as a subject ordained by God for our enlightenment, a living creation that "must be read like a book, not dismantled like a machine."[13] In this subject-subjects model, nature as a whole as well as particular, individual creatures certainly do not have intrinsic value: they are not subjects in their own right. Medieval people did not pay attention to nature in order to care for it better, nor did they have a romantic desire to bond with it. On the contrary, nature for them had a higher calling—in fact, the highest calling. Like the Bible, it was a book, the book of nature, which humans were to learn to read rightly in order to find their way to God.[14] But the natural world was certainly not an object either; it was not a commodity that people could use and destroy at will. Rather, it was a way God had chosen to lead humans into the divine presence. Thus, its subjectivity, its *persona*, its particular individuality in whole and in its parts, was symbolic: *it signified God for humans.* While we might see this as highly anthropocentric (as well as anthropomorphic), it nonetheless meant that nature was a subject of great importance to human beings. If the way to God was an extroverted, not an introverted, way, then human beings had to look outside themselves to nature in order to find God. If the way to God demanded reading these natural signs rightly, then one had to pay attention to nature in order to get the meanings right. In other words, one had to live *in* nature and *with* nature: the relationship was a close one and a very important one.[15]

But how was this manifest among ordinary people? A common and an uncommon example might be illuminating. The common example is emblemism, the widespread practice of seeing animals and flowers as allegories for human enlightenment and betterment. (Grimm's fairy tales, in which animals display human virtues and vices, are one of the few remaining contemporary reminders of this practice.) Thus ants and bees, with their cooperative colonies, teach us good governance; the fox symbolizes cunning while the goat stands for lust and the lion for courage; horseflies exist to encourage us to develop our wits in order to avoid them; singing birds are created to delight us; the fly is a reminder of the shortness of life; and the glow-worm signifies the light of the Holy Spirit. "The mole symbolized the blind Papist, unable to see his own way out of error; and the caterpillar was the emblem of the Resurrection."[16] Every creature had a purpose *for us,* and ordinary medieval men and women lived close to these creatures, both literally and symbolically. The animals often occupied the same dwelling as the people and they served as a lesson book on moral and theological matters. God and God's law for humans were brought close through the animals.

The same was true with plants. Many of the most colorful names for wildflowers come from the Middle Ages. Before Linnaeus created proper Latin names for them (thus distancing ordinary people from plants), common people created a vast set of correspondences between themselves, nature, and God by means of the names given to wildflowers.[17] Some are straightforwardly religious—Christ's Ladder, Star of Bethlehem, Solomon's Seal, St. John's Wort; many connect plants to features in animals—Coltsfoot, Goatsbeard; others show correspondence with parts of the human body—Maiden's Hair, Old Man's Beard, Dead Man's Finger; or with items of clothing—Bachelor Buttons, Ladies' Slipper; some are indelicate, even a bit gross—Naked Ladies, Pissabed (Shitabed), Mare's Fart, Priest's Ballocks. In a time when plants were medicine as well as holy instruction, their importance was central. The common names suggest they were, however, not distant or "objective" forms of medicinal or divine knowledge, but close companions, which could also be the subjects of ribald humor. Human beings were, at the very least and in important ways, *attached* to plants.

A second and uncommon example of the close encounters between human beings and nature is illustrated in the remarkable life and writings of Francis of Assisi. As the patron saint of Christian environmentalism—perhaps the only one—Francis is often lifted up

as evidence that Christianity is not the ecological terror it is sometimes cast as being, that within this tradition there are other possibilities. Be that as it may, the interesting thing about Francis for our
purposes is that he suggests a step beyond emblemism, another way
to understand the subjecthood of nature. Like emblemism, Francis's
attention to things as natural symbols was a form of extroversion.[18]
He looked to the world, not to his own psyche, to find the presence
of God. But unlike emblemism, which tends to see animals and
plants entirely in terms of their usefulness for the human journey to
God, Francis had double vision—horizontal as well as vertical. His
earliest biographers indicate that while he saw things as symbols of
God, he also saw them as valuable in themselves. Thomas of Celano
writing in 1229 states that Francis "admired in everything its Author
and in all events he recognized the Creator. . . ." But Bonaventure
says that "he was filled with a greater gentleness when he thought of
the first and common origin of all beings, and he called all creatures,
no matter how small they were, by the name of brother or sister,
because he knew that they all had in common with him the same
beginning."[19]

Francis's celebrated poem praising the sun, moon, stars, wind,
water, fire, earth, and even death is not an allegory in which the elements signify something useful to humans; rather, they "sing to God
for the fact of being what they are."[20] Francis took that step, which
the emblemists did not take, of letting things *be what they are:* wind
is wind (not only the breath of the Holy Spirit) and death is death
("from whom no living man can escape").[21] Francis, of course, sees
all things as also symbols of God—the sun "gives us light" and also
"bears a likeness to You, Most High One," but his extroversion has
taken a step toward appreciating things *in themselves.*[22] In his study
of Francis as a "model of human liberation," Leonardo Boff claims
that his uniqueness lies in his novel understanding of poverty.
"Poverty is a way of being by which the individual lets things be what
they are; one refuses to dominate them, subjugate them, and make
them objects of the will to power," says Boff. "The more radical the
poverty, the closer the individual comes to reality, and the easier it is
to commune with all things, respecting and reverencing their differences and distinctions. Universal fraternity is the result of the way-
of-being-poor of Saint Francis."[23] Something very close to this
understanding of poverty is what I mean by "super, natural Christians"—the willingness to let things be, "respecting and reverencing
their differences and distinctions."

The closeness that medieval people had with nature—as a means to closeness with God—is redirected by Francis toward seeing nature as intrinsic subject. Its subjecthood was not solely a sign for us; its being was for its own sake—and as praise to God. Water, wind, sun, and stars, the entire earth and even death, are natural symbols, singing the praises of the creator *by doing their own thing*, not by being the symbol of a doctrine or a moral lesson for human beings.

Francis was certainly not the only one with double vision in the Middle Ages. Medieval sacramentalism owes its roots to the dual Greek heritage, the two traditions of Plato and Aristotle, the one focused on the otherworld and the other on this world.[24] While Plato saw nature as patterned on what lay beyond it, the eternal forms, Aristotle began the process of horizontal connections among earth's lifeforms: we were related to the plants through the nutritive soul, to the animals through the sensitive soul, and to other humans through the rational soul. Both forms of Greek thought on nature were hierarchical and potentially dualistic (for instance, Aristotle conflated the natural and the normative in his insistence that males were "naturally" superior to females). Although Augustine's Neoplatonism certainly stressed the vertical, introverted direction, Thomas Aquinas's allegiance to Aristotle qualified it with horizontal, extroverted motifs: natural law, secondary causation, grace as perfecting rather than replacing nature. Thus, a twentieth-century follower of Thomas, novelist Flannery O'Connor, came down solidly on the horizontal side of the sacramental sensibility when she answered a question on how one writes a good *religious* novel with the reply that, first of all, you have to write a *good novel*. Each and every creature and entity in the created order has its own intrinsic distinctiveness, value, and penultimate goal: it is not just good for something else, but good in itself and for itself. The Thomistic universe is a panorama filled to the brim with different reflections of divine being, each imaging that glory *in its own way*.[25] Any balanced picture of medieval sacramentalism must take the analogical character of created being very seriously; each creature has its being, its existence, in a manner appropriate *to it alone*. The world of created being is not a lump of clay; rather, it is a theater populated by individual, unique, distinct, different beings.

Nonetheless, the emphasis from the beginning appears to be on the vertical, not the horizontal, on nature as a way to God and not on the value of individual, different things and creatures. Thus, one commentator on the study of early Eastern (Irenaean) as well as

Western (Augustinian) Christianity concludes: "Nature was glorious in idea; it was demeaned in fact."[26] The interior, vertical route that starts with Augustine continues into the Reformation, especially in Martin Luther as well as into the twentieth century, epitomized in Existentialism. Nature falls into the background, serving as a backdrop or stage for God's important work: redemption. Nor did things fare much better in post-medieval Roman Catholicism. Counter-Reformation Catholicism was anti-nature, seeing divine action as limited to the supernatural, with nature as a mere foil for grace.[27] Even the greatest of the Catholic sacramental poets, Gerard Manley Hopkins, succumbs to the vertical direction. Hopkins, a nineteenth-century Jesuit, was famous for his notion of "inscape," the unique distinctiveness of each and every entity and creature. Nonetheless, he illustrates the attraction of vertical vs. horizontal sacramentalism. A close examination of his writings shows that the true inscape of all things is Christ. "Inscape" is not a natural doctrine, but an incarnational one: to the extent that a person or thing fulfills its true being, it does so only in Christ. Things and people are diverse, unique, and particular only *as* they praise God and only *in order to* praise God. Each person:

> Acts in God's eye what in God's eye he is—
> Christ. For Christ plays in ten thousand places,
> Lovely in limbs, and lovely in eyes not his
> To the Father through the features of men's faces.[28]

What is true of human beings—that in their unique particularity they reflect the divine incarnation—is true also of all natural beings: "Glory be to God for dappled things," for "whatever is fickle, freckled (who knows how?) . . . He fathers-forth what is past change: Praise him."[29] Hopkins states his position clearly: "God's utterance of himself in himself is God the Word, outside of himself is this world. Therefore its end, its purpose, its purport, its meaning, is God and its life or work to name and praise him."[30] The balance is a delicate one: how to hold onto the "things in themselves" while *also* seeing them as "news" of God? Although Hopkins veers in the direction of subsuming matter to spirit, the physical to the mystical, the natural to the supernatural, he nevertheless continued the multi-dimensionality of the medieval world: things are not just themselves—they signify more. But Hopkins was an anomaly at the close of the nineteenth century and even more of one now: few people beyond the seventeenth century had his integrated sensibility, the ability to see the natural and the supernatural worlds *together*.

The Renaissance and the rise of science collapsed those two worlds into one—into the secular world, which would mean nothing beyond itself. The most notable victim of this collapse would be nature. Nature became a mere object with no meaning or vocation beyond its utilitarian value to human beings.

The Present: Our Loss of Nature

Our world now is literalized. What was once rich in meaning, a subject responsive to many deep and sublime interpretations, becomes nothing more than an object to be analyzed, dissected, and commodified. Everything interesting, meaningful, and living moves into our minds: "I think, therefore I am"—with these fatal words, nature loses its subjecthood:

> The gloriously romantic universe of Dante and Milton that set no bounds to the imagination . . . as it played over space and time, had now been swept away. . . . The world that people had thought themselves living in—a world rich with colour and sound, redolent with fragrance, filled with gladness, love, and beauty, speaking everywhere of purposive harmony and creative ideals—was crowded now into minute corners in the brains of scattered organic beings. The . . . world outside was a world hard, cold, colourless, silent, and dead, a world of quantity, a world of mathematically computable motions of mechanical regularity.[31]

It is difficult for us to conceive the disorientation this change brought about for people living in the Renaissance: it meant, most basically, *solitude*. Whereas people in the Middle Ages had lived in a world as subjects among many subjects, animal and plant ones (as well as angelic and demonic ones, with *the* Subject, God, presiding over everything), human beings were now alone. And we still are. The difference is that we have grown used to being alone. Our ecological crisis at the close of the twentieth century is but the last stage in this long deepening of human solitude. We now live in a world in which we have eliminated all other subjects; is it, then, such a crime to get rid of their bodies?[32] Grim as this may sound, it does reflect the common modern (Newtonian) view of reality: the split between the internal, subject, human world and the exterior, object-like, natural world. The old easy commerce between the interior and the exterior, between the human and natural worlds, with both sharing similar qualities of imagination, subjectivity, purpose, and meaning (though in different ways), has long since broken down; and we are left alone, locked into our own minds. Any inkling of such qualities as evident in other creatures or natural entities is considered romantic or anthropomorphic—or worse.

As reality goes, so goes language. Since we no longer believe that nature is alive, significant, important to us, or important in itself, our language about it flattens:

> The cosmos of premodern man was multi-storied; nature was rich in symbols, its objects could be read at many levels and evoke emotion-laden response. Science by contrast strives to reduce the possibility of multiple readings. A traditional world has the ambiguity and richness of ordinary and ritual speech. The modern world, on the other hand, aspires to be transparent and literal.[33]

The language of science has become nature's language, the only language in which it is acceptable to speak about nature. Nature writing, a form of expressing one's relationship with nature—a kind of writing that is both subjective and poetic (as well as scientifically informed)—is seen as a lesser genre, not considered as really telling us about nature. The only language that can do so is one that is quantified, "objective," and assumes that the natural world can be studied exhaustively by the inductive, empirical method. With the seventeenth-century reduction of knowledge about nature to the appearance of objects, language followed suit. Whereas the Middle Ages had need of a rich symbolic language in order to track the many similarities among God, humans, and nature, after the Renaissance a literal, one-dimensional language was sufficient. Metaphor, symbol, and image were now seen as mere decoration, not as necessary in order to suggest the complex ontological connections among all levels of being.

And yet—and yet—nature will not stay put. It refuses, again and again, to obey our decision that it is "nothing but" an object, a machine, reducible to mathematical formulae and DNA. It insists on creeping into our unconsciousness and into our language. This is evident in common expressions describing nature: the way we use our own bodies to describe the world. Like our medieval forebears we see our bodies as the fulcrum of the world: where nature and humans meet—but now it is done unconsciously and with dead metaphors. We speak of the "brow" of a hill, the "eye" of a potato, the "mouth" of a river, an "arm" of the sea, the "face" of a mountain, the "flesh" of fruits, the "bowels" of the earth.[34] Do we mean anything by these dead metaphorical expressions? These common expressions are a silent and largely unconscious reminder of our loss: the loss of a relationship, our reciprocal partner in nature. Thomas Berry speaks of the color, beauty, and sounds of nature as giving human beings a language with which to praise God that we would not have if we lived on a desolate lunar landscape.[35] True enough. But without the color, beauty, and sounds of nature we do not have a rich interior life either. Many of us act as if we live in such a sterile, dead, unresponsive moonscape and scarcely measure the consequences. We do not see the natural world for what it is: the exterior to our interior, the partner in our pilgrimage, another who influences us and whom we influence.

Nature writer Barry Lopez speaks of the relationship between the exterior and the interior "landscapes," how the shape and character of one's life "are deeply influenced by where on this earth one goes, what one touches, the patterns one observes in nature. . . ."[36] He says that he is not concerned simply with facts about nature but with the relationships among the various elements in nature. The order and integrity of the exterior landscape, which can subtly affect our interior landscape, can be small or large. He offers an example of a small instance. "Perhaps a black-throated sparrow lands in a paloverde bush—the resiliency of the twig under the bird, that precise shade of yellowish-green against the milk-blue sky, the fluttering whir of the arriving sparrow, are what I mean by 'the landscape.'"[37] The influence of such a landscape is beyond our ability to express and yet, claims Lopez, over a period of time it does affect us. A larger example, the ways in which the art, architecture, metaphysics, ritual, and ethics of Native peoples are patterned after different landscapes, illustrates this phenomenon. Among indigenous people, the order of their personal and cultural worlds is derived from long, patient attention to the exterior landscape.[38] The "beauty way" of the Navajo, for instance, is "a spiritual invocation of the order of the exterior universe," which is understood to possess an integrity that is unimpeachable and beyond human analysis.[39]

I believe Lopez is right: we are influenced deeply, widely, and permanently by the exterior landscape. Children who grow up in asphalt city ghettos have a very different exterior landscape than what Lopez is speaking about. And they will be profoundly influenced by it. Moreover, they will have no clue that the natural world is a subject that both affects them and is responsive to their acts.

They will indeed live on a moonscape, with all its consequences, both for themselves and for nature.

So nature is important—important to us, however much we may deny it. We describe it with metaphors from our own bodies; it makes us feel lonely when we realize how we've isolated ourselves; it influences us subtly yet deeply in ways we scarcely know or acknowledge. Subliminally, it still has some subjectlike qualities for us. At some level, we are not sure it is just an object. The central issue is becoming clearer: can we recognize its importance *and* "let things be what they are?" In other words, can we avoid cannibalizing nature for our own purposes? Are we the only subjects, or can we seriously allow subjecthood to these others? Can we be super, natural Christians, who, in the Franciscan sense of poverty, respect and reverence all things in their differences and distinctions while seeing them also as brothers and sisters? Can we be extroverts in regard to nature, pay attention to the natural world in itself, for itself, *and also* see all things as interdependent?

This is the main question, and we are a long way from being able to give it a positive answer. Our principal difficulty is introversion: we take everything into ourselves. We can illustrate this by how we look at animals. Since animals are our closest relatives in nature, they are an important test case for our attitude toward the natural world. Once upon a time, when our species lived in caves, animals were the first subjects of human expression: the cave paintings, the earliest human attempts at symbolization, were not of other humans (or of gods) but of animals. They were our "other," our primary relation; they were the ones through whom we first reflected ourselves and reflected upon the world. It is difficult to imagine greater importance. Their importance is seen in creation stories, from early etiological ones to Charles Darwin's theory of evolution: animals were (are) the pathway to our beginnings. We came from them; we would not *be* without them. Up until the seventeenth century, as we have seen, the importance of animals was in various ways acknowledged; as both like and unlike us, they were mirrors for knowledge of ourselves.[40]

But no more. John Berger, writing about how we look at animals, mentions two places where contemporary people typically do so: at the zoo and in the home, at caged animals and pets.[41] The respectful, wary gaze of the primitive human being at the wild other, the animal who was physical sustenance as well as spiritual symbol has become the colonizing eye of the Sole Subject surveying objects under his or her control. The caged animals at the zoo are spectacles for the viewer's pleasure, similar to framed pictures at a museum. One advances from cage to cage, commenting on the cute or clever antics of the imprisoned, or expressing annoyance if they try to hide from the peeping-Tom stare. But if zoo animals are not our other, another subject worthy of our respect, neither are our pets. Americans now spend billions of dollars annually on high-grade food, first-class medical care, hotel-like boarding kennels, and elaborate funeral arrangements for their pets. Many think of them as children and treat them accordingly. But these ways of regarding them reduce them to possessions; they are not subjects in their own right. Interestingly, St. Francis did not call the sun, water, and fire his children, but brother and sister—he addressed them by the only familial terms that indicate equality. Reverence and respect for differences and distinctions demand a little distance.

A personal example will illustrate the point. I recall encountering a raccoon on one of my morning walks. It was about fifty feet away from me, foraging in a swamp. It stopped and looked up at me; I looked back. For a few moments, our eyes locked, mine with interest and pleasure, the raccoon's with wariness and perhaps mild interest. I didn't stare nor was my gaze colonizing nor parental: the raccoon was certainly not subservient to me nor was it my possession. I didn't want to cage or pat it. I felt privileged just to have the chance to look at it. As much as a wild animal in a city park could be, it was a subject in its own right. It was engaged in its own business; it could walk away from me when it chose—and in a minute, it did so. Annie Dillard writes about a similar experience with a hawk on a Galapagos island:

> The wild hawk is tame. The Galapagos hawk is related to North America's Swainson's hawk; I have read that if you take pains, you can walk up and pat it. I never tried. We people don't walk up and pat each other; enough is enough. The animal's critical distance and mine tended to coincide, so we could enjoy an easy sociability without threat of violence or unwonted intimacy.[42]

Since the seventeenth century the Western attitude toward animals has wavered between objectification and sentimentality, with zoos and pets examples of each. Both are forms of introversion: in both cases we internalize, possess, colonize these others for our own purposes. In neither case do we look at them as external to us, as subjects in their own right with desires and projects of their own. Two even more extreme cases of animal introversion are evident in the concept of "animality" (or bestiality) and Walt Disney cartoon animals: the one a negative and the other a positive form of introversion.

Animality is evident in an expression such as "drunk as a skunk." Skunks do not, in fact, get drunk—people do. But human beings have used animals as a way of dealing with what they find most repulsive *in themselves*: rampant sexuality, gluttony, violence.[43] It is only human beings who rape, overeat, and murder, but by claiming it is the animal (the beast) in us that drives us to such acts, humans can avoid responsibility. More seriously, animality has been used as a way of grading other people: blacks, primitives, infants, women, the poor, and the mad have been perceived as animalistic and hence could be treated as such. For instance, it was imperative that black slaves in the United States be perceived as animals in order to justify their enslavement.[44] The internalization of animals, the use of the concept of animality/bestiality in order to clear one's conscience or subjugate other human beings, is an extreme example—and a highly edifying one—of the objectifying zoo mentality. Animals become objects: not just objects to control in cages but also concepts for self-justification and the mistreatment of other persons. The animals themselves are no longer "other"; in fact, they have completely disappeared. They are now only thoughts in the mind, figments of the imagination.

A more positive internalization of animals, but one that also denies them their own reality, is the Disney cartoon syndrome. This syndrome includes not only television and film cartoons but the use of animals in advertising (cute animals sell products), animal picture books, petting zoos, stuffed animals, and animal calendars (the ones with mournful-eyed baby seals). All fall into the warm, fuzzy category: animals are cute, cuddly, safe, and friendly. What these have in common is depiction of animals as caricatures (cartoons) of themselves. They are projections of the human desire for connection with the other; they foster but a twisted, sentimental connection that has little relation to the real lives and needs of actual animals. They are a sad commentary on our solitude, a perverted recognition of the isolation from the planet's other subjects that we have brought upon ourselves. We now want them back, but we resurrect them in bodies and spirits of our own fantastic, sentimental projection. Occasionally one finds interesting, complex projections, such as Maurice Sendak's dark creatures of the night or the inimitable spider Charlotte, who saves Wilbur the pig, but the more common projections are Mickey Mouse, the Lion King, cuddly fleece bears, and llamas tame enough to be petted.[45]

We have been considering how we can let things be what they are in themselves while at the same time acknowledging their importance to us. Like indigenous peoples and medievals, we too should be extroverts: seeing nature as other, as a subject like and unlike us that influences us, as we also influence it. But our contemporary posture before nature is not this way—we are introverts, we internalize nature for our own purposes. To the examples of zoos, pets, animality, and caricature we can add a final, more grandiose, and peculiarly American case of introversion: the use of nature as justification for its self-image of Manifest Destiny. Whereas great nations of the past—France, England, Germany—could base their superiority on historical links to the classical cultures of Greek and Rome, America based hers on nature—the primordial, magnificent wilderness of the new world. In studies ranging from Perry Miller's picture of the American continent as the paradisaical Garden before the Fall, to Barbara Novak's depiction of American landscape painting as an "iconography of nationalism," and most recently Simon Schama's thesis that the giant sequoia trees gave the United States larger and older ruins than the Parthenon—all of these point to America's use of nature as a substitute for the history it did not have.[46] Nature *is* antiquity and its prehistoric panoramic sublimity provided the United States the optimistic, patriotic moral uplift that the young giant needed as it jockeyed for dominance with its European parents. Moreover, nature provided an egalitarian route to God: the book of nature could be read by all, giving every person direct access to the divine. Patriotism and religion joined hands to create Yosemite, our first national park: it was created in order to protect the Big Trees—*not* because they were valuable in themselves but because they were icons of America's manifest destiny. As Simon Schama notes: "It was the aura of heroic sanctity, the sense that the grove of Big Trees was some sort of living American monument. . . . Suddenly Yosemite became a symbol . . . , a primordial place of such transcendent beauty that it proclaimed the gift of the Creator to his new Chosen People."[47]

Throughout these reflections we have traced our loss of nature, our increasing solitude, our isolation as the only subjects in a cold, dead world. We have seen a movement from the extroversion of primitive peoples for whom nature was other, to the vertical extroversion of medievals for whom nature was a symbol of the divine, to our own introversion for whom nature is objectified and made part of our own psyches in order to fulfill various needs and desires.

We are looking for another way, a different way—a way back to a reciprocal, subject-subjects relation with nature, but one that is extroverted and horizontal, that respects nature's differences and lets things be what they are. In letting things be what they are, we will learn how to care for them more appropriately. We will also begin to see how interrelated and interdependent all of us are. Perhaps we will glimpse as well how these others are, now and then, images of the divine, even as we are. If we could develop such a sensibility, we might become, following Francis of Assisi, super, natural Christians. Developing this sensibility, we will suggest, involves the "loving eye," the eye that sees ourselves and others, including earth others, as profoundly related while at the same time able to respect real differences. Perhaps we can find clues to this sensibility as we consider the "arrogant eye," the eye that underlies the present-day Western way of knowing and relating to nature.

The Arrogant Eye

Knowing Nature as Object

Tʜᴇ Wᴇsᴛᴇʀɴ ᴡᴀʏ ᴏꜰ ᴋɴᴏᴡɪɴɢ ɪs ʙᴀsᴇᴅ ᴘʀɪᴍᴀʀɪʟʏ on one of our faculties—the eye. We do not smell, taste, touch, or even hear our way to knowledge of the world. We see our way. Since Plato, who called vision the eye of the mind, sight has been the privileged sense, in part because it alone is "of the mind," free of the messy bodiliness of the other senses. Sight gives the viewer distance, objectivity, and control: one can see without being seen, without being touched, without being heard, without being detected. All the other senses involve the knower with the known at a bodily and personal level. Even hearing demands that we wait and listen for the sound coming from the other. Touch, taste, and smell, the most basic senses upon which life depends, place us in a receptive, passive, accepting position with the others we would touch, taste, or smell. But vision appears to free us from these bodily involvements: we can see the other upon our own initiative and remain totally independent of what we see, uninfluenced by it. Whereas the other senses make us aware that we live in a world which we influence and upon which we are dependent, vision gives the illusion of individualism, distance, objectivity, and control.

Nature: Landscape or Maze?

Two images might make the contrast clearer: a landscape and a maze. Imagine standing on a hill overlooking a valley with a stream running through it. The vista is laid out before your eyes for you to survey: you are at the center and everything appears in relation to you. Westerners are accustomed to seeing nature this way, especially since the development of perspective in Renaissance painting. In medieval painting, nature and human beings are intermixed on a flat surface, and there is no privileged point of view from which to view the painting.[1] The spectator is not the center. But with the introduction of perspective, human beings (generally) disappear from paintings about nature and the only human being left is an invisible one, the spectator. The point of view—the place from which to see the natural world—is that of the invisible spectator who is outside the canvas. She or he surveys nature, now become, appropriately, a landscape, or scenery. The nineteenth-century American Hudson River school, which featured large romantic vistas of mountains, lakes, and valleys, is an illustration, but so are popular nature calendars picturing snow-capped mountains, breathtaking waterfalls, and rainforests (none of which the spectator must actually climb or cope with but can simply look at). The image of nature in paintings, pictures, and film *as a spectacle*, as something that an individual sees from a distance and as oriented toward the viewer, determines also how we experience nature, when we occasionally do so. Most Westerners want their cameras along when out in nature, in order to capture nature as spectacle, to frame and solidify our classic experience of nature. It is a good case of life imitating art, for we Westerners see ourselves as the spectator of a nature scene laid out before us. It appears as an object; it is at a distance; it exists *in relation to the observer*.

But let us imagine being in a maze—a clever set of impenetrable hedges set in irregular circles (a rainforest floor would also work, but more of us are acquainted with mazes). Both landscape and maze are models of nature; both are constructions, but which one, we must ask, is closer to a realistic assumption of where we human beings fit into the scheme of things? Are we the spectator of nature or in its midst? Do we control it or are we part of it? The experience of nature in a maze is totally different than in the landscape model: there is no center (or, if there is, it certainly is not me); subject-object thinking is irrelevant (if anything, I feel more controlled than controlling); closeness, not distance, is my basic awareness; involvement and not my individuality seems paramount. To find one's way about in a maze, a different kind of vision must come into play: one must pay close attention to detail. Objectifying, distancing, controlling vision is useless; rather, one must notice small, particular differences. Did I go by this hedge a few minutes ago? Am I getting closer to the center or to the margin? Can I locate myself by the sound of the fountain? One begins to feel like an animal, using all one's senses to maneuver one's way around this strange environment. One is inside nature, not outside it. One is part of it, not in control of it.

Which image—landscape or maze—is the more accurate expression of our relationship to nature? Certainly the landscape has been the dominant one during most of Western history. It is even prevalent today in environmental circles: beautiful nature as spectacle for human pleasure. Nature as maze, as encircling us and in many ways controlling us, is disorienting and perhaps scary. But it is also an interesting image, especially for us Westerners who feel distanced from nature, who have lost nature and its lifeforms as our other. Nature as maze is nature up close and close by, nature as enclosing us—as in Ming Dynasty paintings of small human figures set amid huge mountains and trees that appear to encircle them. In the maze, we may not feel entirely comfortable, but we feel more in touch. We may not be able to fathom the mysteries of nature, but we feel connected. We are aware of nature's otherness, its independence, its dangers, its complexities and nuances. It sparks our interest and awakens all our senses. To deal with *this* nature, we need to pay attention.

Scurrying around on the ground, sniffing and touching, listening for clues, eyes darting from detail to detail: is this a picture of noble *homo sapiens*, the crown of creation, the *imago dei? Are* we in a maze? Surely not! The Western tradition, both the Hebraic and Greek strands, insists on the nobility and superiority of our kind. We are the ones who stand on the hilltop surveying the earth, confident in our knowledge about it and our control of it. Like the all-powerful God who sees and knows all, who surveys the entire earth from the privileged perspective of heaven, penetrating even into the innermost secrets of each and every creature, so we, made in the divine image, see and know all from our lesser but similar stance. This caricature of the Western God provides the classic model as well as absolute validation for visual knowledge that is objectifying, distancing, and controlling. God sees all and knows all—and so do we. But a disquieting note enters, for such a God (and such a human being) is on a continuum with George Orwell's fantasy of the end of Western culture: Big Brother, who personifies total and totally controlling surveillance.

Would a different understanding of God suggest a different way for Christians to relate to nature? Would, for instance, a radicalizing of Christian incarnationalism—God with us, in the flesh, in the earth, here and now—imply that the maze is better, from a Christian point of view, than the landscape? That it is all right to smell the earth, touch the fur and leaves and scales of its lifeforms, tastes its fruits, listen to its cries and songs—and see, with attentive, interested eye, the earth others who are here? Yes, the maze metaphor might be closer to Christian incarnationalism; in fact, it might be quite appropriate.

We turn now to a closer study of the arrogant, all-seeing eye. We take this kind of vision and its accompanying knowledge so much for granted that we must look carefully at its history (how did it come about?) and its nature (what are some of its distinctive features?) if we are to have any chance of changing it for another way of seeing and knowing. Ways of seeing and knowing, like everything else human beings do, are constructed. Note that both landscape and maze are creations: they are not only models we construct for understanding our relationship with nature but often also literal constructions that mold nature into specific forms, as in landscape gardening or the maze in a botanical garden. Neither is natural. To take myself as subject and everything else as object (as one does who stands on the hill surveying the world) is a model of knowledge. It is also possible to see myself as a subject in a world of subjects (as moving about at eye level with others, trying to become acquainted with them). This too is a model of how we know. Our task now is to understand the dominant Western model of knowledge—its history and nature—as a prelude to suggesting a different model, one that will, I believe, help Christians to love nature with the radical, inclusive love with which we are supposed to love other human beings.

We begin with comments on the deceptiveness of sight and then move into a brief analysis of knowledge as sight in Plato and Descartes. We turn then to the importance of perspective in Western art, especially as it undergirds the arrogant eye in the depiction of nudes. We will note the intensification of sight as distancing, objectifying, and controlling with the rise of the camera, illustrated in phenomena as diverse as *The National Geographic* and pornography. Finally, we reflect on the consequences of the arrogant eye: the subject-object dualism it creates between knower and known, resulting in the loss of awareness of interdependence as well as the refusal to acknowledge difference, and eventuating in an objectifying, controlling "gaze."

Knowledge: The Eye of the Mind

Sight as Mirror of Nature

Touch is our closest sense; sight the most distant. When we touch something we are in immediate contact with it; we become more distant as we climb the ladder of the senses—from touch, taste, and smell to hearing and sight. Nature as landscape involves only sight; nature as maze involves all our senses, including sight, though not the panoramic sight of the landscape metaphor. It is the "maze" sight, the sight of the loving eye, of the attentive eye, of the relational eye, that is important to super, natural Christians. But first we need to look at sight generally as well as within the landscape metaphor, which is the major way it has been understood in the Western tradition, in contemporary science, and commonsense.

Sight is the most magnificent and the most distinctive of our human senses. It is also the most deceptive. It is the basis of language and abstract thought, for by it we can detach an image from an object. The distance that sight gives us from the object, the ability to make a distinction between the thing itself and our image of it, is the basis of symbolic and hence of theoretical thought.[2] Smell, taste, and touch connect us to the earth, but they do not give us sufficient distance to think about it. Hearing is the intermediary sense, giving both distance and closeness, demanding both initiative and waiting: those who can hear but not see are obviously capable of language and abstract thought. The remarkable cases are those, like Helen Keller, who have neither sight nor hearing, but nonetheless are capable of breaking through to the human realm. When Keller realized that the sign for water spelled out on her hand by her teacher was also a symbol, a word that could be detached from its object (the stuff that came out of the pump), she joined the human community. For most of us, however, this journey depends on sight, and hence sight is the most magnificent and distinctive of the human senses.

But it is also deceptive, and it is its deceptiveness that will occupy us in this chapter. The deception of sight is epitomized in the metaphor of the mirror. We are easily deceived into thinking that what we see is reflected back to us directly, purely, objectively—as in a mirror. The eye mirrors the world: what we see is simply what is there. The eye is a camera, a template, a recording machine giving an exact replica of nature. We "do nothing" when we see except allow images to fix themselves on our brains through the neutral conduit of the eye. This is the myth of sight as innocent, epitomized in the common expression, "I saw it with my own eyes," to verify the truth of a reported event. It also lies behind the classic Western way of knowing, the subject-object dualism: I, as subject, know this object before me, which is passive and open to my knowing. I can mirror this object authentically and faithfully, because as subject my eye is simple and innocent (as a mirror is) and as object the thing is laid out before me, more like a dead machine than like another living subject.

In spite of the popularity of this paradigm for knowledge in both ordinary as well as scientific circles, it is profoundly false and dangerously deceptive. Sight is not the most realistic of the senses—the one that mirrors nature accurately; rather, touch probably is. Touch alone offers resistance, the resistance of other real bodies occupying real space. Sight is the freest of the senses, as illustrated by its role in symbolic and theoretical thought. In the mind's eye we can separate the thought of a grizzly bear from the real thing; if we are touching one, that option is not open to us. Sight is not a realistic sense, but the primary imaginative one and as such, it is our most distinctive *and* most deceptive sense.

Annie Dillard notes that we see only what we expect to see. She describes searching for a frog in Tinker Creek, a frog which she expected to be, of course, green. She couldn't find one. What she eventually saw was a *brown* frog.[3] Our eyes always come ancient to their task; we cannot, as Dillard says, "unpeach the peach," simply see patches of color (as an infant or a newly sighted person might).[4] We can hardly imagine such a world. Infants and small children give us glimpses of it. British writer Penelope Lively, describing her own childhood, captures what she calls the "unadulterated vision" of childhood versus our vision:

> No thought at all here, just observation—the young child's ability to focus entirely on the moment, to direct attention upon here and now, without the intrusion of reflection or of anticipation. It is also the Wordsworthian vision of the physical world: the splendour in the grass. . . . A way of seeing that is almost lost in adult life. You can stare, you can observe—but within the head there is now the unstoppable obscuring onward rush of things. It is no longer possible simply to see, without the accompanying internal din of meditation.[5]

Autistic savants, as studied by Oliver Sacks, also provide glimpses into unadulterated vision. Stephen Wiltshire, a young autistic artist, had the ability, after a brief glance at a building, to draw it in detail with a kind of instant transference, almost as if from photographic memory. Sacks notes that he had the capacity to render an object as perceived, rather than conceived. "Stephen Wiltshire draws exactly what he sees—no more, no less."[6] Other artists, whose minds are full of the symbols of the history of art, cannot do that.

These people on the margins of human existence—infants and autistic savants—see the way the rest of us think we see, but don't. The case of the newly sighted, also studied by Sacks, is closer to the truth of sight. Sacks tells the story of Virgil, a fifty-year old man, blind almost from birth, who regained his sight. Rather than the "Hurrah! I see" that we might expect from such a miracle, however, the man was in acute confusion and bewilderment and eventually disillusionment and pain—he preferred his blind existence (a reaction typical of other similar cases). The newly sighted Virgil had not entered our world, but one closer to the "unpeached peach" of the infant or the autistic savant. It was not a world he found attractive. His world, his human, adult world, was one interpreted and given meaning by his other senses, not by sight. But for the always-sighted, as Sacks notes, "when we open our eyes each morning, it is upon a world we have spent a lifetime *learning to see.*"[7]

It is this lifetime spent learning to see that makes both the commonsense and the scientific belief in sight as a mirror of reality naive and dangerous. Feminist philosopher Lorraine Code states the case and its critique concisely.

> Standard philosophical theories of vision represent it as a "bare," primitive quasi-foundational, innocent mode of perception; which provides direct, untainted access to reality. Hence they obliterate all traces of the developmental, constructive processes—all the learning—that is implicated in even the most apparently simple forms of seeing. They ignore the extent to which even seeing is culturally, historically, and ideologically shaped.[8]

If even seeing a peach as a peach (and not just a patch of color) is a complex interpretive exercise, then how much more are our theories of nature as well as our judgments about its role and importance, its beauty and value, its power over us and relevance to us? Whatever we say about nature from our observations of it is, necessarily, reflections from the eye of the beholder and not merely pure and simple mirror images of it.

Sight as Light of Reason: Plato and Descartes

Nevertheless, belief in knowledge of the world as dependent on sight, on unadulterated vision, is old and deep, going back to Plato and coming up into the modern world through Réne Descartes.[9] In both Plato and Descartes, vision is kept pure and true by *disembodiment*. The eye can mirror its object because the eye in question is the eye of the mind not of the body—and the other senses, the maze ones, have a minor role in knowledge. The goal of knowledge is not the world in all its wonderful, messy, unutterable particularity and detail, but the essence of things, universals, the "thing in itself." For Plato, sight is the "light of reason," the faculty that illuminates the mind while at the same time disconnecting us from the body. True knowledge is rational, intellectual, noncorporeal: it is the soul's remembrance of when it dwelt with the gods, knowing truth as the gods do. It is not a matter of attending to the world in all its particularities and differences but of the soul returning to its true home with the gods. The differences and particularities of the world are incidental, for true knowledge is a rational not an empirical matter. As Plato says in the *Meno*, when the soul recalls one thing, all the rest can be deduced. While Aristotle was to modify Plato's disembodied view of knowledge with his more inductive, empirical approach, nonetheless sight remained the primary faculty for knowledge— landscape sight, not maze sight.

Two primary features of landscape sight—disembodiment and subject-object dualism—are very evident in René Descartes, the father of the modern notion of objectivity as well as what we are calling the arrogant eye. For Descartes, knowledge was not to be found through a return to the gods, but by a turn inward, to the individual's internal thoughts: "I think, therefore, I am." We know what we need to know, truly and rightly, not by attending to the world or by consulting other people, but by reflecting on our own inner processes.[10] The individual subject is everything; the world and especially the natural world is merely dead matter. It is object; I am subject. The classic paradigm is an *S* knows *O* statement: John knows the tree is green. This is the definition of knowledge in Cartesian (and positivistic scientific as well as commonsense) terms. Nothing about John (who is not a real individual but the universal knower) nor about the tree (which is no particular tree but the prototypical tree) matters. They are both disembodied and related as subject to object in a general, simplistic sense. The criterion for truth has noth-

ing to do with any actual person or tree nor with any significant relationship between them. In fact, if it were claimed that a seventy-
nine-year-old Egyptian man named John knew a particular tree
from his childhood and upon returning to his village declared with
delight that it is still green and doing well—this would not, in the
Cartesian paradigm, be considered knowledge. Knowledge in the
Cartesian mode is neither embodied nor intersubjective; rather, it is
abstract and located solely in the human subject. Of special importance to our project of loving nature, it is also objectifying. The distinctive contribution of Descartes to the Western way of knowing is
the mechanization of nature.[11] Neither Plato nor the Middle Ages
believed nature was dead; Greek and Christian thought, in different
ways, supported the organic, living character of the earth.[12] But with
Descartes, the objectification and mechanization of nature become
a primary feature of Western thinking and, as we will see, a key element in the arrogant eye.

As we criticize Descartes for his understanding of knowledge
based on disembodiment and the subject-object dualism, we must
recall that his goal was "objectivity," the removal of incidental detail
and the attainment of a neutral, unbiased perspective that would
permit us to know the world "as it is." That goal lies at the heart of
contemporary science; and it has given us much that we take for
granted and value, from huge advances in food production to medical miracles. Objectivity need not and should not become objectification, although both in science and in common sense, they are
often confused. Evelyn Fox Keller defines objectivity as "the pursuit
of a maximally authentic, and hence maximally reliable, understanding of the world around oneself."[13] The key word in this definition is understanding—not control. The goal of objectification is
control; the goal of objectivity is understanding. The importance of
this distinction cannot be overstated. The problem with the commonsense and scientific views of knowledge is that they often con-
flate understanding and control: one understands something *in order
to control* it for one's own uses. A disembodied, subject-object dualism allows and in fact encourages that direction, whereas an embodied, subject-subjects model of knowledge does not. The first permits
the arrogant, controlling eye to set the goal for knowledge of the
world; the second supports the loving, let-be eye in its desire to
understand the others in the world. Objectifying, mechanistic
knowledge is actually *subjective:* its goal is the control of the world for
the subject's own purposes. Human exploitation of nature is a case

in point: we desire to know about nature not primarily to under-stand it but for our own self-interest. Such knowledge is not objec-tive but objectifying; hence, it is subjective, seeing ourselves as the only subjects, with the rest of nature as an object for our interests.[14]

Needless to say, scientific knowledge of nature need not be exploitative. The ends of research can be the health of ecological systems as well as their destruction. As long as there is confusion between objectivity and objectification, however, science can hide its objectification of nature under the cloak of objectivity. One way to help the shift from the arrogant eye to the loving eye occur is to recognize and underscore that science is not the only objective study of nature. If objectivity is concerned with understanding, then many different enterprises, from Native cosmogonies and alternative medicine to nature writing and Georgia O'Keefe's nature paintings become relevant. There is not just one way to understand the natural world. Science does not mirror nature; rather, like all serious knowledge enterprises, it understands the natural world through dominant metaphors and models. For instance, "law" is a different metaphor for understanding nature than is "order."[15] The first, from physics, encourages the search for one, total law that will explain everything. Here nature is imagined to be inert, dead, obedient, and simple. The second, from biology, allows nature to be generative and resourceful, an active partner in a reciprocal relationship with the observer. Stephen Hawking, whose life goal is the discovery of the one law that will explain the universe and put God out of business, represents the first option, while Barbara McClintock, a Nobel prize winning botanist, who spoke of her work with corn plants as having a "feeling for the organism," represents the second. Both are considered good sci-ence, but they rest on different basic models of nature.

The main point here is that nature is too complex, mysterious, vast, rich and intricate to be circumscribed under any of our limited ways of knowing. It is indeed more like a subject than an object, more like a fascinating, multidimensional, complex human being than like a dead, simple object. If we accept the fact that in order to understand Shakespeare (as well as one's favorite aunt), a variety of knowledges are necessary (historical, literary, religious, anthropo-logical, sociological, medical, psychological—as well as personal and familial), why should we refuse many approaches to understanding nature—or grade one as true, best, etc., and the others as soft or inferior? Nature is the most complex, vast, highly detailed and different entity of all, far more so than any individual human being; yet our tendency is to reduce it to an object. Molecular biology is the most extreme example of this drive. It has become for many in science and outside as well *the* tool to explain the natural world. Its accomplishments are indeed astounding, as the current genome project, which is graphing all the genes in the human body and is already beginning to make links between specific genes and medical disorders, clearly manifests. But genetic knowledge is not the only knowledge of ourselves that matters—nor is it the only knowledge that matters in regard to the rest of nature. A tree is not just its DNA any more than we are. It is also a subject in its own world: a rich, complex subject, showing tenacity and ingenuity in the way it survives and prospers in symbiotic relationship with the many others—including the human others—who live along with it. To understand such an intricate, complicated subject as a tree, many different kinds of knowledge will be needed. In none of these knowledges, however, should there be an absolute difference between subject and object, for the tree is also a subject, one which we cannot begin to know unless we acknowledge its complex multidimensionality: its refusal to be just an object.

Acknowledgment of nature as subject is the first step away from the arrogant eye of Western objectification and toward the loving eye of objectivity—toward an authentic and reliable understanding of nature. It is toward an *ecological model* of knowledge in which complexity, embodiment, intersubjectivity, partiality, and understanding are the main constituents.[16] The ecological model relies on the maze view of nature, our place *in* nature along with and close to all the others whom we rub up against, smell, reach out to touch, hear calling us, and see beside us. In the ecological model, we give up the privileged place high on the hill from which to view nature as landscape, recognizing that place as a false and dangerous one, both to ourselves and to the earth. We use our eyes, our embodied eyes—not the eye of the mind—to learn more about the others in the maze, accepting that our eyes are not mirrors reflecting them but valuable instruments by which we can become better acquainted with the others in all their remarkable diversity and difference. The human eye not only has long-distance vision but also remarkable abilities for attention to detail and differences. It can survey a hillside of daffodils but also peer into the heart of one daffodil—and be astounded by what it finds.

Nature: The Mirror of the Mind

Perspective, the Nude, and Landscape Sight

The Western way of knowing believes that the eye mirrors nature: the eye is a camera, taking snapshots of the world, directly and innocently. But, as we have seen, this is a false and dangerous belief, for we learn to see. Only very young infants, the newly sighted, and a few autistic savants have direct, pure vision. Nonetheless, the supposition that we know nature, that our eyes can reflect it accurately to our mind, results in nature's objectification: nature *is* what is mirrored in the mind. It is not a complex subject—indeed, millions, billions, of subjects; rather, it is what is reflected to our minds, as a mirror or camera reproduces an image. In the eye-mirror-nature paradigm, nature is neither subject nor my world or home. It is mainly an object which is out there for me, for my pleasure and use. This is the way the arrogant eye, the Western eye, sees nature most of the time.

The reasons for the Western objectification of nature are old, deep, and complex; our task here is not to study these causes but rather to note their consequences. We are interested in becoming super, natural Christians and hence in learning how to grow in sensitivity toward nature. If Christian spirituality means developing appropriate relations with self, others, nature, and God, then a crucial task for us—and one neglected by most Christians—is overcoming Western objectification of nature. To overcome objectification, one must understand and *feel* its depth. It is not principally a self-conscious attitude; rather, it is our implicit, conventional, pervasive, taken-for-granted, "natural" temperament or sensibility toward nature. It is just how we Westerners *are* when it comes to nature. And because of this, it is difficult to recognize the depth and pervasiveness of our objectification of nature.

Our *felt* view of nature is, I am suggesting, expressed by the metaphor of landscape, not of maze. Whether we view nature in terms of the metaphor of landscape or of maze is not incidental when we begin to see the relationship between *distancing, objectification, and control.* For instance, it does not appear to be a mere coincidence that the development of perspective and the portrayal of nudes appeared at the same time in Western art. Let us contrast Renaissance perspective with medieval "cathedral" (or maze) vision in order to see this connection.

Perspective is unique to Western art; it arose in the Renaissance and radically changed how people viewed nature and themselves in relation to nature. As John Berger notes, "Perspective makes the single eye the centre of the visible world. Everything converges on the eye as to the vanishing point of infinity. The visible world is arranged for the spectator as the universe was once thought to be arranged by God."[17] This contrasts with the portrayal of nature and people in pre-Renaissance and so-called primitive art, which represents them in the way that best shows their characteristic features— for example, in Egyptian art where the head and legs of a person are presented in profile while the eyes and torso are shown frontally, so that all the features can be seen. In the perspectival view, the object, whether natural or human, is rendered only as it is seen from one point of view, that of the invisible spectator or the painting. The "better view" that perspective gives, as spread out panoramically before us, also brings with it psychic distance—we become disengaged from the scene before us rather than participants in it as our medieval forebears were. Reciprocity diminishes with the introduction of perspective; this is not a normative or moral judgment—it is simply what happens when we view something panoramically from a distance. When the point of view is ours, then we cannot be included in what we see, for we are spectators of it, not participants in it. It is important to underscore this point: in the Renaissance, a basically different place for human beings emerged—not *in* the earth, but as viewers *of* it. This was a profound change in sensibility, manifested in seeing the earth in mechanistic rather than organic terms, in the rise of science and technology, in the Enlightenment's confidence in human rationality. It is not an idea about human beings, but a profound change at the feeling level of what it is like to *be one*.

We can grasp this change if we contrast Renaissance landscape perspective with being in a Gothic cathedral. When one enters a Gothic cathedral, one is surrounded by it. One does not look at the cathedral, one is part of it (even from the outside, it is hard to get a full view of it, as cathedrals were usually set in villages and surrounded by houses). To become acquainted with a medieval cathedral, one must move from place to place inside it, investigating its many parts and details. There is no privileged position—no perspective—from which to view it. As Yi-Fu Tuan writes of this experience:

> The Gothic cathedral baffles modern man [*sic*]. A tourist with his camera may be impressed by the beauty of the nave, aisles, transepts, radiating chapels, and the span of the vaults. Should he seek a position to set up his camera, he will find that there is no privileged position from which all these features may be seen. To see a Gothic inte-

rior properly one has to move about and turn one's head. . . . The medieval cathedral was meant to be experienced; it was a dense text to be read with devout attention and not an architectural form to be merely seen.[18]

If we also recall what might be considered the ultimate landscape shot—the NASA whole-earth image from space—we may be able to sense the difference between these two sensibilities: the medieval and the modern. When we view the whole-earth image, we look at the earth from a distance of thousands of miles, not as if we live and move and have our being in it. While we might feel uplifted by its beauty and sad for its vulnerability, these are still emotions of spectators viewing an object from both actual and psychic distance.

How, then, are the development of perspective and the appearance of nudes in Western painting related? The portrayal of nudes epitomizes the distancing, objectification, and control that characterize the arrogant eye, the eye that has developed from perspective. Nudes are portrayed from one point of view, that of the (presumably) fully dressed male spectator of the painting. Paintings of nudes, usually female, are so frequent in post-Renaissance art that we often do not notice how odd and disturbing they are. For example, Manet's "Luncheon on the Grass" (1862–63) depicts a nude female having a picnic with two completely—and elegantly—dressed men! What this painting shows explicitly, the female body for male eyes, is the implicit message of all nude art. Often the male eye is not in the picture; nonetheless, the presumed spectator, the main protagonist, from whose point of view the nude is seen, is the invisible person, presumably male, who is looking at the picture.[19] "In the art-form of the European nude the painters and spectators were usually men and the persons treated as objects, usually women. This unequal relationship is so deeply embedded in our culture that it still structures the consciousness of many women. They do to themselves what men do to them. They survey, like men, their own femininity."[20] As nude, woman becomes the looked at, the surveyed, the objectified: what matters is her appearance, how she looks to the male eyes. This legacy is very much with us in the portrayal of women in the media: in television situation comedies and talk shows as well as in advertising.[21] The objectification of women through nudity or through a focus on their appearance, is one that they internalize. "Men look at women. Women watch themselves being looked at"—captures a profound and disturbing example of the pervasive dominance of the arrogant eye in Western culture.[22] If women also do to themselves what men do to them—survey themselves as objects to be controlled—is it too extreme to suggest that the female body is open to becoming "colonised territory"?[23] The prevalence of sexual abuse and rape seems to indicate that it is not.

The depiction of female nudity is a key marker in the development of the arrogant Western eye toward *nature* because of the old, deep, and pervasive relationship between women and the natural world. The identification of women and nature as well as similar cultural attitudes toward and treatment of them both is by now a platitude. But this platitude takes on new life in the stunning example of the relationship between perspective and nudity: the construction of the painted, female, nude body for the gaze of the invisible, clothed, male spectator. Here we see objectification of and control over body in a powerful, profound way. If this bit of nature, the female body, can here be understood as "colonised territory," cannot such an understanding also extend to nature more generally? As one commentator remarks on the development of the nude and of perspective in Western art: "The attitude toward women in this art—toward the central image of the nude in particular—is part and parcel of a commanding attitude toward the possession of the world."[24]

The landscape sensibility, then, the way of seeing the world from a privileged, distant, objective point of view, can slip easily into a position of surveillance and control. Subtly and in ways that appear innocent, we Westerners—women included—stand in the shoes of the white, Western, male spectator who looks at the world as if it were a framed picture, showing everything from his point of view. We see the world as an object—whether it be a woman's body or a natural scene—available for control.

If female nudity is an example of the arrogant eye, the eye that objectifies in order to control, so also are zoos—places where human beings can observe animals in a way similar to viewing nudes in an art gallery. Zoos collect animals, especially exotic ones from faraway places, as spectacles for human viewing. Visitors move from cage to cage, much as one moves from painting to painting: in each case, the point of view is that of the spectator (who is often annoyed if the animal hides, refusing to be the spectacle one paid to see). Whereas animals used to be our significant others, the ones we related to at the most basic level (even when we killed and ate them), now they are mere objects whom we use in experiments for our improved health, eat without reverence, and domesticate in zoos and as pets. Zoology has been called "the science most like the looking glass,"[25] for how we relate to animals is an indication of how we relate to our own bodies. As animals are objectified, so also are those human beings seen as mainly body—women, Natives, children, the homeless, the disabled. The animals we refuse to acknowledge as subjects return as bestial qualities we project onto other people—or that we fear in ourselves. How much better it would be to acknowledge—and admire—animals as genuine others! The objectification of animals, as epitomized in zoos and pets, is a loss not only for them but also for us. Our arrogant eye has diminished our own world. "There is something tedious and narcissistic about a totally human world. . . . Nonhuman Otherness is not merely degraded now, but absent; and so, in a sense, are we."[26] What has happened that we have allowed this to occur? Mary Midgeley, speaking of young children's "cosmological" urge, their reaching out to life, notes that "animals, like song and dance, are an innate taste."[27] If this is true, we of the arrogant eye appear to be losing one of our basic human traits.

The Eye of the Camera: Scopophilia

These sobering examples of nudes and zoo animals cause us to ponder our "natural" way of viewing the world, as a mirror of the mind, as reflected back to us as an object from our own perspective. But we need to go deeper still, to the eye of the camera, where distancing, objectification, and control merge in new and extraordinary ways. The camera appeared in 1839, a development that has had a revolutionary effect on how we see the world.[28] Its uses are innumerable: portraits, police work, war reporting, pornography, family photos, anthropological reports, postcards, tourist snapshots, planetary probes, military reconnaisance, x-rays of the body, nature calendars, etc. The camera deepens the perspectival way of seeing the world in some profound ways; most notably, it gives us pictures that appear documentary and not interpretive. The distant, objective, controlling eye of the perspectival viewer is now validated by the eye of the camera. Unlike painting, stories, memoirs, journals, or letter-writing, the camera seems simply to record what is there, free of any subjective comment. It supports the Western view of knowledge: seeing is believing. It accounts for the enormous success of magazines such as *Life* and *The National Geographic*—what matters in both these publications is the pictures (few people, it appears, read the text). Reality via the camera is delivered to us in spectacles and in bits and pieces: we now see the world as a series of pictures that are only incidentally related. Whereas stories, memoirs, and letter-writing relate incidents to one another through narrative and interpretation, pictures give an episodic, atomistic, disconnected sense of the world. Contrast, for instance, taking snapshots as a tourist with keeping a daily journal of the trip. The snapshots give instant appearances, pretty sights, and a sense of immediacy, but they supply no connections between the events or their significance to the tourist that a diary provides. But it is almost impossible for contemporary Westerners to stash the camera and go with a journal, for photography has a magical sense for most of us. As Susan Sontag in her now-famous essay on photography comments, "Having a photograph of Shakespeare would be like having a nail from the True Cross."[29] For us, photos are "a trace, something stenciled off the real, like a footprint or a deathmask."[30] We treat them like the Bible or the flag: we do not step on them or throw them away.

Because of the prevalence and importance of the camera (and its offshoots television, film, and state-of-the-art computers), we need to be careful and discriminating in assessing its impact. Visual learning has become primary in our society. The eye, not the ear, indeed the eye as related to pictures or pictures plus text rather than to text alone, is now dominant. We are not primarily a generation of hearers or readers but of viewers, and viewers now not even of the world directly. Our relation to the world, and especially to nature, is increasingly secondhand: through film and computers, we know a virtual world, while the other one—the old one of people, trees, animals, hills, and water—seems to slip away from us. Our deeper study of the dominance of vision as the Western way of knowing the world has eventuated in eliminating its object—our world—in some significant and disturbing ways.

This is the startling conclusion of our path toward distancing, objectifying, and controlling the world through vision: we are now in danger of losing it as we substitute pictures for the real thing. A small, daily, and telling example will make the point. As recently as one generation ago children spent their free time out of doors "doing nothing" in vacant lots and small city parks. How many children today spend their free time looking for tadpoles in ditches of water, versus the number of children glued to the television set or home computer—even if they are watching a nature program on television or calling up pictures of frogs on the computer screen? Is this important? Does the "extinction of experience," the experience *of* nature by both children and adults, matter, either to us or to the natural world?[31]

There is, then, an underside to the camera. Not to undercut the many positive aspects of photography, we need to see how it contributes to the arrogant eye. Susan Sontag compares a camera to a gun: one loads, aims, and shoots it, and the result is a snap "shot." Photography is, she claims, an act of aggression: "To photograph people is to violate them, by seeing them as they never see themselves, by having knowledge of them they can never have; it turns people into objects that can be symbolically possessed."[32] While one may object to the gun analogy as overstated, even a tourist camera can turn people into objects. In a newspaper article entitled, "Sometimes cameras really do steal souls," the writer, a recent tourist to the Mbuti pygmies in Semliki Valley near the Uganda-Zaire border, noted that the pygmies were a prime target for tourists hoping for "a National Geographic moment." But the pygmies "were not as small as expected, and, in faded, tattered Western clothes, nobody's romantic idea of the noble savage. When the passengers had first entered their village they noticed a few pygmies in Western clothes bolt into their huts and emerge moments later in traditional dress. A brief dance was performed, but it lacked heart."[33] The tourists did not get their National Geographic moment, but they did manage to steal some souls, as the writer comments: "These lovely people were ruined . . . by being stared at as if they were in a fishbowl or a zoo."[34] Perhaps this is the way the camera is like a gun, destroying life by stealing souls.

Staring at others as if they were in a fishbowl or a zoo: this is what Sigmund Freud called scopophilia—subjecting other people to a curious, controlling gaze, seeing them as objects. Scopophilia lies at the heart of the arrogant eye; scopophilia defines the arrogant eye. There are many forms of it, and it is so prevalent that we often do not recognize it. Commercial Hollywood films, for instance, present one example in their depiction of women. Feminist film critics claim that the point of view of most Hollywood films is male: he alone is subject and his gaze controls the world of the film. The male is the active protagonist (the one with whom the audience, both male and female, is meant to identify), and the male gaze, especially as aimed at women, is the dominant one, created by various cinematic techniques.[35] Actresses frequently complain that there are few roles for them as protagonists and the roles that are available often portray women as either victims or temptresses. A film such as *Thelma and Louise*, presumably about two strong women, actually puts them in the position of the male—in this instance, as masculinized guntoters, who treat others (men) as objects. The gaze, while presumably now from female eyes, is still that of the male. This is certainly not to suggest that all men treat women as objects, either in real life or in films; rather, it implies that scopophilia, the objectification of others, is deeply ingrained in our culture and that it is the predominant point of view of the seemingly most realistic of our media—film.[36]

The most extreme example of scopophilia is, of course, pornography: the objectification of others for the purpose of stimulating erotic feelings. Pornography is principally a visual activity, pictures and film being the main contributors to this radical example of the arrogant eye, the eye that distances, objectifies, and controls others for one's own pleasure or benefit.[37] The close connection between pornography and sexual abuse, especially of women and children, is well documented and serves as a grim reminder of the consequences of the objectification of others. Voyeurism is a variation on the pornographic arrogant, "the erotic gratification of watching someone without being oneself seen, i.e., the activity of the Peeping Tom."[38] While voyeurism may at first appear to be a failing only of those at the margins of society, it is in fact a common variation on the dominant subject-object spectator gaze. In a poignant remark in his *Letters and Papers from Prison*, Dietrich Bonhoeffer bemoans the prurient nature of slow-motion films showing the growth of plant life: there is, he says, "something indecent in prying like this into the secrets of life."[39] I suspect that few of us feel like voyeurs when we watch nature films that, with the increasing power and sophistication of zoom lenses, can capture for our gaze the moment of copulation as well as of birth within the nests and dens of even the most secretive, nocturnal birds and mammals. Does it even cross our minds that we should respect their privacy—that they are subjects in their own worlds and not just objects in ours?

A final example of the arrogant eye and a particularly telling one because it is seemingly both objective and benign is the *National Geographic Magazine*, the third largest publication in the United States (right behind the *TV Guide* and *Readers' Digest*), which reaches 37 million people per issue and probably many more via doctors' and dentists' offices.[40] It is revered by Americans as both scientific and objective; one must be a member of the Society to subscribe; and people often save issues in attics or donate them to hospitals rather than toss them out. The *Geographic* is something of a national icon and with good reason, for if one studies its pictures (and the pictures *are* the *Geographic*), from its beginning in the late nineteenth century to the present, one gains a fairly accurate sense of the

American image, both of itself and of others. A recent study of the *Geographic* characterizes its version of the American national vision as classic humanism, one that shows that "human values are basically the same around the world" and these values as implicitly American.[41] Put more bluntly, the *Geographic*, as Chester Nimitz once said, "promotes Americanism throughout the world."[42] This is certainly not a militaristic promotion; rather, it is a cultural one, and of a subtle sort—it assumes that others, even the dark-skinned, exotic others with minimal clothing, are basically "like us."[43] The all-time favorite *Geographic* photograph is of an elderly, Middle-Eastern man (with a photogenic leathery face and sensitively warm expression) embracing his young granddaughter: for its audience, it reveals the universal nature of human, especially parental, love. Nothing else about the two people is important—not their economic, cultural, or social conditions and certainly not their names. They are not subjects but types, in a way similar to the much-loved photos of parents and children in Edward Steichen's famous 1955 exhibit, "The Family of Man."

In spite of its reputed objectivity and scientific character, the point of view of the *Geographic* is American and specifically, middle-of-the-road American. In the post-Vietnam era, the *Geographic* moved away from its earlier romantic, nostalgic photos of natives in exotic places toward a more realistic vision, evident, for instance, in its depiction of environmental deterioration. Pictures now regularly appear of garbage on beaches and clear-cutting in rainforests, but even in the most severe cases of environmental degradation, the tone of the *Geographic* is always upbeat, mirroring the mixture of denial and optimism that one finds on environmental issues in the American public.[44] The "two sides" of any environmental issue are presented "in balance," seldom if ever in terms of gross greed or error on one side. "Life goes on" is the larger message: "The magazine thus preserves the sense that it has a grip on reality, while retaining its message that all is fundamentally right with the world."[45]

This kindly, upbeat, universalizing, tolerant American gaze as epitomized in *National Geographic* and oriented to the others (who are not American) is one of the more benign forms of the arrogant eye. It claims that others really are like us (under the skin, even dark skin); these others are not, however, seen as *subjects in their own worlds*. They are, to the extent that we know and care about them, assimilated to the one Subject, the American one. What is different about them (their color, culture, history, etc.) is accidental; what is similar to us is what matters. Subtle as it is, it is still a form of arrogance: it objectifies and controls others for one's own pleasure, peace of mind, and interests.

If we have difficulty, as we seem to, in taking other human beings seriously as subjects in their own worlds, in all their differences and particularity—how much more difficult do we find it to take other lifeforms and nature in general this way? And here we find ourselves returning to the notion of virtual reality. Is reality, life in the maze, too difficult? Is an alternative reality, one in which we deal with people (and other lifeforms) only at a distance preferable? In a symposium on the way the Internet is shaping our sense of reality, four experts shared their thoughts on the subject.[46] At the center of the discussion was the extent to which the virtual world of computing is replacing the world we live in—and the loss that entails (as one commentator remarked, "a cyberkiss is not the same as a real kiss").[47] For some, the balance is shifting toward mediated worlds:

> Growing up in the Fifties, I felt I was living in a very real place. The terms of human interchange were ones I could navigate. . . . More and more of the interchanges that are being forced on me as a member of contemporary society involve me having to deal with other people through various level of scrim, which leaves me feeling disembodied . . . I do believe that we gain a lot of our sense of our own reality and validity through being able to hear an echo, by getting our words back, by being mirrored. And community, in the old-world sense, was about being mirrored immediately. You know, you yell for Clem, and Clem yells back, and you understand the terms of your world.[48]

Similarly, in an article entitled "Nature has no 'virtual' equal," the author describes a television commercial depicting a young boy suited up for a hockey game. The viewer presumably imagines the boy heading off to a pond or river, perhaps pausing along the way to listen to the sound of winter birds. But the commercial never even lets the boy get outdoors; rather, in the author's words, "In the final clip of this lunatic version of happiness in the late 20th century, we see him bounding around in a mindless frenzy in front of the video screen. Some hockey game. Some life. Jesus wept. So should we all."[49]

The distancing, objectifying, controlling eye that began with Renaissance perspective may eventuate in the loss of the world of smell, taste, touch, hearing—and close, detailed perception of the other. "You yell for Clem and Clem yells back" is from the world as maze, not as landscape.

Dualism and the Arrogant Eye

The loss of the natural world and its replacement by virtual nature has been *allowed* to occur, for as mere object, nature is expendable. The subject-object dualism that lies behind the arrogant eye values only the first member of this dualism. In fact, given the Western way of knowing—which privileges the eye of the mind, reason, as the mirror of nature—*the* fundamental dualism of Western culture is reason vs. nature.[50] This dualism illuminates most of the other dualisms: whatever falls on the top side of a dualism has connections with reason and whatever falls on the bottom side is seen as similar to nature. Thus, male/female, white/people of color, West/East, heterosexual/homosexual, educated/illiterate, rich/poor all illustrate the reason/nature dichotomy. In each case, characteristics associated with reason (progress, rationality, order, initiative, control, culture, development, civilization) adhere to males, whites, the West, heterosexuals, the educated, the wealthy, while traits linked to nature (the body, sex, emotionalism, chaos, lack of control, primitivism, nudity, passivity) are connected to females, people of color, the East, homosexuals, the illiterate, the poor.[51] Val Plumwood, a feminist philosopher of nature, describes the reason/nature dualism of the West as an ideology, "the politics of nature," which has resulted in a colonizing attitude by the masters, those who fall on the reason side, toward everything on the nature side. The key point for our purposes is that, as Plumwood puts it, "the category of 'nature' has been above all a political category, one that has allowed its occupants [slaves, women, the homeless, the disabled, the mentally ill—and the natural world] to be erased from consideration as others to be acknowledged and respected. . . ."[52] In other words, whatever falls into the nature side of the dualism is not a subject; rather, it is merely an object for the use or pleasure of those who fall into the reason category. This is the final outcome of nature as merely the mirror of the mind, of knowledge as the eye of the mind: the dualism of reason vsersus nature—a separation so intense that intimacy, mutuality, and interdependence are impossible.[53]

The key features of dualistic thinking illustrate this outcome.[54] First, in dualism *the subject denies its dependency* on the other; thus, masters deny their dependence on slaves, men on women's work, humans on nature's finite limitations. In point of fact, however, those in the "background" are essential to the foreground subjects, who could not exist without these unacknowledged others. Second, *the other is polarized through hyperseparation*; while only a small difference may separate the two parties (skin color or gender, for instance), radical exclusion is necessary in order to treat the other as object. Differences are not seen as a matter of degree, but as absolutes. For instance, that humans and chimpanzees are 98 percent the same genetically is an uncomfortable fact for dualistic thinking to deal with. Third, *the bottom side of the dualism is incorporated into the top side* by being defined in terms of it: it is merely a "lack." Its being is defined in terms of lacking what the top side has; thus, other lifeforms in nature are graded on a scale of their proximity to or distance from the ability to reason. For instance, a giraffe is merely a human being *manqué*.[55] These three features of dualistic thinking—denial of dependency, hyperseparation, and incorporation—result in instrumentalism (permission to use the other to serve one's own purposes) and stereotyping (since the others are not subjects, but mere types, their own particular needs and wishes need not be taken into consideration).

The relevance of this analysis to the typical Western attitude toward nature is painfully obvious. While we have made some progress in our sensitivity toward other human beings—women, children, the physically challenged, homosexuals, people of color—as evident in the fact that their subjecthood is now at least a matter of discussion, the subjecthood of nature has not advanced very far. If one of the features of the post-Enlightenment has been moving the line of ethical regard beyond Immanuel Kant's rational man (the only other that Kant believed deserved one's moral consideration) to include a larger and larger number of human beings in various conditions, then we now have to ask: Does the line stop with us? Are human beings the only subjects? Is everything nonhuman merely object? Can we survive if we deny our dependency on nature, radically separate ourselves from it, and define it solely in terms of ourselves? Should we Christians accept this dualism? Is a utilitarian attitude toward creation, one that uses it for our own ends, one that is deaf, dumb, and blind even to *its* own needs and interests, right from a Christian perspective? Does Christian spirituality, the development of sensitivity toward others (God and neighbor), include also sensitivity toward nature—its needs and interests?

This is the major question we are asking ourselves. Before we turn to consider a possible answer to this question, let us close our reflections on the arrogant eye with a final and very disturbing example. In the eighteenth century, the philosopher Jeremy Bentham, in an essay entitled *Panopticon* (total vision), imagined the ideal prison, one in which the inmates could be constantly and economically under surveillance. In his fantasy a perimeter prison building in the form of a ring would contain cells open front and back so that from a tower in the center of the structure a single guard could see into the daylight cells and continuously observe the prisoners. As Michel Foucault, commenting on this metaphor as "the eye of power," notes, the surveyed, aware of the other's controlling eye constantly surveying them, eventually will turn the eye inward and survey themselves, becoming their own jailers. "There is no need for arms, physical violence, material constraints. Just a gaze. An inspecting gaze, a gaze which each individual under its weight will end by interiorising to the point that he is his own overseer, each individual thus exercising this surveillance over, and against himself."[56] The controlling eye subdues and trains the surveyed until finally the eye from above becomes the eye from below; the other is broken, disciplined to do the bidding of the gazer. Subjects become enmeshed with the eye of power and participate in their own oppression. Eventually the desired attitudes and behavior become normal, everyday matters, accepted as ordinary and customary.

Those of us who believe we live outside of the arrogant eye of Western culture need perhaps to think again. Have we internalized the landscape eye, the dualistic eye, so completely that it *is* our eye? Have we become prisoners in our own egos, no longer realizing that we have lost our significant other, the natural world? Do we participate willingly in our own oppression, as well as in the oppression of nature, no longer seeing our own dualistic way of being in the world as wrong, unhealthy, un-Christian, but simply as what we must accept and discipline ourselves to support? Have we trained and broken *ourselves* to see the world with the arrogant eye?

5

The Loving Eye

Knowing Nature as Subject

In Touch with the Others: A Radical Suggestion

THE FIRST THING THAT MAMMALS DO WITH their newborns is touch them. Animal mothers lick their young to form the bond necessary to their offspring's life, and human parents instinctively know that touching and holding their baby is essential to its happiness and well-being. Our prenatal existence is also one of touch: our entire bodies float in amniotic fluid, surrounded by the walls of the womb. Surely, touch must be our first sensation. Young children want to touch other people and everything else as well. "Look but don't touch" is deeply unsatisfying to them. Touch is a primary need that puts us in contact with the world, situating us in relation to others. Babies that are not touched and allowed to touch do not develop normally. Human beings can exist without their other senses, but we could not exist without touch: unless we are touched and can touch, we have no way of knowing that we even *do* exist—where, for instance, I begin and end, what is me and not-me.

If our understanding of the self, of who we are in the scheme of things, were to begin with touch (as our experience of actual selves does), rather than sight, we would have a *basically different sense of self.* Abandoning the Western subject-object dualistic sense of self would reveal an ecological self, a relational self, a self that would not, could not, exist apart from others. It would be a sense of self as relational and responsive. It would not be an individualistic self that decides to form relationships, but a responsive one that from its prenatal existence on is created by relationships. It would not be an abstract, rationalistic sense of self ("I think, therefore I am"), but a concrete, embodied sense of self ("I am touched and touch, therefore I am").[1]

If touch were accepted as our primary sense, we would have a radically different understanding of the self and others than we do in the Western paradigm. This understanding would affect how we *see* the world. The conversion from the arrogant eye to the loving eye must take place at a basic level, at the most basic level: how we understand ourselves in the scheme of things. Are we the lone, isolated individual standing on a hill looking out on the world as if it were a landscape, laid out for our pleasure and profit? Is the subject-object dualism that emerges from this sense of self the appropriate, the right—and the Christian—way for humans to be in the world? Or is it more appropriate to see the self as coming from the womb, licked and touched into existence, oneself reaching out to touch and responding when touched: created, surrounded, and supported by others, by other people, other lifeforms, other things? Do I exist as one subject among many other—and different kinds of other—subjects, ones whom I influence and who influence me? Is the subject-subjects paradigm of the self and world that emerges from touch a better model—a more realistic one, a more humane one, perhaps even a more Christian one?

These are some of the questions we now want to try to answer. Our assumption is that how we see the world, whether with an arrogant or a loving eye, depends upon our deepest, most basic sense of self in relation to the world. Our thesis is that a sense of self coming from touch rather than from sight gives us a way to think about ourselves as profoundly embodied, relational, responsive beings, as created to love others, not to control them. This chapter will unpack and expand this proposal in several ways. First, we will explore how a model of self and world based on the sense of touch rather than sight changes how we know the world and act toward it, underscoring once again that models are constructions, not descriptions. We will then reflect on the marks or characteristics of the subject-subjects model, beginning with some comments on Martin Buber's I-Thou model, and then turning to feminist understandings of the self and the other. In the third section, we will consider how the subject-subjects model of being and knowing can be extended to nature. Since the model is based on relations between human beings, how can it apply to nonhuman entities, both living and nonliving? Can a tree, a mountain, or the earth itself be considered a subject, or are they only objects? Finally, we will reflect on how we might develop the loving eye that should be the result of this paradigm of human being and knowing. Educating the loving eye is a lesson in both appreciating the difference and particularity of the others as well as cultivating empathy with them.

Our Primary Sense: Touch

We begin our exploration of the ecological model of the self with two key points: understanding how the sense of touch as the primary sense grounds the model and recognizing that it *is* a model, a construction. On the first point: a number of features of touch are critical to the model of the self and world that we are trying to develop.[2] Touch is related not just to one organ (like the eye, ear, nose, tongue) but to the whole body. It relates us directly to the physical environment, giving us an immediate rather than a mediated awareness of it. It involves being touched as well as touching—unlike sight, it is two-way, for one cannot touch without being touched. Touch reveals the world to be both resistant (other people and things are there, taking up space) and responsive (the world affects me—the wind feels cold, this human hand feels good).[3] These are the reasons why touch is the most basic, realistic sense, why we cannot exist without it, why we would not know that we *do* exist apart from touch. Touch gives us an immediate sense of our bodies as existing in a world composed of other resistant bodies—other people, other animals, other things. It is a total sense of existing, of being alive, affecting all parts of us, but a sense of being that is also totally relational and responsive: I cannot touch *without being touched.*

If we were to take touch as the primary sense that defines who we are in the scheme of things, it would also affect how we understand the other senses, especially listening and seeing. They would be on a continuum with touch. Thus hearing, another responsive sense, would gain higher status than it presently has. The Western way of knowing, as we have suggested, is based on the eye and in particular, on the distancing, objectifying, controlling eye. It has been also "a thinking primarily anchored in saying—without—listening."[4] The eye that objectifies and controls is supported by the mouth that speaks: ours is "a logocentric culture" anchored in "assertive discourse."[5] Western knowing orders and explains, with little use for receiving and listening. The former is the domain of the active individual grasping, mastering, and using the world, while the latter is seen as a lesser (and often female) role—that of the open, responsive receiver, wanting to learn more about the world. When touch is seen as primary, listening and hearing gain in importance, for the ear is one of the major ways we exercise our relational, responsive selves.[6] Apparently the loss of hearing makes people feel more unhappy and more cut off from the world than does the loss of sight. Listening puts us immediately into a responsive relationship to others; in fact, hearing depends on waiting until the other speaks or makes a noise. We relate to the other directly, as listening to someone tell a story, versus watching a television adaptation of the story, illustrates.

But the primacy of touch also affects the way we *see* the others in the world. This will be a central point throughout our reflections, because sight is, for human beings, a central sense (in part due to our upright posture, which makes smell less possible!). We are bound to see, so how should we see? If sight is understood within the context of touch, it will not be the distant, disembodied, objectifying, controlling arrogant eye of subject-object dualism. Rather, it will be "in touch" vision, a relational, embodied, responsive paying attention to the others in their particularity and difference. The eye of the body is not like the eye of the mind. The eye of the body respects and admires the physical, the concrete, and the diverse, rather than searching for the abstract, the general, and the same, as does the eye of the mind. The others known by the embodied eye will not be fitted into categories and types but seen as particular, embodied others that offer both resistance and response. They cannot be cannibalized by the appropriating eye but must be granted their otherness, their unavailability, their difference, and even their indifference to us. Touch provides us with our first sense of *limits:* other bodies resist when we push or pull them. Touch suggests that the intimacy of responsiveness must be balanced by the boundaries of resistance. Touch reminds us that reality is made up of others; touch is a lesson in "objectivity." This will be a *very* important point in our reflections on modeling the relation between self and world. For, unlike the arrogant eye, the loving eye, schooled by its relationship with touch, will insist that others are real, that my own self is limited, that boundaries are necessary, and that the particularity and differences of the others must be central in my seeing and knowing them. Here nature is not the mirror of the mind. Rather, it is composed of many different and surprising others to whom I must pay close attention if I am to know them at all. The goal of the embodied eye, the loving eye, the eye that sees the other as both responsive and resistant, is what Evelyn Fox Keller calls the highest form of love, "love that allows for intimacy without the annihilation of difference."[7]

In *Pilgrim at Tinker Creek*, Annie Dillard introduces one of her major metaphors for how human beings should conduct themselves in the strange, surprising world in which they find themselves—one should "explore the neighborhood." She quotes a woman who once said to her, "Seems like we're just set down here . . . and don't nobody know why."[8] Dillard suggests a first step should be "exploring the neighborhood," beginning with a small bit of it, like Tinker Creek, "to discover at least *where* it is that we have been so startlingly set down, if we can't learn why."[9] The world as neighborhood, as a place where one listens and looks in order to learn who one is, who the others are, and how all fit together in one place: this is a nice summation of an "in-touch" model of being and knowing. The neighborhood encloses us within a particular space where many live together, inviting us to pay close attention in order to learn more about our neighbors.

In summary: our first point is that if we understand ourselves to be in touch with others, touching them and touched by them—if this is our basic sense of who we are—we will have taken an important step toward an ecological model of being, a model that says we exist only in interrelationship with other subjects.

Constructing the Subject-Subjects Model

A second key point in regard to the subject-subjects model is recognition that it is a model. Like the subject-object way of knowing, it is a construction. It is not a description of how human beings know the world; it is not the only way that we can know it. Rather, it rests on a decision, a judgment, that this is a good, appropriate way. The subject-object way of knowing, because of its widespread acceptance and use, appears to be the "natural" or the only way. But it also is a model. It is based on imagining everything that we know to be like things, like lifeless objects, while the knower alone is alive and active. The subject-object model could also be called the agent-thing model. The subject-subjects model could be called the agent-agents model. Neither model fits perfectly all the different entities in the world, but the question to ask is, which model is better? Recall how Lorraine Code answers this question. "It is surely no more preposterous to argue that people should try to know physical objects in the nuanced way that they know their friends than it is to argue that they should try to know people in the unsubtle way that they claim to know physical objects."[10]

Is it better to think of people as objects or to imagine all of non-human reality to be on a continuum with ourselves? Since both subject-object and subject-subjects ways of knowing are models, we have a choice. Which model fits the data better, and which model helps us live more humanely on the planet? The subject-subjects model appears to be preferable on both counts. It fits the data better because, according to the postmodern view of reality, agency, activity, and influence are characteristics not just of human beings but of all animals, of trees and plants, of oceans and winds, of mountains and of the earth as a whole. These terms fit different entities in different ways. But to understand everything we know as alive, as having relations of interdependence with others, as changing others and being changed by them, is closer to the contemporary understanding of reality than is the subject-object model, which claims that only the human knower is alive, active, and influential while everything else (and often other people, to the extent that they are objectified) is dead, passive, and unchanging.[11] The ecological model of knowing rests on the assumption that the world is composed of living, changing, growing, mutually related, interdependent entities, of which human beings are one. None of these entities is a mere object; all, in different ways, are subjects. For example, this model can accommodate the poignant reciprocity between two subjects such as an elderly, isolated man and his cat and only companion: the subject-object model is obviously not sufficient to account for this relationship. The model can also make sense of the relationship between painter Georgia O'Keefe and the Southwest as one of genuine mutual interaction: the Southwest changed O'Keefe in profound ways as she related to it as an alive, active entity. The subject-subjects model can even include the NASA whole-earth picture: our feelings for the vulnerability and fragility of the earth as well as its rare beauty fit better into the subject-subjects model than into the subject-object one.

Not only does the subject-subjects model appear to fit the data of our world more closely (according to the present picture of that data), but it is also a better model for the world's well-being. We have seen the results of the subject-object model: the objectification of other people (those who fall into the category of body—women, children, people of color, "primitives," the disabled, the poor and the homeless, etc.) as well as of the natural world (as a resource for our use). What would be the results of the subject-subjects model—might it be the "subjectification," rather than the objectification of others? If we were to use the model of subject-subjects for all our knowing, assuming all others were *in some sense* subjects, how might we treat other animals as well as trees, plants, mountains, oceans, and the earth itself? Presumably, we would treat them more like subjects than like objects. The suggestion is revolutionary. But the model would also revolutionize how we treat other people: the objectification of other people would no longer be condoned. The subject-subjects model is not a reversal of the subject-object model, but a different model. It is not a dualism but a continuum: everyone and everything is somewhere on the subject continuum. The knower and the known are more alike than they are different.

As a construction, the subject-subjects model is a way of relating to other people and other entities that can help to return us to our primal world, the in-touch world of infancy and childhood—but now with a second naiveté. We cannot return to that world innocently or directly, nor should we want to. We cannot return to the womb and the breast nor fuse with nature, as children do (and deep ecologists and romantics would like to).[12] The subject-subjects model gives us, however, a way to a mature, nuanced sense of self and world as intimately, dynamically related—but a relationship that respects others as separate, complex, and marvelously diverse. The model gives us many of the pleasures and comforts of coming home but also the realism that we can't go home again. It helps us along the way to a mature love of others, as Keller said, a "love that allows for intimacy without the annihilation of difference."[13]

Being and Knowing: The Ecological Model

Some Preliminary Reflections

The final outcome of subject-object thinking is the death of the self. The subject that set out to know the world as object, to colonize and control all others, ends by being itself destroyed. The isolated, superior, individual self surveying the world as landscape with the arrogant eye is self-destructing in the late twentieth century, because this model of the self and the world is too far from reality. Like other myths that are innately false—Nazism, for example—it is finally being acknowledged as the lie it is. Human beings cannot live in the world this way because the world is not set up to accommodate the behavior that issues from such arrogance, as deterioration of the environment, for instance, is proving.

To admit this is not to fall into naive realism. It is not a denial of "nature" as a human construction (in fact, many constructions, as we have seen). But it is a denial of idealism: that nature is whatever our minds make of it. An ecological model of self and world acknowledges that the natural world is "there" (apart from our interpretations, indeed, apart from us, for it would go along nicely were all human beings to disappear tomorrow). This model of self and world also accepts that our constructions have limits: according to the evolutionary, ecological picture of reality now current, we cannot act on certain interpretations of nature without dire consequences. If, for instance, we act as if nature's resources are unlimited, we will pay a price. Hence an interpretation of human beings as the only subjects—as the Subject—appears to be inappropriate and dangerous.

A tempting alternative is to flip the coin: from one subject to no subject, from the objectification of the world to the submersion of the subject into the world. This is, essentially, what romanticism, back-to-nature movements, and deep ecology are about. Since we cannot and should not control nature, let us become one with her (the feminization of nature as well as sexual fusion with nature are typical expressions of this alternative).[14] The problem, however, is that then we disappear as subjects, and so do the others. Deep ecologist Arne Naess describes human beings as well as other lifeforms as "organisms" which "are knots in the biospherical net."[15] In this way of thinking, the model contains just one Subject of which we are all parts, equal parts.[16] The principal difficulty with this model in terms of our issue of how Christians should love nature is that the other *as other* is not taken seriously. Differences, complexity, and diversity are sacrificed to oceanic feelings of oneness with the earth. Elimination of the other is as problematic as its objectification. What we need is a model that helps us to love nature, not objectify it or fuse with it.

Neither hyperseparation nor fusion will do—what we need is a model of self and world that, while acknowledging as Martin Buber says, "In the beginning is relation," also recognizes the otherness of the other.[17] Most postmodern models of being move in this direction, whether from process thought, phenomenology, existentialism, Zen Buddhism, or feminism. In different ways and with differing emphases all of these contemporary movements are critical of subject-object dualism, both its claims concerning who human beings are in the scheme of things and how we act on the basis of those claims. Each insists that, fundamentally, we are social beings, and most would agree with process philosopher A. N. Whitehead that "there is no possibility of a detached, self-contained local existence"; with phenomenologist Maurice Merleau-Ponty that "the world is not what I think, but what I live through"; with Zen Buddhist Thich Nhat Hanh that being is "interbeing endlessly interwoven"; with phenomenologist Martin Heidegger that human beings live within the earth as a "sheltering agent" and should practice "attentive dwelling within the sphere of things"; with existentialist Martin Buber that "all real living is meeting"; with Jungian Thomas Moore that homelessness means estrangement from a sense of belonging to the earth; with feminist Caroline Whitbeck that "a person is an historical being whose history is fundamentally a history of . . . *lived* relationships"; and with philosopher of science Donna Haraway that we are "boundary creatures," transgressing the borders between the human, the natural, and the technological, and as hybrids are always unstable and changing.[18] What these various statements suggest is a basic change in sensibility from the modern post-Enlightenment confidence in the individual who, as rational man, is set over against the world, which he can both know and control. The new sensibility understands human beings to be embedded in the world—indeed, in the earth: they are social beings to the core, and whatever they know of the world comes from interaction with it. The goal of knowledge is not control so much as it is healthy, humane existence for all parties concerned—not progress and profit but sustainability.

As widespread as this new sensibility is among postmodern thinkers, it has not become the current view in most of our cultural, political, economic, educational, scientific, or even ecclesiastical institutions. Rather, the old subject-object dualistic view, which privileges the enterprising individual who uses the world for his or her own ends—including such worthy ones as scientific discoveries or a closer relationship with God—is still the dominant one. This is the sensibility that *functions* in our society, even though well-meaning people will claim that a relational view should function and that they themselves believe in it. The critical issue, however, is which model actually functions in society. Which model, the ecological or the subject-object one, is the implicit and determining assumption upon which decisions at all levels and in our major institutions are being made? We are not asking which idea is more interesting or important, but which way of understanding who we are actually shapes our society. Few would claim, I think, that the relational, subject-subjects model is the functional one in Western culture at the turn of the millennium.

Yet it should be and it needs to be. It should be because it is closer to reality as currently understood than is the alternative model. And it needs to be because the future of our species and the well-being of our entire planet depends on embracing it. As liberation theologian Leonardo Boff says, "When reconciled with ourselves . . . we can, without coercion, live with our own kind (social ecology), and also with all other creatures (environmental ecology), as, indeed, brothers and sisters."[19] "When reconciled with ourselves" is the chilling proviso: can we be reconciled so that we will be free to be the social beings we were created and meant to be? Christian faith has some important contributions to make to this all-important question, but so does the ecological model. If Christianity can tell us *how* we might become reconciled, the ecological model can help us see *what* such reconciliation looks like in our time.

A Case Study: Buber's I-Thou

One of the most interesting and suggestive examples of the ecological model is Martin Buber's I-Thou relationship. It is a helpful case study as we try to define our subject-subjects model, because Buber's view is similar to ours, though at one point significantly different. Like the Scottish Church Council's definition of spirituality, Buber's subject-subjects model includes developing a relationship not only with God and other human beings but also with nature. His insistence that we can and should have an I-Thou relationship with a tree often meets with astonishment if not ridicule, but he means it seriously:

> The tree is no impression, no play on my imagination, no value depending on my mood; but it is bodied over against me and has to do with me, as I with it—only in a different way.
>
> Let no attempt be made to sap the strength from the meaning of the relation: relation is mutual.
>
> The tree will have a consciousness, then, similar to my own? Of that I have no experience. . . . I encounter no soul or dryad of the tree, but the tree itself.[20]

The goal, however, of this I-Thou relationship is not just a relationship with the tree. Buber's main thesis in his famous book, *I and Thou*, is that in what he calls "uncanny moments," moments of intense, present awareness, one can glimpse the eternal Thou in and through the human and the natural Thous of this world: "Every particular *Thou* is a glimpse through to the eternal *Thou*. . . ."[21] The goal of I-Thou relationships, whether with other people or with nature, is mystical union with God.

On one reading of Buber, the momentary, fleeting I-Thou relationships with a tree or a person are the means to an individual's union with the eternal Thou.[22] Thus, Buber could be accused of religious utilitarianism: using the things of this world as stepping-stones to God. But such a reading would not be fair: the passage on the tree, for instance, is introduced by Buber's comment that in the I-Thou relation we are "seized by the power of exclusiveness."[23] The tree is not a figment of my imagination, nor does its value depend on my mood. Rather, it is "bodied over against me"; the relation is mutual, and therefore it is in some sense a subject. It puts itself forth in such a way that "I encounter . . . the tree itself." While Buber does indeed see all things *in* God, he does so in a way that tries hard to retain the intrinsic value of all the Thous through whom we meet the eternal Thou: "If you hallow this life, you meet the living God."[24] He wants "to give the world its due and its truth," while at the same time including the whole world in the eternal Thou, God.[25]

Yet one gets the impression from Buber that the I-Thou relationship is superior to the I-It; in fact, the common—and erroneous—interpretation is that the I-It relation objectifies things. Nonetheless, the intense moments of connection, of real relationship, between Thous are fleeting and rare; most of the time we live in the I-It world, the world of individuality, difference, and use. Buber sees this as necessary: I-It relations are simply what compose ordinary, everyday experiences of perceiving, knowing, willing, or feeling things. This kind of knowledge, however, does not contribute to our real, I-Thou relationship with others, which appears to be immediate and mystical. The I-Thou relationship is quite separate from knowing the other in its embodied, concrete, particular otherness. The real relationship, the relationship that through each thing unites us to God, is not based on concrete, embodied, particular beings and things in their individuality but on mystical connection. Even in the passage on the tree, Buber does not speak of *a* tree (one with a history of its own as well as perhaps a history with him), but of "the tree itself"—does he mean the essence of treeness?

For all his helpfulness in extending spirituality to the natural world as well as his insistence that our relation with nature be one of subject to subject, Buber comes very close to a nature-supernature dualism. What we know about others—their individuality, their embodied differences, their concrete reality—does not contribute to their real being as intimations of the Divine. Buber does not intend this dualism, for he says clearly that he sees all things *in* God; but the *particularity* of things does not appear to contribute to their divine role as conduits of God. The I-It and the I-Thou—individuality and real relationship—are two tracks. "The aim of self-differentiation is to experience and to use. . . . The aim of relation is relation's own being . . . through contact with every *Thou*, we are stirred with a breath of the *Thou*, that is, of eternal life."[26]

Buber's subject-subjects model deserves attention because it is close to the one that seems appropriate for super, natural Christians. It is a clear and well-known subject-subjects alternative to the dominant subject-object model. It includes nature as one of our three primary relationships. And it goes beyond secular subject-subjects models in that it relates everything, both the human and the natural worlds, to God. It appears to do everything right—except one thing. It does not allow us "to hold on hard to the huckleberries."[27] Buber's mystical eye sees through the forms of things and people to their divine ground. A model of being and knowing that begins with touch will forever resist this maneuver: it will insist on being bonded to skin, fur, and feathers, to the smells and sounds of the earth, to the intricate and detailed differences in people and other lifeforms. It will want to hold on hard to the huckleberries. It will insist that intimations of the divine be seen in the color purple and in the heart of a daffodil, in this particular woman dying of AIDS, in this Native village that has conquered alcoholism, in this economic plan for dealing with third-world debt. The ecological model for super, natural Christians must be one that allows us *to be* super, natural: a model that shows that, as the incarnation insists, God is found in the depth and detail of life and the earth, not apart from it or in spite of it.

Another way to express the difficulty that Buber's I-Thou model presents to super, natural Christians is its introversion and verticality. The powerful mysticism of the model turns the eye inward and upward toward the One Thou who includes all other Thous. Unlike the medieval model, which was extroverted and horizontal, inclining the eye to look outside the self and toward other creatures for signs and symbols of the divine, Buber's subject-subjects model is, at base, a model of one individual with God: I and Thou. It arose within twentieth-century existentialism and bears the marks of that cultural milieu. An ecological model is closer to the medieval view than to existentialism: it suggests a cosmology, not just a psychology, a way of being in the world rather than a way for an individual to find God.

Our ecological model is beginning to come into sharper focus. Let us take stock of our reflections so far. We began with the assumption that how we know and behave toward others depends on who we believe we are in relation to them: knowing and doing depend on being. We then suggested that touch, not sight, is our primary sense and that an ontology that begins with touch tells us some critical things about who we are in the scheme of things. We are subjects living among many other subjects whom we influence and who influence us. All of us, human beings included, are bodies—concrete, particular, different bodies—that both resist and respond to others. We learn a lesson in objectivity from these others, who, while interdependent with us, also provide limits to our self-aggrandizement and egocentricism. We are both similar to and different from others in the world, both human and nonhuman others—hence, we exist on a continuum with them rather than in a dualistic hierarchy over against them. And finally, therefore, neither hyperseparation nor fusion describes our relation to others, but rather a subject-subjects, mature relationship, one that is able to respect difference while embracing intimacy. Further, like the medieval model of self and world, which was extroverted and horizontal, we believe the ecological model also helps us to look outside of ourselves and toward others, for it too suggests a cosmology, a way of being in the world, and not just a psychology, an understanding of the self. Our reflections have been oriented toward finding a *functional cosmology*, an understanding of self in the world, not just a self with self, or the self with (human) neighbor, or even the self (alone) with God. And we need a cosmology that for our time is functional, that works, one that can become the implicit paradigm within which we make our personal decisions and our culture makes its corporate ones.

Marks of the Ecological Model

The subject-subjects model is based on human relationships. Can it, should it, be extended to the natural world? Should we treat other lifeforms and the earth itself as being on a continuum with how we treat other human beings, other subjects? The Western subject-object model of being and knowing assumes that human beings are so radically different from all other earthly creatures (by virtue of the reason/body split) that we can and should treat the natural realm in a radically different way: as an object. But the ecological model, grounded in touch, does not allow us that option: in this model the self is not just related to nature; rather, nature is constitutive of the self. Whatever we are has its roots in nature; moreover, we begin in the womb as a fertilized cell and we end in the grave as a decomposing body—we *are* physical. If nature is part of us, so we are part of nature; that is, not only are we body, but nature is spirit (or subject, soul—whatever we call that part of ourselves that we consider "more than" nature). The "more than" part of ourselves may be realized differently in various dimensions of nature, but it is also there (if, that is, we want to claim it is in us). The in-touch model of being and knowing insists on a continuum between "them" and "us": we are not just over against them, but they are part of us as we are part of them.

We turn, then, to a missing part of our subject-subjects model to consider how nonhuman beings can be considered subjects. We will look to feminist epistemology for insight, especially to feminist treatments of the mature self that can tolerate both intimacy and difference, that can avoid both fusion and dualism. From an analysis of the self that can relate to other people in a mature way, refusing either to be submerged in the other or to cannibalize the other, we will see how this same maturity can be a model for human-nature relations.

One of the main contributions of feminist epistemology is its critique of the dualized self and its proposal for a relational self. Psychoanalyst Jessica Benjamin speaks of the self as developed through the "dance of interaction," by recognition of both kinship and difference, by "both asserting the self and recognizing the other."[28] Theologian Catherine Keller criticizes the stereotypically male "separative self" as well as the female "soluble self," suggesting instead the "connective self."[29] Ecofeminist philosopher Val Plumwood believes in neither hyperseparation, which results in egotism, nor incorporation, which results in altruism. She espouses the relational or ecological self that can desire the well-being of others for their own sake as well as one's own, as, for instance, a mother desires her child's health.[30] Scientist Evelyn Fox Keller argues for "dynamic autonomy," which "reflects a sense of self . . . as both differentiated from and related to others, and a sense of others as subjects with whom one shares enough to allow for a recognition of them as subjects. . . ."[31] She claims that this sense of self allows for "dynamic objectivity," a kind of knowledge of others that, because it recognizes both distance from and connection with others, results in a greater objectivity or truer understanding of them than does the objectivity of subject-object dualism.[32] Psychologist Caroline Whitbeck insists that the actual development of the self is not dyadic but multiple: we are formed by interaction with many others, some similar and some very different from ourselves.[33] Philosopher of science Donna Haraway claims that the end of the dualized self allows us to refigure relations between humans, nature, and machines in novel, cross-boundary ways, in ways other than hierarchical dualism and incorporation.[34]

This sampling of feminist views of the self suggests a number of characteristics that will help us fill out our notion of the subject-subjects model of being and knowing. First is recognition of the fragility of the human self. It tends on the one hand to fear absorption by others and hence to hyperseparate from them, resulting in subject-object dualism. On the other hand, it tends to fear alienation from others and hence to incorporate into others, resulting in romanticism, deep ecology, and the conventional feminine loss of self.[35] The alternative model of the self and others that feminists propose is a mature one. A self in this model is able to bear these fears and not succumb to them, able to embrace intimacy (and not slide into incorporation or fusion) and to recognize differences (and not retreat into hyperseparation or dualism). Maintaining this balance is difficult: it demands acceptance of who one is at the deepest level. One must be at home with oneself. It is, as we will suggest, beyond our capabilities to achieve on a sustained basis. While an analysis of the self can help us see the model of self and world we need, analysis cannot bring it about. A conversion of the heart and acceptance of ourselves as both loved and limited is needed; it requires, in other words, what in Christian circles is called "justification" by God. We will come to that eventually, but an ecological understanding of self and world *can* help us see in some detail what it would mean to relate to others—and even to nature—as subject to subject. Hence the first point is that a relational self-world model is difficult; it demands maturity and the refusal either to fuse with others or retreat from them.

Second, the model is not dyadic but multiple; it is not oppositional, but interactive. It is not a landscape model, where I stand surveying the other as object, but a maze model, where I am moving about in the world, being touched by and touching many others. The model assumes that I am formed by many relationships of many different sorts with others, some of whom are like me and some unlike me in various ways. In other words, the ecological model assumes multiple relations with many others, who are related to the self analogously along a continuum. For example, let us look briefly at the life of John Woolman, the remarkable eighteenth-century Quaker and abolitionist who in his *Journal* writes of the many influences that made him the person he became.[36] They range from a boyhood incident in which he killed a mother robin, causing him to realize the consequences of an evil act (he must now kill the chicks), to his decision to walk hundreds of miles rather than use post horses, which were being mistreated. Woolman saw the interdependence of relationships and acts; for instance, he noted that because of the expensive lifestyle of slave masters, slaves became a "necessity," whereas frugality also had a rippling effect, resulting in a fairer distribution of goods to all people. The self he became was influenced by and dependent on many different others—from robins and horses to slavemasters and slaves. Our experiences with the others in the world make us who we become: we are both continuous with them and different from them in complex ways. The relationship with these many others is certainly not a subject-object dualism; rather, it is more like an interaction with subjects of various sorts (robins, horses, slaves, slavemasters) who influence one another in rich, diverse, multiple ways. Donna Haraway summarizes this point well. "The knowing self is partial in all its guises, never finished, whole, simply there and original; it is always constructed and stitched together imperfectly, and *therefore* able to join with another, to see together without claiming to be another."[37]

Third, because the relational model sees a continuity between the self and others, it knows them differently—not as objects, but objectively. Because it is (presumably, hopefully) mature, able to deal with intimacy and difference, it is not afraid of the other (the different) but can see it as it is with love, with the recognition that the other exists for itself and not just for me.[38] Recall Iris Murdoch's enigmatic statement (which perhaps is now becoming clearer), "Love is the extremely difficult realization that something other than oneself is real. Love . . . is the discovery of reality."[39] Love is being objective, the recognition that reality is made up of *others*. The relational self can feel a close connection with others as subjects who live in their own worlds with their own interests (as I do), without wanting to fuse with them. Rather, the relational self desires to know these others, to understand and appreciate them. Thus, the ecological model of the self, the self defined by its connections with others, results in knowledge of others that could be called "loving objectivity. "It is a kind of loving attention that friends might give to each other, in which the goal is the well-being of the other, or that a father who wishes the best for his offspring might bestow on his child, or that a naturalist might exhibit for an old-growth forest's health, causing her to learn as much as possible about it. This kind of knowledge assumes that one knows another subject, but knows them "objectively." In fact, loving the other as subject—that is, as one who, like myself, has a world and interests—is the very reason for desiring the knowledge to be objective: to be what is best for *this* subject in *its* world.[40]

Finally, the relational model of self and world, built as it is on a flexible, fluid boundary of self and others, means that self-interest and altruism are not always opposed; in fact, they often converge.[41] Just as one rejoices when a friend or a child gets a good job or an award (since one's own self is formed and nurtured by these relations), it is also imaginable that we would rejoice when a marshland is preserved for migrating birds or a pocket-park bill is passed in our city, if we believed that our interior landscape is formed by the exterior landscape. If self and world are not oppositional but connected, so that who we are is profoundly related to who the others are—including the others in the natural world—then well-being becomes a more common term; in fact, one's own well-being could not come about apart from the well-being of others.

In sum, then, the ecological or relational subject-subjects model of being and knowing calls for a mature self, one able to be intimate with the other while appreciating its difference; for multiple, interactive relations with many different kinds of subjects; for a loving objectivity toward others whose connections with the self make it possible for us to find our own self-interest in the interests of others.

The Subject-Subjects Model and Nature

Can we extend this model of the self and the world to our relations with nature? In one sense, the question is redundant, if not absurd. The ecological model of self and world is *derived* from the workings of natural systems: we are interpreting the human self's relation to the world as one instance of ecological interrelationship and interdependence. But, in another sense, the question is a real one because the subject-subjects model is based in *human* relationships. Our answer is yes: it can and should be extended to nature. Actually, it is easy to do so. Because the model began with touch and throughout stresses the multiplicity of subjects, their diversity, and their continuity, the model is open to the natural world. In fact, our attitude toward nature can be seen as the test case of the first feature of the model—maturity to embrace intimacy with the other while also acknowledging difference. The hyperseparation of the subject-object model comes about principally because of human fear of being anything like nature. A mature self can feel profound closeness with nature without fear of being absorbed into it, can recognize that we and the chimpanzees are genetically 98 percent the same yet different in interesting and significant ways. The second characteristic of the subject-subjects model is its inclusion of multiple relations with many different kinds of subjects, all related to each other analogously. This opens the way to speak of animals, trees and plants, mountains, oceans, and even the earth as a whole as subjects, as agents which both influence others and are influenced by them. We will presently deal with this issue in more detail. The third feature of the model underscores the "in itselfness" of each entity we know: that objective knowledge of others means desiring to understand them in their own worlds. Other species, then, should not be defined in relationship to us; they are not human beings *manqué;* they do not simply lack what we have. Perhaps there is no greater significance of our model than this point: it overturns knowledge of nature *as object,* as for or against human beings, and insists we know it *objectively,* in terms of its own subjecthood. Finally, since the subject-subjects model understands all beings and entities to exist on a continuum of similarity and difference, the dualistic opposition of my good and their good breaks down. Thus, we human beings cannot deny our dependence on nature, as masters have denied their dependence on slaves, men on women. The model supports a holistic understanding of well-being: the health of nature and my health—as well as the health of other human beings—are interrelated.

Let us now pick up one crucial aspect of the subject-subjects model as extended to nature: how can we speak of the other (non-human) lifeforms, of the land, and even of the earth as subjects?[42] Marilyn Frye speaks of "the health and integrity of an organism [as] a matter of its being organized largely toward its own interests and welfare."[43] An object cannot, does not, do that: it does not have a center that influences and organizes its environment toward its own flourishing. The ability to do so suggests something like agency or intentionality: remember the wood tick who will wait eighteen years for the right combination of light, sweat, and heat to complete its lifecycle? It is a subject living within a defined world, even as we are. The point is not that we find this world narrow or the goal of the subject minimal. Rather, the point is to recognize that the wood tick is not merely an object in *our* world (for instance, an annoyance if lodged under one's clothing), but *a subject in its own world.* It is an agent; it has an intention, though not necessarily a conscious one. Val Plumwood gives us a helpful definition of nonhuman others as subjects. "The ecological self recognizes the earth other as a centre of agency or intentionality having its origin and place like mine in the community of the earth, but as a different centre of agency, which limits mine."[44] She notes that to some animals we can ascribe awareness, choice, imagination, and emotion (missing a companion, choosing the wrong way, learning a new technique) and to a larger class sentience, pleasure and pain, and volition. In any case, similarity to or distance from *our* form of subjectivity (which is marked by consciousness and reason) ought not to be the standard. Rather, Plumwood claims that there is an unfolding, development, and directedness inherent in all natural processes. "The plant world includes fully intentional others whose strivings, interactions and differences in life strategy are intricate, amazing, and mysterious."[45] "To all living creatures we may clearly ascribe a teleology or overall life-goal, for the sake of which its parts are organised. . . . Intentionality is common to all these things, and does not mark off the human, the mental, or even the animate."[46] Here teleology means growth, flourishing. Mountains, for instance, are the products of a long, unfolding natural process, with a specific history and a particular trajectory for further change. Forest ecosystems are wholes, "whose interrelationship of parts can only be understood in terms of stabilizing and organising principles," which are intentional in the sense of directed toward the growth and flourishing of the forest.[47] In these terms, then, it is possible to speak of the integrity of the land and even of the whole planet—that they are, in this sense, subjects whose intention is their own healthy flourishing.[48]

We search for appropriate language here, language that will underscore that "we are like them" and "they are like us" without either reductionism or anthropomorphism. The language of intentions, goals, purpose, direction—even of health and flourishing— refers first of all to us. We use it metaphorically of the earth others, not knowing how it applies but finding it better and more appropriate than its opposite. Another way to make this point is to note that the language of intentions and goals revives the medieval belief after several centuries of Cartesian disbelief that nature is like us. An evolutionary, ecological picture of reality supports this claim, for since we are born from nature, our "mother" must be *something* like us.

At the very least this means problematizing the boundaries between self and other, subject and object, extending autonomy, agency, and creativity beyond our own species. Evelyn Fox Keller's notion of "dynamic autonomy," the recognition that the human sense of selfhood is formed from interaction with others (including earth others) is at the same time an acknowledgment that these others are also subjects, agents that both influence and are influenced.[49] In fact, as Keller notes, we cannot even know another "objectively" (as it is in itself) unless we consider it to be a subject. As object it simply fits too easily into our preconceived notions of what it is, but as subject its particularity must be attended to in order for us to know it as it is.[50]

The Cartesian dualism that has plagued us for several centuries is loosening its grip. The rigid boundaries between subject and object, self and other, mind and body, humans and nature are being questioned. "Postmodern philosophy is beginning to discover the body in the mind, the mind in the animal, the body as the site of cultural inscription, nature as creative other."[51] For example, Donna Haraway's way of speaking of the fluid boundaries between humans and nature includes the notion of nature's agency. She suggests that agents or actors are not just human. "We need a concept of agency that opens up possibilities for figuring relationality within social worlds where actors fit oddly, at best, into previous *taxa* of the human, the natural, or the constructed."[52] Or, as she puts it concisely, "Actors come in many and wonderful forms."[53] She suggests the metaphor of "coyote" or trickster for nature's agency because, while not a subject in the same way humans are, nature is (as seen in Native cultures) "genuinely social and actively relational."[54]

The subject-subjects model is also a boundary-crossing notion, refusing the antagonistic opposition of humans versus nature. Hence, when we extend the subject-subjects model to nature, we are doing nothing more than recognizing our roots in nature and nature's incarnation in us. Within the evolutionary, ecological story, we are not and cannot possibly be utterly different from all the rest. This story claims that we are all similar, even at the point of what we consider our most distinctive endowment—our value as subjects. The others also have this endowment, at some level and in some way.

Super, Natural Christ.

p 69, 70.   p 75
76, p 84, Scopophili
85,

David Korten –
Globalizing Civil
Society; Reclaiming
our right t

1-800-596-7437

...py about this: we are not sug-
...conscious, purposive subjects,
...to be objects for us. They are
...nconscious ones, oriented to
...ents, influence, often in broad
...is means, among other things,
...sons we should take the earth
...e they are centers of value in
...subjects they can and do alter

...ty of other lifeforms, the land,
...ical to embracing fully the sub-
...ge in breaking down the polar-
...ver nature that has plagued us
...we accept this ontology—that
...fferent—then the way we know
...em will also change. We will not
...se of controlling or using them,
...nderstanding them better both
...ill, of course, also use earth oth-
...e will do so remembering that
...knowledge of all others, then,
...ons, rather than how we know
...ns, unlike knowledge of objects,
...her is, is not merely the creation
...penness of the known as well as
...g eye of the knower.[58] The best
...also fine naturalists, understand
...that genuine knowledge of these
...k information about them but
...ss, and the willingness to be sur-
...le, had a healthy respect for the
...hat her great love, the sea, pre-
sented her with. She did not ... romantic attachment to it nor did
she think of it as a mother, but rather as "a rewarding, awesome,
albeit unruly, and always surprising acquaintance."[59] Feminists often
use the example of friendship (rather than one of our blood relationships) to illustrate this kind of knowledge: friendship insists on
detailed, careful acquaintance which can happen only through interactive, reciprocal relations between the knower and the known.[60] It
assumes an ecological base for both ontology and knowledge: we *live*

and *learn* in relationships. The goal of this knowledge is practical: it is to help create a better world, one fit for habitation by human beings and the earth others.

Finally, the subjectification of the world (in contrast to its objectification) creates in us a different, basic sensibility toward it. Thomas Moore expresses this sensibility with his notion of "soul-ecology"—a sensibility that sees other people, animals, mountains, and even city buildings as presenting themselves to us vividly, each in its own particularity, independence, and subjectivity. It is the recognition, similar to the notion of the *anima mundi* in medieval times and the early Renaissance, that other things have life and vitality. The world is alive, not dead; it is like an organism, not a machine. Soul-ecology is not, however, about a general sense of life and vitality, but a particular sense of them. As he notes, "An animal reveals its soul in its striking appearance, in its life habits, and in its style. The things of nature similarly show themselves with extraordinary particularity. A river's power and beauty give it an imposing presence. A striking building stands before us as an individual every bit as soulful as we are."[61] Moore sums up soul-ecology by claiming it is "the capacity of things to be close to us, to reveal their beauty and express subjectivity."[62] In post-Enlightenment modernity we have lost the capacity for deep connection to other entities, both living and nonliving, in their concrete individuality. "It's a simple idea: if you don't love things in particular, you cannot love the world, because the world doesn't exist except in individual things."[63] Indeed, it does not—and with this insight we turn to our last point on the ecological model: what it can do for the Christian wanting to be super, natural. It can help us become lovers of, friends with, nature by teaching us to pay attention to it in all its concrete individuality, otherness, and difference.

The Loving Eye

Paying attention to another person or thing with a loving rather than an arrogant eye is not easy. We can only see and know others rightly, that is, as selves with interests of their own, if we are relatively mature, relatively confident of our own boundaries, being neither egocentric nor self-denying. In childhood we often experience closeness with others—human, animal, and plant life—with a kind of "world-openness," a deep pleasure in exploring the world for its own sake.[64] This first naiveté is an unself-conscious interest in nature, a wide-eyed curiosity about it, as well as identification with it. It is not a state to which we can return, much as romantics and deep ecologists wish we might. Rather, our task is to attempt the second naiveté, a return to connection with others that recognizes distance and respects differences. Often we do not or cannot manage this measure of maturity. We either fall back into merging with others (the so-called feminine pattern), or we distance ourselves entirely from them (the so-called masculine or the subject-object pattern). The subject-subjects model asks for something much more difficult of us: that we relate to all others as subjects, which means affirming connections and recognizing boundaries. In other words, the ecological model of being and knowing says that we should see others with a loving eye.

Those who have written most perceptively on the loving eye all insist that it has two major notes: an appreciation of the difference and particularity of others as well as an empathetic connection with them. It is as if the world-openness of childhood, that sense of interest in and closeness with all others, had now gone to school; it is to be educated to understand how difficult it is to really know others in their otherness and also to feel genuine bonds of affection for them—*as they are.* Elizabeth Spelman speaks of "the strenuousness of knowing other people, even people very much like ourselves."[65] Consider, then, knowing people not like ourselves as well as knowing other nonhuman subjects, *very unlike* ourselves, and the need for education becomes clear.

Let us look at each of these notes: the otherness of the other and ways we can become close to the other, as other. On the first point, because the arrogant eye, the eye that objectifies and cannibalizes, is so dominant, we need to undergo stern discipline in letting the other "be." A critical part of our education is to focus on the distance, the difference, the particularity, the uniqueness, the "in itselfness," the indifference, the otherness, of the other. We need, for a while, to bracket all connections and simply try to appreciate others as other. This is the aesthetic mode of perception and is expressed in a statement by Rainer Marie Rilke: "In order to have an object speak to you, you must take it for a certain time for the only one that exists, the only phenomenon which, through your devoted and exclusive love, finds itself placed at the center of the universe."[66] An exercise in *detachment* is a necessary preliminary to attachment, for we must attempt to see others as they are, in themselves, for themselves, as subjects.[67] We are often shocked by this exercise. It seems both impersonal and useless (as art is often considered to be in our culture). What the aesthetic mode of perception, however, helps us do is pay attention to individuals in all their particularity: we look at a sunset, a building, even another person simply to appreciate them in their difference and detail. Iris Murdoch puts it this way: "The greatest art is 'impersonal' because it shows us the world, our world and not another one, with a clarity which startles and delights us simply because we are not used to looking at the real world at all."[68] The aesthetic mode "holds on hard to the huckleberries," compelling us to stop, look, and listen to this thing, that person, this event: to pay attention. It is the mode of perception that appreciates the color purple in a field somewhere and that wants to look into the center of a daffodil. It also pays attention to the differences in people's faces. It rejoices in everything being separate and other and special and its own thing. The reason why aesthetic detachment is a necessary first step in developing the loving eye is because, as Murdoch says, it brings about "the extremely difficult realisation that something other than oneself is real," it brings about "the discovery of reality."[69] We cannot connect appropriately with real others, in their real differences from us, until we acknowledge who and what they are in their own worlds with their own wishes and needs.

It appears that one of the chief obstacles to developing this aspect of the loving eye—aesthetic distance—is fantasy.[70] We imagine who or what the other is, rather than taking the time to find out. Elizabeth Spelman contrasts imaginative thinking, which can easily slide into fantasy, with perception, and quotes Jean-Paul Sartre to illustrate her point:

> When I perceive Peter I can always approach him closely enough to see the grain on his skin, to observe his enlarged pores, and even the theoretical possibility of my examining his microscopic cells and so on to infinity. This infinity is implicitly contained in my actual perception, it overflows it infinitely by everything I can specify about him at each moment. It is this which constitutes the "massiveness" of real objects, but the nature of Peter as an image is to be "thinned."[71]

The thinness of imagination versus the richness of perception: this is a fascinating point since so often imagination is praised as more important and profound than mere perception. The attentive eye, the eye that wants to educate itself about the other in all its thickness, detail, and difference depends on perception, not imagination. There is, of course, a hermeneutical issue here. We have insisted that there is no such thing as an innocent eye, that we always see from particular contexts, that all sight is embodied (the eye of the body versus the presumably pure eye of the mind). Nonetheless, as we shall see from some of our finest nature writers, a combination of scientific knowledge, empathy, and aesthetic distance can join to produce sketches of natural subjects in their own worlds that are closer to these worlds than would be works of either imagination or science.

Spelman concludes from her exercise in the importance of perception that to know another truly, one must become an *apprentice*. Here we move into the second note necessary to developing and educating the loving eye: the appropriate *connection* between knower and known. A mature relationship with others, especially others very different from ourselves, demands modes of connection that acknowledge difference. We cannot slip back into the innocent child's eye nor the merged eye of the romantic; rather, we should become apprentices or world-travelers, enter into modes of connection that privilege the other as teacher and guide, with the knower taking the position of listener, novice, foreigner.[72] It will not be easy to develop a mature, affectionate relationship with others while taking full account of their real, and often radical, differences. We will often feel as one does when beginning a new kind of work or traveling in a foreign country: one does not "know one's way about." Trying to discover who another person is as a subject in their own world, especially if the person is of a different race, class, or country, demands time, patience, openness, attention to detail, and the willingness to be surprised. It demands educating the eye: it is not enough to feel a sense of oneness with others; in fact, wanting closeness without respect for differences is usually a mask for one's own way of life or agenda. For example, some women of color resist the notion of the sisterhood of all women, finding this blood relationship a poor metaphor for taking into account the deep differences among women: it assumes an intimate relationship to be already in place when it is not.[73] "Friendship" is often seen as a more viable metaphor: it is not a given, but something that must be worked for.[74] The loving eye of friendship is not the taken-for-granted eye of blood relations, but the educated eye, which realizes that understanding the other in his or her unique particularity is the necessary prerequisite to helping the other.[75] If the goal of friendship is the well-being of the other (one likes a friend and wants them to prosper), then becoming an apprentice to the friend, learning to travel in his or her world, is a prerequisite.

Again, we extend our model to nature as subject: we should become friends with nature. The way to make our eye able to love nature truly—not fuse with it or control it, but respect it in its differences while feeling empathy for it—is to educate ourselves. Nature writers, who combine information and empathy, respect for particular worlds of plants and animals studied with loving attention, illustrate how the model can be extended. For example, the early twentieth-century American naturalist John Muir's special gift was listening to plants, which "included analytical scrutiny, along with sensitivity to the plant's environmental relationships. Muir's listening to a plant also involved cultivating empathy—that intuitive projection by which we imagine the character of another. Together these techniques create the kind of understanding we hope for in human relationships: recognition of another's living integrity."[76] Muir himself wrote, "I could distinctly hear the varying tones of individual trees—Spruce, and Fir, and Pine, and the leafless Oak. Each was expressing itself in its own way—singing its own song, and making its own particular gestures. . . ."[77] Muir neither sentimentalized nor objectified nature: rather, his intention was to understand plants better by paying loving attention, patient, careful attention, to the particularity of these others in their own worlds. On the basis of a lifetime of such attentive love for trees and plants, he spoke out on their behalf, becoming an important voice in the preservation of many forest areas.[78]

The loving eye, then, is the eye of the second naiveté, educated so as to help us embrace intimacy while recognizing difference. This is the eye trained in detachment in order that its attachment will be objective, based on the reality of the other and not on its own wishes or fantasies. This is the eye bound to the other as is an apprentice to a skilled worker, listening to the other as does a foreigner in a new country. This is the eye that pays attention to the other so that the connections between knower and known, like the bond of friendship, will be based on the real subject in its real world. The world of touch, of childhood, of the first naiveté that tells us we *are* all interrelated and interdependent, becomes, through the educated loving eye, its mature, adult realization—the second naiveté. We become able to love all the others, the human ones and the earth others, with intimacy and distance, with affection and respect for difference.

We must now deepen and illustrate this conversation. How can we move from the first to the second naiveté, from the child's innocent, innate delight in other lifeforms to a nuanced, educated, and responsible love of nature? How can we educate the loving eye so that we *can* be super, natural Christians, caring for nature rightly, appropriately, in terms of its own needs? How can faith in God's justification—divine acceptance of our fragile egos—help us to become mature, super, natural Christians? How will Christian faith push the loving eye beyond even the second naiveté, slanting it in a more radical direction? The last two chapters will deal with these issues. In chapter 6 we will take a deeper look at the importance of direct experience with nature, especially for children and city dwellers. We will then consider the significance of mediated experience with nature through the work of nature writers. In the last chapter we will reflect on the ethic of care that emerges from the ecological model as well as Christianity's contribution to this ethic. We will focus on two contributions: the importance of justification as the remedy for sin (our refusal or inability to treat others as subjects) and care of the neediest subjects that emerges from Christian radical, inclusive love. We will close with some thoughts on a new, sober sacramentalism.

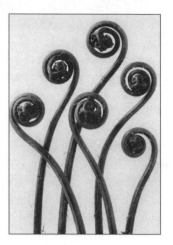

6

Down to Earth

*Close Encounters with the
Natural World*

NATURALIST ROBERT PYLE CLAIMS THAT ONE OF THE major causes for the ecological crisis is "the extinction of experience":
the lack of close encounters with the earth in the lives of many children and adults.[1] It is not just that other lifeforms are becoming
scarce or extinct, but our experience of and with them is, too. The
results are deep and disturbing. We not only learn less about these
earth others; but disaffection sets in, and hence we care less for
their well-being. We do not care about what we do not know. With
the loss of direct experience with nature, a cycle begins: distance
breeds lack of knowledge, lack of interest, lack of concern. Pyle
notes, "People who care conserve; people who don't know don't
care. What is the extinction of a condor to a child who has never
known a wren?"[2]

Our cities are constructed with one species in mind: our own.
The others, the ones that cannot adapt to our habitat, gradually
slip away until they are gone—out of sight, out of mind. A city
block in Chicago or Los Angeles is often composed of human
beings and human-made materials—brick, concrete, macadam,
along with the insects, rodents, and odd blades of grass that can
find their niche. But what happens to nature *and* to us in such
habitats? It is not only nature that suffers; we do as well. And both
are diminished. The ecological model of being and knowing claims
that we only exist in interrelationship and interdependence with
others, and not just human others. An in-touch model insists that
fundamentally we are embodied subjects on a continuum with

many other different kinds of embodied subjects, all of which live together in relations of mutual response. Nature is a major companion in our human journey. Take away all others except the human ones and what happens to us? We are deprived of what E. O. Wilson calls our innate desire to connect with other life-forms—our "biophilia."[3] Often we humans admonish one another to love nature out of a sense of duty in order to conserve and protect it, and we certainly should do so. But those who have spent the most time with nature—the naturalists, biologists, and nature writers—often claim that loving nature comes "naturally" to humans. Gary Nabhan credits his boyhood fascination with herons along the Lake Michigan shoreline with his decision to become a naturalist.

> I did not realize until later that it was not a *new* career; the vocation of being a naturalist on one's home ground is truly the oldest profession in the world. Several million years of foraging and hunting by our hominid ancestors had hard-wired into me—into all of us through natural selection—the capacity to see the world as a naturalist. I was preadapted to give my full attention to those herons.[4]

If we are hard-wired, preadapted to close encounters with the natural world, then the loss of such experiences is a deep and damaging one—to *us*. We are less because of that loss. As we turn now to consider in more depth how the loving eye might be educated so that we, as Christians, can love nature more appropriately, the first thing we must note is that it is not just an obligation. The ecological model, based in touch, is a reciprocal one: we touch and *are touched*. The first naiveté of childhood, that rush of interest and joy in insects, tadpoles, weeds, puppies, and creeks, is a clue to who we are in the scheme of things: we belong with these others and feel good when we are in their company.

This chapter will investigate in more depth the first and second naiveté: the grounding in childhood experiences of a love for nature and the education of that love through the mediation of nature writing. Nature writing illustrates the basic components of the loving eye: appreciation for the otherness of the other (through aesthetic distancing) and appropriate bonding with the other (through apprenticeship, listening, and friendship). While there are certainly other forms of mediation between humans and nature, nature writing, we will suggest, is a particularly helpful one.

Do Touch: Experience, Place, and Wildness

If we are biophiliacs, creatures who desire to connect with other
creatures, then we can understand Robert Pyle's statement that to a
child, "a face-to-face encounter with a banana slug means much
more than a Komodo dragon seen on television."[5] People who, as
adults, have a love and concern for nature usually develop it as children through direct experiences in particular locales that have the
feel of wildness. There is often a ditch, a small park, a creek, an abandoned railbed where one could wander, collecting bugs or chestnuts,
chasing squirrels—or whatever. The place need not be large, and
certainly not a wilderness, but it should be wild; that is, undomesti-
cated, potentially surprising, inviting us to meet earth others as subjects. A television nature film or even a self-interpreting nature trail
will not do: the experience must be direct, it must be in a particular
place, and that place should be wild. For a five-year-old these criteria can be fulfilled quite satisfactorily by a handy ditch; for a ten-year
old, by a vacant lot; for an adult, by a wooded acre or two.

Let us look more closely at these components of close encounters
with nature—direct experience, locale, and wildness. In her book,
An American Childhood, Annie Dillard comments on her own awakening to the wonder of being alive: "Children ten years old wake up
and find themselves here, discover themselves to have been here all
along. . . . They wake like sleepwalkers, in full stride; they wake like
people brought back from cardiac arrest or from drowning. . . ."[6] Her
awakening came about as she roamed Frick Park, a small wooded
area in residential Pittsburgh, where she imagined herself a pioneer
searching for panther tracks, pried under rocks in creek beds to find
salamanders, collected buckeyes. She began to identify birds in the
park with the help of a field guide, started to draw pictures of the
animals she encountered (which helped her to see them better), collected rocks until she had over 340 of them, and checked out the
Field Book of Ponds and Streams from her local library (which she
notes had also been checked out by many other people in the black
ghetto area of the city where she lived). Her parents bought her a
microscope, which opened another level of connection for her to this
amazing world that literally stunned her. Her astonishment at seeing
an amoeba through the microscope for the first time, her rushing to
share this wonder with her parents, and her continuing sense of
being constantly surprised by the world around her epitomizes the
first naiveté: "Month after month, year after year, the true and bril-

liant light, and the complex and multifaceted coloration, of this actual, historical, waking world invigorated me."[7] Her direct experiences in her "wild" city park woke her up to the world about her. These childhood experiences gave her a permanent sense of living in a rich, interesting, responsive environment of which she was a part, as was everything else. She became, quite literally, awake to the world. Everything, everyone interested her (as we might say, as subjects, as others): "Everywhere, things snagged me," she writes, "One took note; one took notes."[8] Every baby interested her, but so did tetanus shots, tennis balls, city pebbles, violin makers, fishermen, Islamic scholars, vials of air, bats, and even muddy rawcuts left by Pittsburgh road builders. She was interested in people, things, events, other lifeforms just because they were themselves, they were here, they were different—and fascinating. As she states, "What is important is anyone's coming awake and discovering a place, finding in full orbit a spinning globe one can lean over, catch, and jump on. What is important is the moment of opening a life and feeling it touch—with an electric hiss and cry—this speckled mineral sphere, our present world."[9] This sense of awakening to the world, of seeing it alive and oneself alive in it and toward it, is what could be called a conversion to the earth. It is a conversion that, if begun in childhood, can last a lifetime. Dillard comments that at her present age she wakes up again and again every day, "And still I break up through the skin of awareness a thousand times a day, as dolphins burst through seas, and dive again, and rise, and dive."[10]

The first naiveté, the sense of both wonder at and connection with other living things, is magnificently captured in Dillard's account of her childhood. Is this mix of direct experience with nature in areas of relative wildness still possible for our children and ourselves? Is it even necessary or important? Is second-hand knowledge of nature through books, television nature films, interactive computer simulations, and school nature programs not enough? These mediated sources are certainly important, as we will see when we look at one of them—nature writing—in more depth. But there is, nonetheless, no substitute for the real thing. Biologist Stephen Jay Gould, lamenting the emphasis that some modern science museums place on interactive displays and computer games, notes that nothing stirs the imagination like bones do. "The real bones [of a tyrannosaurus] send shivers down my spine, for I know they supported an actual breathing and roaring animal some 70 million years ago."[11] The reason why the real thing, the direct experience with other earth creatures in places of relative wildness, is important to both children and adults is that only in this way do we *feel* in touch with these others. Only in this way do we become aware again and again of our deep connection with them. This is not an oceanic experience of connection with nature in general. Rather, it is an interest, a fascination with others, often one other, that develops from focused attention to particular things in special places. It comes from small beginnings in local places with some concrete, embodied other.

A luminous time in my own childhood will provide an example. My family owned a small cabin on a Cape Cod lake, and from the time I was about eight or nine years old, I was allowed to go alone in a rowboat, with its half-a-horse-power motor, to the third lake (the one furthest from the cabin) to hunt for sun turtles.[12] I often went early in the morning, which increased my enormous sense of adventure: to go alone to this—to me—remote area to hunt, indeed, stalk turtles was a privilege around which I could scarcely contain my excitement. I spent hours hunkered down in the boat, creeping up, with the help of a canoe paddle, to the sleeping turtles sunning themselves on lily pads. I seldom netted one, but occasionally I succeeded. The real success, however, occurred at another level: the sense of being on an adventure in a wild area, an adventure in which I was in a close encounter with a mysterious and fascinating other species—as I found turtles to be then and still do—gave me a sense of intimate connection with them. For years I kept turtles as pets, until I realized the cruelty of this practice; then I started a collection of stone, wood, and glass turtles; and even now I will stop my car and come close to risking my life to rescue a foolhardy turtle attempting to cross a highway. My early experiences with this wild other, these reptiles, with their ancient lineage, impressive longevity, ingenious skeleton, and immense difference from my own species, have made it my link to nature.[13] It is as if turtles opened up a pathway for me into the natural world—giving me a bridge to pass over into that other world. Turtles were then and still are my animal "other," the one with whom I feel a special connection, a special empathy. Whenever I see the peculiar shape of a turtle—the humped back and stretched-out neck—even just the shadow of it or from a distance down a road, I feel a visceral reaction: my attention is immediately and totally riveted on it. Peculiar? Perhaps, but a witness to the power of the first naiveté, to the bond with the natural world characterized by curiosity, fascination, wonder, and attention that can awaken in a child and continue, albeit in different forms, throughout life.

Was the opportunity to hunt turtles when I was a child a significant cause in my becoming an ecological theologian? Did the fact that I have returned to the natural world with a second naiveté, an educated, loving eye, come from these early experiences? Who can say? I suspect there is a connection; at any rate, I do believe that in order for people, both children and adults, to see themselves and nature within an ecological model, hands-on, down to earth, close encounters are essential.

But how possible are they? According to some recent statistics, 57 percent of third-world children live in urban slums, and 25 percent of American children do. In the U.S. most Anglo as well as Hispanic and Native children gain what knowledge they have of nature through television and other secondhand media.[14] Yet many naturalists maintain that the middle years of childhood, from seven to twelve (before the inner turmoil of puberty sets in) are the window of opportunity when openness to and fascination with nature is at its peak—the time to load "the ark of the mind" with other species.[15] Many children, especially city dwellers—and to an even greater extent, poor city children—are being deprived of critical experiences with nature, the loss of which may affect them in profound ways. It will certainly affect how they think of themselves in the scheme of things, a scheme that will not include nature. That lack will diminish them as well as diminish nature. A chilling example makes the point: in a PBS interview after the 1992 Los Angeles riots, a young man from the area correctly identified six automatic weapons by their sound alone.[16] In another time and place he would have been able to identify six common species of hawks and owls by sound alone. The interior landscape *is* influenced by the exterior. The environment in which a child develops matters: whether that environment includes nature or is defined by weapons influences who that child becomes and what she or he cares about.

We have been claiming that local, close-by, available wild places are necessary for people and that such places give them the direct experiences with nature that help to create a sense of belonging to nature and caring about it. Such experiences are central to our ecological model's becoming a *functional* one for people. But is this just out-of-date, nostalgic, utopian thinking? Is it also elitist? Are such experiences now only possible for the well-off few who can escape the concrete jungles of our cities for the few remaining wilderness areas?

Some would say so, but let us recall that wildness is not the same as wilderness. "Wildness" is a place to be visited on its own terms; it

is not necessarily a vast track of land, but a place available for exploration.[17] Wildness means accepting the place and those who live in
it as other, as others—it is not the size or remoteness of the area that
matters, but the opportunity it presents to meet earth others as subjects. Wildness can be found in a piece of near-by nature: a small city
park, of course, but also what one naturalist calls "hand-me-down
habitats," "unofficial countryside," "shreds and scraps of the natural
scene"—free places for pottering, netting, catching, and watching.[18]
It can include derelict railway land, ditchbanks, abandoned farm
land, cemeteries, the grounds of a city museum, bankrupt building
sites, old gravel pits, embankments, margins of landfills, and vacant
lots. "A miniscule ecosystem pinched off between two interstates
near downtown Kansas City is a wonder of varied habitats, from
swamp-loving cattails to towering oaks and sycamores."[19] Wildness
can even, if pressed, be found in a terrarium or an aquarium, an
apartment balcony garden, house plants, or a goldfish named Ellery.
"Try the old trick of marking off a square yard and exploring just there
with as much attention as you would a Rocky Mountain meadow."[20]
One can practice one's stalking skills and be surprised by the unexpected in a tiny natural place—provided one approaches the place
with a sense of expecting to meet a surprising other. Is wildness,
then, in the eye of the beholder? Yes, of course, in part it is. For some
people the Rocky Mountains are not wild; a tourist with camera in
hand can domesticate those mountains very easily. For other people
that square yard of backyard dirt is a veritable treasure trove of
strange and wonderful creatures.

But we in America have a long history of finding wildness only in
wilderness. In his study of nature in American culture and literature,
Leo Marx makes the case that the pastoral ideal, the flight from the
city (the domain of the machine) to the country (the place of the
garden) has defined our sensibility.[21] Nature means wilderness; it
means escape from the ordinary life to the extraordinary, the primitive, the good and the pure. The call of the wilderness is evident in
the writings of Mark Twain, Ernest Hemingway, or Robert Frost; in
the paintings of nineteenth-century American Romantics; in television Westerns or advertising (cigarettes, beer, and cars sell better if
depicted against snow-capped mountains). One finds nature by
escaping the filth, corruption, and mechanization of the city. The
industrial revolution drove Americans into the city, while confining
nature to the countryside and wilderness areas. We were to earn our
living and raise our children in the denatured cities and then escape

to the country for rest and recreation. This dualistic ideal served neither nature nor us well. The post-World War II suburban compromise is not, however, an improvement; in fact, it lost both the diversity and excitement of a city as well as the wildness of nature. Miles of individual but similar houses bordered by manicured lawns have created a sterile and boring environment. What we need is vibrant, interesting cities of diverse human populations with wildness built or rebuilt into them. Only 2 percent of Americans presently live in rural areas; the rest live in cities or surrounding urban areas, and this trend seems likely to continue. Whatever happens to American as well as worldwide population growth in the foreseeable future, it will increase and much of that increase will be in cities.[22] Hence, the question arises: Can we make our cities places where we can encounter wildness? The American pastoral ideal, which sends the upper middle class off to hike in the Rockies and the middle class escaping out to the suburbs, is both out-of-date and elitist. It takes care of the few while neglecting the many, and even so does not assure that the few will encounter nature's wildness. The domesticating camera's eye and the manicured lawn are able tamers of wildness.

As a theologian, I cannot be of much help with city-planning—which may be only to acknowledge how interwoven theological issues are with economic and political ones. The possibility of human beings living appropriately with other lifeforms on our planet—what we have called the ecological model—is not simply, or even mainly, a theological issue. It is one that must be tackled in many different ways by many different people. All I can do, as a theologian, is to suggest why as Christians we support this model and how as Christians we can help bring it about. As Christians we support the model because loving nature as subject is an extension of loving other human beings that way; as Christians we can help bring this model about by insisting that we need both wilderness to protect biodiversity and wildness to encourage real encounters between human beings and nature. In other words, the radical, inclusive love of others, especially the most oppressed others, which is at the heart of Christian faith, demands two things of Christians. It demands that we support the preservation of wilderness areas so that nature, the new poor, can grow and flourish. It also demands that we work for pockets of wildness in our cities, so that ordinary people, especially poor people, can experience nature directly. Of course, it also demands zero tolerance for environmental racism, but just as Gustavo Gutiérrez said that the poor have a right to think, I would add that they also have the right to the joy of being in nature. Christian faith does not have one nature policy for the elite (enjoyment of nature) and another for the poor (freedom from pollution). In sum, then, as a theologian, I am claiming that it is not just "nice" to have parks and wooded areas in cities for our leisure hours; rather, it is essential to have them—for everyone—so that we can learn who we are in the scheme of things. We are, at the most basic level, from and with these earth others. They are not just casual acquaintances to whom we can choose to be related. Rather, they are our relatives, our kin, the network of life from which we came and to which we will return. We *all* need to awaken to this reality; in this sense, "bird-watching" is not just a hobby but part of our vocation.[23]

But that reality is abstract and useless unless it is felt, reborn, in every person. The conversion to the earth, the awakening to who we truly are, occurs most often, it seems, through immediate encounters with particular wild others. Strange as it is, small, seemingly inconsequential meetings—with herons, amoeba, and turtles—can be the occasion for world-shaking changes in our sense of self and our species in the scheme of things. This is why as a theologian I believe that the way cities are constructed is critical to the future of our species as well as of other species. Of course, it is not *the* answer; it is simply one small piece in the vast, complex agenda spelling out how we can live humanely on this planet with all the others. I cannot stress often enough the many different changes that we first-world Christians (and others) need to undergo if the planet is to survive and flourish. The development of a Christian nature spirituality is merely the beginning step, the conversion to earth others, that should result in many kinds of changes (economic, political, legal, ecclesiastical) at many different levels of society, both national and international. Our focus here, however, is on a change in sensibility, a change in the sense of *who we are*. This change takes place locally and personally, but its reach can be—and must be—global.

By way of illustration, let us look at a few examples of how people and nature might interact in small places, such as cities. It is commonly acknowledged that cities people like are ones sprinkled with many patches of green space: Paris (famous for its parks), Rome, London, Vancouver, New York come to mind. New York City, for example, has 26,000 acres of parkland in addition to Central Park (in fact, those 26,000 acres are equivalent to 31 Central Parks!). That is astonishing and immediately makes one realize the potential within one of the most populated American cities for urban wildlands.

Ninety-five percent of New Yorkers believe that the parks are important to their lives; moreover, creating pocket parks out of vacant lots has given vitality to neighborhoods. "For New York neighborhoods desperately staving off collapse and abandonment, creating parks can be a salvation: clearing and planting a vacant lot lets a community prove to itself that when people work together they can breathe life and safety back into a place."[24]

Let us look a little more closely at some experiments in creating city wildlands in the United States as well as an African case of putting local people in charge of conservation projects. From an article appropriately entitled "Wild Times in the City" with a subtitle "Urban Preserves Meet the Needs of People and Nature," we get a glimpse of ways that a number of American cities are building wildness back into their parameters. From Tulsa's Arkansas River Least Tern Preserve, which is a bird sanctuary entirely within the city limits, to Chicago's 150,000 acres of prairie, oak savanna, woodland, and wetland, only thirty minutes from the city center, awareness is growing that such areas not only serve the needs of nature's biodiversity but also the desire of human beings for close encounters with nature. Four thousand people have volunteered to help clear brush, monitor rare species, and pull weeds in the Chicago reserve; children also come in droves. "'It's an eye-opening experience,' says parent-volunteer Amelia Howard. 'Kids used to the inner city don't know what fresh air and open space is. This gives them a better respect for nature.' Blindfolded kids are told to hug a tree, feel its bark and figure out where the sun is. 'We teach them about being quiet . . . about listening to the wind, feeling the sun.'"[25]

Off the New Jersey coast is a small, forty-five acre island, a shipbuilding graveyard and eyesore. Recently it was turned into an egret rookery.

> There are 700 nests on the island now, and the birds—great and snowy and cattle egrets, black-crowned and yellow-crowned night herons, green-backed and little blue herons, glossy ibis and numerous seabirds and waterfowl—commute to the city like everyone else. In so doing, they bring a breathtaking touch of nature to the lunchtime crowd in Central Park or school kids visiting Brooklyn's Prospect Park or almost anyone riding a bus or ferry into or out of Manhattan.[26]

These few examples are simply a taste of what is happening—or could happen—in many cities in the United States. As the article notes in closing, "Urban preserves, then, may be the most valuable reserves of all. How many among us, after all, will ever visit Denali or the Serengeti? Urban preserves not only protect biodiversity, but they are close at hand, and it may be the wilderness at home that feeds and satisfies what Thoreau called 'the primitive vigor of Nature [with]in us.'"[27] Moreover, if the poor have a right to close encounters with nature, that cannot occur for most unless nature is *close to them*.

Another and quite different example of reconnecting humans with nature comes from Africa, where experts call attention to "Trouble in the Garden of Eden." "When local people are excluded from conservation activities in the world's wilderness areas, the very goals of conservation are threatened. In fact, the concept of wilderness as a pristine area untouched by humans is an urban myth."[28] Two-thirds of protected areas in Africa exclude people, allowing them no use of the wild plants and animals. Yet flora and fauna are part of these people's lives and culture: people understand and value them. Moreover, when local people are excluded from their traditional lands, resentment grows, as does poaching, poisoning of animals, and deliberate burning of forests. Where an alternative vision has emerged—one which recognizes that humans and animals can live in symbiotic relationships—and therefore puts local people at the center of conservation, the results have been very different. Community wildlife schemes in Africa, in which people derive direct revenue from wildlife, are increasing. And in India a system of joint forest management has resulted in 800,000 hectares of forest partly under the control of local people. Neither deep ecologists nor conservation professionals are happy with these schemes, but there is evidence that the only projects that will succeed in the long run are ones with local control. As the authors pointedly ask: "Whose interests are served first and foremost? Big and often wasteful . . . bureaucracies? Or local people's, whose livelihoods depend on conservation and enhancement of biological diversity?"[29]

To sum up: close encounters between humans and nature come in many forms. Increasingly, however, they should not be wilderness experiences for the first-world elite and cannot be jungle or rainforest experiences for tribal peoples. Nature and people lived together in one way in the past—mainly on nature's turf—whereas today and in the future, nature and people will continue to live together, but it will have to be mainly on our turf. There is no returning to the pristine wilderness (it does not exist), nor is the city/country split a healthy one for either party; rather, in addition to preserving vast tracks of wilderness for the earth others, we need also to build nature into our new cities and rebuild it into those cities that have lost it. We need to do this for nature's sake and for our own.

Nature Writing: Mediating the Second Naiveté

Passing Over to the Other: The Nature of Nature Writing

Our close encounters with nature need not, however, always be immediate ones. We can learn a lot through the experience of other people. The movement from the first to the second naiveté, from the innocent eye of childhood's encounters to the educated, friendly eye of adulthood, can especially benefit from nature writing. Good nature writing combines experience, place, and wildness in ways that are particularly useful for educating the loving eye: it gives us concrete examples of people who have learned to pay close attention to nature. These examples are personal testimony of coming alive to the otherness of particular creatures and places. Nature writing is the ecological model in practice; it shows us how the loving eye develops.

Nature writing has, therefore, some interesting similarities with religious autobiographies. Both are mediating forms: both connect a subject (the writer) with a strange other—nature or God.[30] And further, both of these mediating forms connect the reader to nature or God as well—through the experience of the writer. In a religious autobiography, the reader learns how one person experiences a religious tradition, tries to live it, works out his or her beliefs in actual practice. A religious autobiography provides a hands-on, concrete, practice-oriented introduction to what can often be abstract and baffling: the history and doctrines of a religion. A religious autobiography is thick description; a showing rather than a telling; a story of how a particular person has discovered a religious tradition, made sense of it, and incorporated it into their life. Whether it be Augustine's foundational *Confessions*, Roman Catholic convert Dorothy Day's *The Long Loneliness*, Mohandas Gandhi's *Experiments with Truth*, or former slave Sojourner Truth's *Narrative*, each work invites us into a world where a *subject experiences a strange other*. The autobiographical genre allows us, to a certain extent, to experience that also. It is a mediating form that does not focus solely on either the knower or the known but on both together, on the subject in the process of learning. When one reads a religious autobiography one "passes over" to the point of view of the author, one experiences with the writer, one is taken along on the author's journey.

The personal narrative has some obvious advantages when dealing with difficult, abstract, or mysterious subject-matter, such as God or nature. One immediately sees the point by comparing religious autobiography with theology or nature writing with science. While religious autobiography will include some theology, just as good nature writing depends on science, in each case we have a personal, interpreted, concrete *experience* of the subject-matter, with no pretensions to being anything else. Whereas some theology parades itself as God's Word and reductionist science claims nature is a dead object, a mere resource for human beings, the mediated forms are a more modest type of reflection. They say: "This is how it has been for me; this is my experience, my interpretation, of living with God or nature; let me invite you to share these reflections—and judge for yourself." I am not suggesting that religious autobiography and nature writing are the only genres or even the best ones for learning about a religious tradition or nature. Scriptural study and the history of doctrine are certainly central for knowing a religion; hard science and philosophy of science are critical to knowledge of nature. But on the matter of *becoming acquainted* with God or nature, the mediating forms are helpful. They "let the material speak": they are subject-subjects forms. It is no accident that the first Western religious autobiography, Augustine's *Confessions,* is in the form of a prayer to God: the entire work is a dialogue in which Augustine speaks and listens to God— two subjects interacting. What is kept before the reader at all times is the mystery, the richness, the aliveness of the Other to whom Augustine is attempting to relate. Likewise, in good nature writing we see a human subject relating to other lifeforms as interesting, mysterious, surprising others. Nature writers are students of relationships; what excites them is not just another species, but relating to it—in other words, "responding to the earth as a living subject."[31]

As we approach nature writing, then, we do so with the expectation of passing over to another's point of view, another's interpretation of relating to some aspect of the natural world. As an embodied, concrete kind of writing that places human beings in touch with nature, it fits well with the ecological model of being and knowing. It does not hyperseparate from nature nor wish to fuse with it; it recognizes the otherness of nature; it gives us a maze, not a landscape kind of knowledge; it acknowledges the knower's particular inter-

pretive limitations; it welcomes the influence of the exterior landscape on the interior one; it seeks intimacy with the other but only
by way of aesthetic distance and scientific accuracy—it really wants
to *know the other as other*. Therefore, while other mediating forms
such as field guides, science textbooks, nature films, and museum
displays are certainly useful for educating the loving eye, nature writing gives us privileged access to nature via another—and usually
well-informed—human being's experience with nature. Nature
writing, then, may be one of the best ways to educate our eye to
nature as subject.

But the analogy of nature writing with religious autobiography
does not tell us all we need to know about it. Gary Nabhan's description of a nature writer brings together several crucial features.

> The bent of personality that makes for a natural history writer comes
> from a need to write, a love of landscape, insatiable curiosity about
> the details of life in that landscape, a dedication to accuracy in under-
> standing the details, devotion to language and image rooted in imag-
> ination rather than science, and a desire to ponder one's relationship
> to the earth—qualities that could come together in anyone, but
> surely are rooted in childhood.[32]

There are similarities here with the features characterizing close
encounters with nature (the first naiveté): place, wildness, experience. Nature writers do not write about nature in general but about
a particular locale, a place they care about, a place that has influenced them, that they want to know intimately and share with others. They recognize and celebrate the wildness or otherness of this
place in two ways: through accuracy and imagination, through a
naturalist's scientific attention to detail and a poet's aesthetic attention to particulars. Finally, the experience which is both theirs and
shared with the reader, the experience of the wild other(s) in this
place, is a second naiveté experience. It is not the direct, innocent
encounter of the child, but a mediated account, a well-informed,
imaginative interpretation by an adult.

Place, wildness, and experience: let us look briefly at each through
the second naiveté eyes of nature writing. Nature writers fall in love
with a place; in fact, conversion experiences are not unusual. Joseph
Wood Krutch, well-known Southwest nature writer and former
drama critic and professor at Columbia University, is an interesting
example. He had published a book in 1929 entitled *The Modern
Temper* in which he used the metaphor of the desert to describe the

despair he sensed in modern life: to him nature was obviously inhuman and impersonal.[33] But then he visited the Southwest desert for the first time and had a conversion. He describes it "like love at first sight" or, even more interesting, as a cat's first contact with catnip— a primal, irresistible attraction. He comments: "Suddenly, a new, undreamed of world was revealed. There was something so unexpected in the combination of brilliant sun and earth that my first reaction was delighted amusement."[34] The experience of this place changed Krutch's life. Eventually he moved to the Southwest, switched from writing drama criticism to nature books, and worked to preserve the area. But the most interesting aspect of this conversion to the land for our purposes is that it did not result in a sentimental attachment but rather a naturalist's love for it. He educated himself about the particularities of its flora and fauna, so that he might understand them better and share his learning with others through his nature writing. Krutch's experience, while somewhat extreme, is not unusual: the conversion to a place with the accompanying desire to learn more about it, share its wonders with others, and care for it is a common theme among nature writers. As Krutch illustrates, nature writers can, in William James's terms, be second-born as well as the first-born who come to love nature as children.

What these writers care about is wildness, the otherness—or what we have called the subjecthood—of their place. It is the sense that trees, animals, creeks, a prairie or desert or forest are what they are: themselves. Nature writer Gretel Ehrlich discovered this wildness in sheep.[35] In her book, *The Solace of Open Spaces*, she writes of moving to a sheep ranch in Wyoming after a devastating personal loss, hoping to lose herself in the land. She was seeking therapy. What she found, however, was very different and much better: the surprising healing power of the other—the vitality and indifference of the arid land, the "stubborn, secretive, dumb, and keen" qualities in the sheep.[36] Getting to know animals very different from herself was the occasion for an expanded sense of their specialness as well as a tough-minded assessment of her own ability to survive and flourish. She writes that "the intimacy with what is animal in me returned." As she elaborates:

> An animal's wordlessness takes on the cleansing qualities of space. . . . Animals hold us to what is present: to who we are at the time, not who we've been or how our bank accounts describe us. What is obvious to an animal is not the embellishment that fattens our emotional résumés but what's bedrock and current in us: aggres-

sion, fear, insecurity, happiness, or equanimity. Because they have the ability to read our involuntary tics and scents, we're transparent to them and thus exposed—we're finally ourselves.[37]

Her interior landscape is changed by the exterior, but only because she related to the other as really *other*, as subject. Sheep, animals that for most of us scarcely fill the definition of wild, became for Ehrlich the occasion for real meeting with an other, a meeting of appreciation for their qualities and of transformation for herself.

Meeting an earth other on its own terms, as it is, with openness and interest, is a recurring theme in good nature writing. It is, in fact, the *heart* of such writing, for it is this that fascinates both the writer and the reader: the surprising, mysterious, and endlessly interesting character of even the simplest creature. E. O. Wilson gives a stunning example with the case of the honeybee's "waggle dance," which is:

> the tail-wagging movement performed inside the hive to inform nestmates of the location of newly discovered flower patches and nest sites. The dance is the closest approach known in the animal kingdom to a true symbolic language. Over and over again the bee traces a short line on the vertical surface of the comb, while sister workers crowd in close behind. To return to the starting line, the bee loops back first to the left and then to the right and so produces a figure-eight. The center line contains the message. Its length symbolically represents the distance from the hive to the goal, and its angle away from a line drawn straight up on the comb, in other words away from twelve o'clock, represents the angle to follow right or left of the sun when leaving the hive. If the bee dances straight up the surface of the comb, she is telling the others to fly toward the sun. If she dances ten degrees to the right, she causes them to go ten degrees right of the sun. Using such directions alone, the members of the hive are able to harvest nectar and pollen from flowers three miles or more from the hive.[38]

Such ingenuity, such complexity—who would have imagined the humble honey bee capable of such feats! Wilson calls the honey bee a "magic well"—the more you draw from it, the more there is to draw. Or as he says: "We are in the presence of a biological machine so complicated that to understand just one part of it—wings, heart, ovary, brain—can consume many lifetimes of original investigation."[39] Knowing any wild other in depth calls up in him a sense of wonder. "Our sense of wonder grows exponentially: the greater the knowledge, the deeper the mystery and the more we seek knowledge to create new mystery."[40] We usually reserve such depths of layered complexity for the human spirit: we are the magic wells. But Wilson and other nature writers find the wild others to be equally deep and complex; they are indeed more like subjects than like objects.

Finally, the experience that nature writers share with us of wild others—whether sheep or honeybees—in particular places— whether the Southwest desert or Wyoming—is a second naiveté experience. It is a highly interpreted experience with several dimensions of interpretation. It is certainly a personal account of nature, an account interpreted through the interests and needs as well as gender, class, and race of the writer, right on down to their tics and idiosyncrasies. And we wouldn't want it any other way: in nature writing we do not get Nature, but Annie Dillard's Ellery, Jane Goodall's apes, John Hay's Cape Cod, Rachel Carson's ocean, Sharon Butala's Saskatchewan prairie, Henry David Thoreau's Walden Pond.

Science and Aesthetics: Two Ways to Educate the Loving Eye

But the experiences of wild places and animals are interpreted in other ways as well: scientific and aesthetic ways. One of the features of good nature writing is the naturalist's eye, its scientific accuracy. Wilson's waggle dance illustrates the point; the wonder that we feel for the honey bee's dance is directly dependent on Wilson's knowledge of it as a scientist. Attention to detail, knowing about the other in its particular, special, unique character and ways, is at the heart of appreciation of it as a subject—that is, as *it is*, as *what it is*. We cannot love what we do not know; we cannot care appropriately for what we do not know. Accurate, detailed, scientific information about other lifeforms as well as whole ecosystems is central to educating the loving eye. Scientific knowledge need not objectify the other. Rather, as we have seen, it can do just the opposite: it can produce appreciation of and a desire to care for the other. In fact, we cannot care for the wild others unless we do know, in detail, in accurate detail, who they are and what they need.

Nature writing, however, has sometimes been seen as romantic, sentimental fusion with nature, rather than well-informed appreciation of it. Novelist Joyce Carol Oates, in a piece entitled "Against Nature" criticizes the overblown rhetoric of some nature writing. It is, she says, full of "Reverence, Awe, Piety, Mysticism, Oneness."[41] Plenty of examples support her critique, but they are not from the best of the genre. The best ones, perhaps paradoxically, are the most scientific. It is the accurate details about the earth others that call forth our wonder—one could almost say that the greater and deeper the detail the more the wonder grows, as E. O. Wilson suggests. Annie Dillard drives home this point with some information on caterpillars and elm leaves. "There are . . . two hundred twenty-eight separate and distinct muscles in the head of an ordinary caterpillar" and "there are . . . six million leaves on a big elm," but that's not all, the six million leaves "are toothed, and the teeth themselves are toothed."[42] There's nothing romantic, oceanic, or uplifting about these statements; they are just the facts—but they fascinate, astound, and call forth our wonder.

So science is necessary for good nature writing. It is one of the main ways our attention is drawn to and learns about the earth others. It is a major form of educating the eye, of becoming an apprentice to nature, of entering into a well-informed friendship with nature that accepts the other as it is in its own world. Science helps us to become travelers to the new world of nature, to replace our ignorance and half-truths with genuine and accurate information.

A second major way that writers interpret their experience of nature is aesthetic: attention to the other through image and metaphor. Just as science is one form of lifting up the concrete particularity of the earth other, so also is art. Nature writers help us to see what we otherwise might not notice at all by arresting our attention, making us stop and take notice. Recall the simple but powerful haiku:

> An old silent pond
> Into the pond a frog jumps.
> Splash! Silence again.[43]

We do not usually pay *any* attention to the splash of a frog. The aesthetic moment most basically is simply when one stops and looks at something for no reason other than interest in it. Aesthetic interest is absorption in the particular, the individual: *this* stone with these *particular* markings which feels *this* way in my hand right now at *this* moment. We have difficulty seeing things this way, stopping and paying attention to something other than ourselves in its own specialness, being present here and now to another in its uniqueness. Art helps us to do this. Nature writer John McPhee describes violent, seismic movement in a mountain range in Pleasant Valley, Nevada, in an aesthetic way, that is with the arresting help of the metaphors of bread, zippers, and a locomotive:[44]

These mountains do not rise like bread. They sit still for a long time and build up tension, and then suddenly jump. . . . This fault, which jumped in 1915, opened like a zipper up the valley, and exploding into the silence, tore along the mountain base for upward of twenty miles with a sound that suggested a runaway locomotive.[45]

If we were driving by such a mountain range, most of us would just see a static (boring?) pile of rocks—as the author notes, "To a nongeologist, it's just ranges, ranges, ranges."[46] But this description by a scientifically informed, imaginative writer makes them come alive. We *see them.* That is what aesthetic attention, arrested attention does. It focuses our eye directly and precisely on the other. However, it does so in a connecting way; that is, metaphors attach us as well as arrest us. The homey images of bread, zippers, and locomotives bring those distant, imposing mountains into our world of reference. Good nature writers focus our attention on the strange earth others by familiarizing them: Dillard calls planet Earth our neighborhood that we should get to know; Rachel Carson speaks of the ocean as a difficult but interesting acquaintance; E. O. Wilson describes the honeybee's strange maneuvers as a waggle dance. The central model of this book—the subject-subjects model—is an attempt to focus our attention on the differences and uniqueness of earth others through the metaphor of subject for nature. A good metaphor first causes shock and then the shock of recognition. "Nature as subject" initially shocks, but, hopefully, it also causes a nod of acknowledgment. Hence, the aesthetic rivets our attention on the other, but in a way that connects us to the other.[47] In other words, an aesthetic response to another is neither subjective nor objective, neither focused only on the self or only on the other, but on the connection of the self to the other. But, and the "but" is crucial here—on the other *as other.* The interest is, as with scientific attention, primarily on the other, not the self.

In sum, then, we have been looking at nature writing as a form of mediating the experience of nature to us, as a way to return to nature. It is, we have suggested, a second naiveté experience of nature, one that helps to educate our eye so that we can know it better and love it more appropriately. Like the first naiveté of childhood, nature writing is characterized by the experience of encountering wild others in particular places. This experience, however, is now interpreted, nuanced, and informed not only by the writer's personal story but also by scientific knowledge and aesthetic imagination.

Nature writing is not a difficult or esoteric enterprise, reserved for an insider elite. Anyone can do it, and in any place, even in one's own backyard. We can educate our eye not only through the writings of others but also through our own reflections, if we are willing to leave the camera home and take the notebook with us! As we turn now to three examples of nature writing, we will see that unlike hard science and academic theology (which often appear to be controlled by the initiated few), good nature writing can be done by ordinary people.[48]

Geography vs. Autobiography: Three Examples of Nature Writing

Nature writing is geo-graphy—earth/writing. It is not auto-bio-graphy—self/life/writing. But as we have seen, it is not geography as we learned it in school: the names of countries, the major rivers, the capitals of states. It is interesting geography: earth/writing by people for people. Geography is not autobiography, but the two are connected: nature writing is about the self *and* the earth other, the earth other as attracting the self, the self as moving toward the earth other. In the three examples of nature writing that we will look at now we will see different versions of this central relationship: Sharon Butala's *The Perfection of the Morning*, Sue Hubbell's *A Country Year*, and Annie Dillard's *Pilgrim at Tinker Creek*.[49] In different ways, each of these books attends to nature as subject; each mediates nature to us through science and art; each is motivated by the desire to be an apprentice to nature and to see it with a loving eye; each is an example of the interactive, relational model of human beings and nature. But each book illustrates the ecological model with its loving eye in different ways and with its own special insights. In some important ways, the books are similar—all are by white, North American, middle-class women—which was a deliberate choice, so that we will not be comparing apples and oranges. On the critical point of the self-other or subject-subjects relationship, we will be comparing three writers from similar backgrounds (and backgrounds similar to the presumed readership of the book). They are all fine pieces of nature writing that have helped me know and appreciate nature better, and it is my reading of them that I will now share.

Sharon Butala

Sharon Butala's *The Perfection of the Morning* is appropriately subtitled *An Apprenticeship in Nature*. It is a book about a thirty-six-year-old woman, adrift professionally and personally, who moves from the city to the Saskatchewan prairie when she enters into a second marriage with a rancher. She knows nothing about this dry, fierce land and feels distant from it and the hardy people who make a living from it. Initially, the reader suspects a self-help, recovery book: nature as therapy for the wounded spirit. And, in a sense, it is a book about recovery, but not in the way Butala had imagined. What is most interesting about this book is Butala's persuasive story of how her attention shifts from herself to the land. She does, indeed, become an apprentice to the land. As she gradually moves her focus from self to earth other, she begins to heal. She starts out, however, where many late twentieth-century privileged, white, North Americans are—inside her own psyche, self-absorbed, dissatisfied, dabbling in an eclectic mix of therapies (Jungian, Goddess traditions, mysticism, Native rituals, out-of-body accounts, dreams). But soon after her arrival on the prairie she begins to take long walks across the stark, stony, arid but beautiful land. At first her reactions are romantic and oceanic; she is searching for "feeling some pure connection to the universe" and has little interest in the details of the land, claiming that it is not her nature "to be obsessed with what natural objects themselves are made of, or how or when, or what their proper names might be."[50] She claims that a "scientific approach" is irrelevant to her reasons for going out into nature; for instance, she values a small rock she found "because it holds personal meaning" for her.[51] She admits that when she walks on the prairie she is often in a reverie, "sunk deep in myself," and realizes "how far removed I often was from the world around me."[52] A significant change begins to occur when, as she puts it, "I tried harder to pay attention." As she writes:

> I began to try to stop thinking about anything else but the dirt on the road, the grass beside it, the stones, the fields spreading out on each side, the hawks circling overhead, the song of the meadowlark or redwinged blackbird, the sound of the wind in the grass, a particular rock high on a hillside. This required concentration, I found, and a constant calling myself back from thoughts of other things to my surroundings at the moment. . . . I did not glance at plants or lichens on rocks or on the ground, I studied them. I practised inner stillness in order to hear, really hear, the wind, the birdsong, whatever else might be in the air. It took tremendous effort and I failed more often than I succeeded, but I persisted out of a sense of discovery and of need.[53]

Shifting her attention from self to earth other resulted in awareness, an awareness in which her own self began to move toward these other subjects. "But this time I had a sense of my 'awareness' going out of me and not of these things *entering* me, but of me going *out* to mingle with them."[54] A fine writer, Butala eloquently portrays her step-by-step journey from self-absorption toward attention to earth others. She takes the reader with her on this journey, convincingly spelling out the small shifts in practice and imagination that move her from being an isolated to an ecological self. She learns this from the land, by being an apprentice to it:

> You have to be still and quiet for these things to happen; you have to release your expectations; you have to stop thinking you already know things, or know how to categorize them, or that the world has already been explained and you know those explanations. You know nothing. You understand nothing. You have only what your own body tells you and your own experience from which to make judgments. You may have misunderstood; you may be wrong. Teach me, is what you should say, and, I am listening. Approach the world as a child seeing it for the first time. Remember wonder. In a word: humility. Then things come to you as they did not when you thought you knew.[55]

The prairie walks that gradually shifted her gaze from herself to the land powerfully illustrate how it is possible to relate to the earth as another subject—in her case, as teacher. The primary insight of Butala's apprenticeship in nature is the influence of the land on us. She saw this in the Crees and in the rural men and women who worked the land: who they were was profoundly affected by this particular prairie with its distinctive sky, rocks, animals, trees, bushes, grasses. As she came to know this place with its flora and fauna, she opened herself to its shaping power and was changed. Rather than losing herself in the land as she had initially hoped and expected, the harsh, arid, beautiful place formed her into a different person—one more like itself:

> Close proximity to a natural environment—being in Nature—alters all of us in ways which remain pretty much unexplored, even undescribed in our culture . . . we should stop thinking, with our inflated egos, that all the influence is the other way around. We might try to shift our thinking in this direction so that we stop blithely improving the natural world around us, and begin to learn, as Aboriginal people have, what Nature in her subtle but powerful manner has to teach us about how to live.[56]

The result of Butala's story is not only that she is healed, but she also now sees her own life as a manifestation of the larger life by which she is surrounded. She sees herself as a social self, related both to other people and to nature in many profound ways. The land that has influenced her so deeply—nourishing, enlightening, and disturbing her—she now wants to protect and care for. An isolated self has become an ecological self. She becomes active in efforts to preserve Saskatchewan farm and prairie life, believing that people must work to provide "the direct link to Nature our species must maintain."[57]

Sharon Butala's account of her apprenticeship in nature is a superb first reader for people who, like her, want to get out of their own heads and become acquainted with nature as a fascinating, sustaining, surprising other. Her story is especially persuasive on how an ecological self can develop, because she begins with a highly individualized, inner sense of self and actually undergoes a transformation over a period of years to an ecological self. She invites the reader to "pass over" to her experience of an arrogant eye becoming a loving eye, from the eye that looked only at herself to one educated through an apprenticeship in nature able to see the land as subject, as a significant other.

Sue Hubbell

Sue Hubbell's *A Country Year* also has an appropriate subtitle: *Living the Questions.* Hubbell has few answers but does indeed try to live the questions with the help of "the Wild Things" to whom she dedicates the book.[58] *A Country Year* is a low-key, wry, keen-eyed piece of nature writing by a divorced, middle-aged, self-taught naturalist and commercial bee-keeper who lives alone in the Missouri Ozarks. In a sense, Hubbell is the opposite of Butala: for her the human self is in the background with the Wild Things (not grizzly bears and whales but cockroaches, spiders, and bees) in the foreground. Her attention is on the things themselves, not on herself: she is there, but usually in the shadows. Just as Butala's book graphs the movement from self to earth others, Hubbell's essay shows the movement in the other direction. In Hubbell's case, the focus is on natural systems and how she already fits into them, not on how she, as an isolated individual, can make contact with an alien land. For example, she reflects on how earning her livelihood from bees puts her inside their circle: they support her while she influences where and how they swarm, mate, and produce honey.[59] Spying a spider one morning behind the woodstove, she notes the similarities between herself and the spider in spare prose and a wry slant on things.

> We are both beekeepers; both of us make a living from the bees. My way, compared to hers, seems excessively Byzantine. I cosset the bees all year long, take away their extra honey, process it, bottle it, truck it to New York to sell to Bloomingdale's, and then use the check to buy the things I need. She simply eats bees. We are both animate bundles of the chemicals common to all living things: carbon, hydrogen, oxygen, nitrogen, sulfur and phosphorus. Both of us have been presented with a set of problems posed by our chemistry and quickness, among them how to grow and how to make a living. Those are big questions, and as is often the case with Big Questions, we have come up with different answers—answers that in turn are still different from those of the honeybee, who is a similar chemical bundle and upon whom we both depend for a living. The honeybee's solutions have more to do with metamorphosis and the nectar of flowers, and those answers are good ones, too. Living in a world where the answers to questions can be so many and so good is what gets me out of bed and into my boots every morning.[60]

This passage is typical of Hubbell's sensibility: she educates our eye by disorienting us. She puts herself, and by implication the reader as well, into the middle of nature, into the inner circle of some small ecosystem, and makes us realize that we *are* ecological beings—similar to and different from others in the system. We are bone of their bone, flesh of their flesh, and faced with the same basic questions.

Another fine example of Hubbell's special combination of the naturalist's eye with the poet's imagination, helping us see the fabric of nature in which we participate, is her description of her chicken coop. Here the mice and phoebes who steal corn are eaten by the rat snake, thus keeping the coop free of thieves and allowing the chickens to prosper. Hubbell, however, upsets the system by occasionally saving a phoebe.

> I like to think of it as a circle. If I take one step out of the center, I find myself a part of that circle—a circle made of chickens, chopped corn, mice, snakes, phoebes, me, and back to the chickens again, a tidy diagram that only hints at the complexity of the whole. For each of us is a part of other figures, too, the resulting interconnecting whole faceted, weblike, subtle, flexible, fragile. As a human being I am a great meddler; I fiddle, alter, modify. This is neither good nor

bad, merely human, in the same way that the snake who eats mice and phoebes is merely serpentish. But being human I have the kind of mind which can recognize that when I fiddle and twitch any part of the circle there are reverberations throughout the whole.[61]

What is disquieting and instructive about Hubbell's perspective is her ability, as a naturalist, to identify *us* with *them*. We are, she suggests more like them (and they more like us) than we care to admit. We all have to make a living, find our way, and our human answers are often not as superior to the solutions of these others as we like to suppose. A main difference between us and them is that we ask the Big Questions, but we have few answers. Like physicist James Jeans, Hubbell believes that we live in a world that is not only queerer than we think, but queerer than we *can* think. She invites us to pay attention to the interesting, resourceful others everywhere around us who, in their own way, live out the questions. We do not have to go far for this instruction: Hubbell's earth others are not lions and tigers, but the homely creatures under one's bed or behind the kitchen sink:

> In truth, I don't mind the wood cockroaches that come in on my fire-wood. . . . Their digestive system and mine differ enough so that we don't share the same ecological niche; they do me no harm, we are not competing, so I can take a long view of them. There is no need to harry them as a bee would, or to squash them as a housewife would. Instead, I stoop down beside them and take a closer look, examining them carefully. After all, having in my cabin a harmless visitor whose structure evolution has barely touched since Upper Carboniferous days strikes me, a representative of an upstart and ten-tative experiment in living form, as a highly instructive event. Two hundred and fifty million years, after all, is a very long view indeed.[62]

Although Hubbell focuses her keen attention on others, a shift also occurs within herself. *A Country Year*, like all good nature writ-ing, is an account of a personal relation to particular wild others. During the twelve years that the book covers, she reaches an inner peace—a quiet delight in the land and the small animals and insects whom she meets. Her account is a kind of parable of one way of answering the Big Question, the question of how to live: do so sim-ply, with trimmed-down needs, close to the earth and with delight in it. It is not *the* answer; it is merely what one hard-working, inde-pendent, reflective woman has learned about living, a learning that involves nature in a central way. She does not overwhelm; in fact, she understates. At one level, she simply admires the color purple, as when she writes that "the river's banks were covered with *Mertensia virginica*, one of the many wildflowers that are called bluebells. The clusters of sky-blue, bell-like flowers were growing so thickly that we could not walk among them without crushing them, so we simply stood and admired."[63] But she also, like Butala, became active in local land preservation; her awareness of the interconnections of all life moved her to political action to care for the place she had come to know and love. But what is most special about Hubbell's nature writing is her encouragement to the reader to go deeper and look at common insects and animals with open eyes and minds, becoming appreciative of their marvelous, complex ways. Some would say, she muses, that bees are "simply a bunch of bugs." "But spending my days in close and intimate contact with creatures who are structured so differently from humans, and who get on with life in such a different way, is like being a visitor in an alien but ineffably engaging world."[64] Hubbell's low-key, understated sensibility and writing style are an invitation to the novice to join her modest journey toward seeing the humblest creatures as interesting others, as subjects. The last paragraph of the book is about caterpillars:

> This spring I often walk along, eyes to the ground, looking for them. There may have been nobler quests—white whales and Holy Grails—and although the Ahabs and Percivals of my acquaintance are some of my most entertaining friends, I am cut of other stuff and amuse myself in other ways. The search for what may or may not be sawfly larvae seems quite a good one this springtime.[65]

Annie Dillard

Like Butala's and Hubbell's books, Annie Dillard's subtitle gives us a clue to her sensibility: *A Mystical Excursion into the Natural World.* Whereas Butala states her antipathy to theology and Hubbell seems indifferent to things religious, Dillard is obsessed by it, especially the issue of theodicy. As a naturalist who knows the grim story of evolution's fang and claw, she insists that the eye trained on and educated by nature be the realist's eye. "We wake in terror, eat in hunger, sleep with a mouthful of blood."[66] And that includes *all* of us. Dillard questions God about this "evolution that loves death more than it loves you or me." "God *look* at what you've done to this creature, look at the sorrow, the cruelty, the long damned waste!"[67] She never gets a clear answer. But she does come to an insight: there is horror in creation, but there is also beauty, there is terror, but there is also glory: "If we describe a world to compass these things, a world that is a long, brute game, then we bump up against another mystery: the inrush of power and light, the canary that sings on the skull."[68]

Pilgrim at Tinker Creek is a rich, multicourse feast for the novice nature sojourner. The first and most important lesson of the book is a wake-up call: it is a call to become alive to the world about us, to become witnesses of its intricacy, its ordinary marvels, its unending fascination (those muscles in the caterpillar's head, those million leaves on the elm tree). All of this can be found in our own back-yards, in a place like Tinker Creek, if we just have eyes to see. But the second lesson, also an important one, is that all the fecundity, beauty, and rich detail of nature is also waste, blood, cruelty, and death. The first half of the book is a hymn to the glories of creation, the second half to its horrors. Butala and Hubbell stop at the first, but Dillard presses us to look below the surface. "The world has signed a pact with the devil; it had to. It is a covenant to which every-thing, even every hydrogen atom, is bound. The terms are clear: if you want to live, you have to die. . . ."[69]

The special thing about *Pilgrim at Tinker Creek* is its steely-eyed, no-nonsense, tough-minded reading of nature. Unlike Henry David Thoreau's *Walden Pond* (to which it is often compared), Dillard's book is a risky, snake-infested trek into the jungle, not a lazy Saturday afternoon reverie at a New England pond. Whereas Thoreau saw God in nature—the pond reflected the divine—Dillard's under-standing of the relation of God and nature is ambiguous and ambivalent. For the most part, God has absconded from nature, leaving us to the waste and death, the unending eat-and-be-eaten round of life's survival game. But not entirely. There is the "canary that sings on the skull," the beauty of the ordinary, what we find if we keep our eyes open and investigate our neighborhoods. And then there are also occasional, mystical moments of direct contact with God, when holiness comes as a force, like "something had unhinged the world."[70] All of this is part of the journey that Dillard takes us on, making her apprenticeship in nature a very complex one. Butala tells the story of shifting attention from the self to nature; Hubbell invites us to see our human selves as already in nature; Dillard press-es home both of these points. By attending to nature, we will be stunned by its beauty; by acknowledging our participation in it, we will be shocked by its brutality.

Dillard's sensibility is an extreme one: she reminds me of the seventeenth-century metaphysical poet John Donne, who joined heaven and earth in outrageous ways:

> Batter my heart, three-person'd God. . . .
> Except you'enthrall mee, never shall be free,
> Nor ever chast, except you ravish mee.[71]

Dillard's perspective is also similar to the early Karl Barth: God only touches the world as a tangent does, a glancing blow, now and then. Sometimes when I read Dillard I think of a "Far Side" cartoon: her point of view is from another dimension, from a place where we do not usually stand to see things. Why is this important in a nature writer? It is important because she helps us to see things *differently* than we do most of the time—in more extreme, less balanced, less middle-of-the-road, but clearer, ways. She sees such beauty in nature that it knocks her socks off ("My God what a world. There is no accounting for one second of it").[72] And she sees waste and horror that make her cringe in outrage and disgust ("Either this world, my mother, is a monster, or I myself am a freak").[73] As a mediator of nature, she helps *us* to see these things too. Most of the time we see with what I would call "middle vision," vision that is neither astounded at the beauty nor shocked at the horror, but formed by the conventions our societies dictate (and most cultures are afraid of both ecstasy and terror). We simply live as though we will do so forever and that the ordinary is not extraordinary, in either direction. When we wake up, when the scales fall from our eyes and we track the details of the simplest bit of nature—goldfish, leaf, spider, whatever—we begin to see differently: the otherness of each and every lifeform in creation comes home to us. The beauty is in the detail, in the intricacy and fringes of nature: we must notice this richness, for we are here to be witnesses to the stunning diversity of nature. "The whole creation is one lunatic fringe," she writes. "If creation had been left up to me, I'm sure I wouldn't have had the imagination or courage to do more than shape a single, reasonably sized atom, smooth as a snowball, and let it go at that. No claims of any and all revelations could be as far-fetched as a single giraffe."[74] The "Far Side" cartoon possibilities are evident here! We also lose that comfortable "middle vision" perspective when we acknowledge the horror of nature. Unless we see *differently,* we do not really see at all; that is, we see neither the glory nor the horror. Dillard's special gift as a nature writer is her "Far Side," Barthian, metaphysical poet's outrageous sensibility. Reading her is like having someone remove bandages from one's eyes and saying, "Look! Look at what a wonderful, incredible, fascinating world you live in (a world with a goldfish as glorious as Ellery and a giraffe past anything you could ask for or imagine). Really, pay attention to all this, learn about it in detail, look at it through a microscope (and a telescope), witness to it, tell other people about it." But when the bandages come off, we also see the other side of things. She seems to be saying, "Look again. All this beauty is at the mercy of blood, decay, struggle, defeat, and death. It's a dog-eat-dog world and you and I are part and parcel of it." *Both* ways of looking at the world, says Dillard, are true, and we must look at it *both* ways.

Dillard never resolves the dilemma; there is no easy answer. And yet, at the close of book, she reaches a kind of acceptance, one hinted at in the beginning when she accuses God of deserting the world. "It could be that God has not absconded but spread, as our vision and understanding of the universe have spread, a fabric of spirit and sense so grand and subtle, so powerful in a new way, that we can only feel blindly of its hem."[75] Faith in a world that takes the realities of evolution seriously is difficult but not impossible. It means, however, dealing with nature on its own terms, as another, which is not transparent to its ground, but more like a mysterious text that must be deciphered, letter by letter. It requires sharp eyes, studious attention, and an open mind if this mysterious other is to be known at all. Dillard does not anthropomorphize nature nor see God in nature: the natural world is, like a subject, finally mysterious and unknowable in its otherness. At the most, we can get to know some bits of it in our own neighborhoods.

Dillard offers us an apprenticeship in nature of both an ecstatic and sobering sort: she takes us higher than Butala or Hubbell and plunges us deeper. She shocks us into attention to nature—both its beauty and its horror. The Catholic novelist Flannery O'Connor (who shared Dillard's sensibility) once said that for the blind you must write in large letters and for the deaf you must shout. That is what Dillard does for us: she wakes us up so that we can become witnesses. Like her we become explorers, stalkers in our neighborhoods. "I am a fugitive and a vagabond, a sojourner seeking signs."[76] This is her greatest gift. "We teach our children one thing only, as we were taught: to wake up."[77]

But Dillard deserves a reading that ends as she does with a slight tilt toward the canary. We should witness to the skull as well as the canary, but in the last chapter of the book, she writes, "Beauty is

real. I would never deny it; the appalling thing is that I forget it."[78]
And on the last page of the book is a statement of gratitude for the
privilege of living that I like very much, believing as I do that gratitude and not fear or guilt is the most basic religious emotion, "I
think the dying pray at the last not 'please,' but 'thank you,' as a
guest thanks his host at the door."[79]

Sharon Butala, Sue Hubbell, and Annie Dillard give us mediated
close encounters with nature. They awaken us to the natural world,
causing us to pay attention to it in ways most of us could not on our
own. They help us also to see ourselves as ecological beings who are
profoundly influenced by nature and in turn affect it deeply. From
such writers we learn that we are *in* and *of* nature; and yet, at the same
time, it needs our attention and care in ways that are becoming fright-
eningly evident. In other words, from good nature writers we realize
that we are in a *real relationship* with nature, one so deep, so total, yet
so demanding of our attention to it and its needs that the model of
subject to subjects seems increasingly appropriate and right.

Halting the Extinction of Experience

Traditionally, naturalists have written about nature as wilderness, far-
off nature, remote mountains and forests. But our three writers—
Butala, Hubbell, and Dillard—found their wild places closer to
home: on a cattle-grazing prairie; in a beehive and a chicken coop;
beside a creek in New England. Nature writing is even moving into
the city. And this is a good thing, for the city is where most of us
live. If we are to avoid the extinction of experience with nature, we
must invite nature back into our cities. Nature writer Robert Pyle
began his journey toward becoming a lepidopterist (a butterfly
expert) after seeing a butterfly in a vacant city lot when he was a
child. From that chance encounter emerged a lifetime fascination
with the birds, flowers, and especially butterflies that flourished
along the banks of the ditch forming the High Line canal, a major
water source running through the city of Denver. From the marginal
lands along this ditch grew his love of nature:

> Even if they don't know "my" ditch, most people I speak with seem
> to have a ditch somewhere—or a creek, meadow, woodlot, or
> marsh—they hold in similar regard. These are places of initiation,
> where the borders between ourselves and other creatures break down,
> where the earth gets under our nails and a sense of place gets under
> our skin. They are the secondhand lands, the hand-me-down habi-
> tats where you have to look hard to find something to love.[80]

His writing is "a love song to damaged lands," signaling a new kind of nature writing and one we need, since damaged land is the reality facing most people in most parts of the world. "Loving nature" can no longer be a romantic bonding with the pristine wilderness; more likely, it will mean caring for spoiled remnants that initially may seem unattractive—vacant lots, abandoned railroad lines, ditches, one's own backyard. Can we love these lands?

Some people in some cities are moving in this direction. Not only is nature writing changing focus from the grandiose and remote to the small and nearby, but city planners, environmentalists, and educators are also realizing the necessity and potential of small gardens, creeks, and wildlife habitats in cities. Many cities are attempting to create greenbelts, corridors of interconnected green spaces, that will encourage plant and animal biodiversity. These ecological quilts can become a green patchwork for flora and fauna as well as pockets of wildness for people. Moreover, detailed instructions are available on how ordinary people with a backyard or even just an apartment balcony can add to the greenbelt by creating their own small patch to encourage plant and wildlife diversity.[81] Some secondary schools have initiated programs in which children create gardens, wildlife habitats, trails, and small ponds, making their own wild place in what was once a macadam or gravel schoolyard.[82] Another way that people and nature are interacting in cities is through the establishment of urban farm plots. A recent United Nations study reported that one-third of the world's produce is grown in cities.[83] These plots take many forms: allotment gardens rented to apartment dwellers, abandoned lots cultivated by neighborhood organizations, institutional gardens created from asphalt parking lots, rooftop gardens for people in public housing. Architect Michael Hough, author of *Cities and Natural Process*, advocates urban farms for a variety of reasons. "There's tremendous potential for helping people who are really in need of food. But there are all sorts of other benefits to the city that occur as a consequence. If you get on top of one of those rooftops downtown and look down, there's a sea of green. The trellised vines produce shade, some social activity, as well as grapes."[84]

These efforts are small and local. They will not restore the wilderness; they will not save the planet if commercial interests continue to degrade it and if consumers do not rein in their insatiable appetites. But local effort by ordinary people to restore nature in their cities is a necessary and encouraging step. It is necessary because if most of us and our children are to experience nature and thereby grow to care about it, nature must be close by. It is encouraging because the future of the natural world will be inevitably intertwined with human beings: we must learn to live *together*. The extinction of nature and the extinction of the experience of nature are profoundly connected. Our encounters with nature can be reminders that we *do* care about these others who are now so frequently out of sight, out of mind. A close encounter with a single butterfly can be a moment of enlightenment, as Robert Pyle suggests:

> In teaching about butterflies, I frequently place a living butterfly on a child's nose. Noses seem to make perfectly good perches or basking spots, and the insect often remains for sometime. Almost everyone is delighted by this, the light tickle, the close-up colors, thread of tongue probing for droplets of perspiration. But somewhere beyond delight lies enlightenment. I have been astonished at the small epiphanies I see in the eyes of a child in truly close contact with nature, perhaps for the first time. This can happen to grown-ups too, reminding them of something they never knew they had forgotten.[85]

In summary: we have been asking how Christians might come "down to earth," how we might learn to pay close attention to it with the help of nature writers. By passing over to the experience of nature through the educated, loving eye of another, we can then pass back to our own experience, but with that experience now more attentive to the others that make up the natural world. The components of our first naive encounters with nature—the experience of wild others in particular places—are still present in our mature, reflective encounters. But we now consciously affirm something we only sensed before our eye apprenticed itself to nature: that the other is really *other*—whom we need to know in order to love.

It is this otherness of the other, the subjecthood of nature, that will guide our final reflections on the care of the earth. The ecological model contains an ethic; just as who we believe we are in the scheme of things influences how we know others, so also it influences how we treat them. Being, knowing, doing; ontology, epistemology, ethics: the subject-subjects model is a total way of being in the world. Christian faith, I believe, supports the ecological model but pushes it to new depths and to new heights—toward the neediest in nature and toward nature as in God.

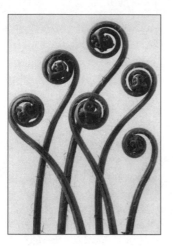

7

Caring for
the Others

NOVELIST ALICE WALKER TELLS THE STORY OF A HORSE named Blue who was boarded in a field beside a house where she lived. The horse, alone in the field day after day was, she says, lonely and bored:

> But then, in our second year at the house, something happened in Blue's life. One morning, looking out the window at the fog that lay like a ribbon over the meadow, I saw another horse, a brown one, at the other end of Blue's field. Blue appeared to be afraid of it, and for several days made no attempt to go near. We went away for a week. When we returned, Blue had decided to make friends and the two horses ambled or galloped along together, and Blue did not come nearly as often to the fence underneath the apple tree.
> When he did, bringing his new friend with him, there was a different look in his eyes. A look of independence, of self-possession, of inalienable *horseness*. His friend eventually became pregnant. For months and months there was, it seemed to me, a mutual feeling between me and the horses of justice, of peace. I fed apples to them both. The look in Blue's eyes was one of unabashed "this is *it* ness."[1]

But soon the visiting horse was sent back to its owner, with impregnation completed. Walker says that Blue became "like a crazed person," whinneying and tearing at the ground, and when she looked at his piercing eyes, she adds, "If I had been born into slavery, and my partner had been sold or killed, my eyes would have looked like that."[2] Walker's conclusion is that "we are one lesson." As we treat animals, so we treat people and vice versa. Profound connections exist between oppressing other people and oppressing nature—the arrogant eye is trained on both. Thus "earth itself," as Walker puts it, "has become the nigger of the world."[3] We are all "co-conspirators," those who, literally, breathe together: we are one community, breathing in and breathing out.[4]

The ethic that emerges from the ecological model is care for all those in the community. Because all of us exist together and because we know these others to be subjects, who are more or less like ourselves, the proper way to treat the others is with the care that one extends to community members. This does not mean that we necessarily *like* all the others, or even that we do not eat or kill them. The first dimension of care is simply respect. It is acknowledgment that others exist together with us in a community of subjects, all having desires and goals. The horse named Blue had his "inalienable horseness" and knew when he was flourishing—the look in his eye that said "this is *it*ness."

Since we live in a community of subjects, we, the self-conscious subjects, owe the others, at the very least, respect. Respect means nothing more (or less) than acknowledging the otherness of the other; that the raison d'être of the other subjects in this community of planet Earth is not to be for or against me; that most of these other subjects are indifferent to human beings; that they have their own reasons for living, their own definitions of "*it*ness"; that they are co-conspirators, breathing the air of the planet as we do. Respect is simply the recognition that there *are* other subjects, that the world is not arranged for my well-being or even, necessarily, for the well-being of human beings, or for any other particular species.[5] Our narrow, anthropocentric perspective—what could be called the intrinsically arrogant eye of human beings—makes it very difficult for us to achieve the disinterested point of view necessary in those who genuinely respect others. One must rise above believing that one's own needs and desires are the only needs and desires—and even that human needs and desires are the only ones, realizing that if we really are co-conspirators on one planet with many other subjects, then respect for them is our first response.

In some cases, that is all that we can manage. An ethic of community is not all love and harmony; it is not just mutual enrichment, cooperation, and friendship.[6] On the contrary, it is a very difficult ethic because it claims that the community within which we live and to whom we are responsible does not stop with human beings but includes all the earth others. This is a pleasant thought if we think

of earth others such as butterflies and redwood trees; it is less pleasant if we include killer bees and poison ivy; it is decidedly unpleas-
ant when it reaches to cancer cells and the AIDS virus. Nevertheless,
they are all members of the community, in the sense that their existence has its own ends and is not simply for our benefit, displeasure,
or death. Of course, we may decide to fight and if possible kill cancer cells and the AIDS virus—our own will to survive and prosper
demands it. But even as we do so, our sensibility will be different if
we respect others, even the most difficult cases, as subjects in their
own worlds. At the very least, it will make us realize that cancer cells
and the AIDS virus are not "out to get us": we are not the center of
creation around which everything else is oriented. Respect at this
most basic level simply means acknowledging others for who they
are—subjects in their own worlds. It means, as well, realizing that
our ideas of desirable world are just that—our ideas—and are limited by our perspective (one could call it the Job lesson in world-
design).[7]

   This chapter is concerned with how we would respond to others,
especially earth others, if we were to live within the ecological model.
The answer is that we would respect and care for them. The first half
of the chapter reflects on what such care means, as well as the relationship between an ethic of care and one of rights. The rest of the
chapter will show how a Christian nature spirituality can learn from
the ecological model and its ethic of care as well as deepen and rad-
icalize it.

The Ecological Model and the Community of Care

If the first step is respect, the second step is to accept "community"
as the metaphor within which to understand our responsibilities to
others. The community metaphor is appropriate because it is a subjects expression: synonyms for community are neighborhood,
town, colony, village, city, group, fellowship. It implies a society of
subjects, and is significantly different from the organic metaphor as
used by deep ecologists, which does not respect subjecthood, either
of human beings or other lifeforms.[8] In this model there is just one
Subject, the earth, with many parts.[9] Another alternative ethical
metaphor is the "rights of the individual" from the Kantian tradition.[10] It extends the Enlightenment ideal of individual rights ("life,
liberty, and the pursuit of happiness") to other lifeforms and even
to ecosystems. This position appears to recognize different subjects

(by extending them rights), but the subjects are atomistic and unrelated. Neither of these positions deals with subjects as both different from one another and as intrinsically related to one another. In the organic model, all subjects are fused into one; in the rights model, all subjects are individual and separate. In the first, all differentiation is lost; in the second, individuals are related only by contract. While, as we shall see, both of these metaphors—organism and rights—should be included within a community model, each is problematic when standing alone. In contrast, the model of community allows different subjects to be related to one another through respect and care.

An Ethic of Care

We have suggested that respect is the first response—sometimes the only response—that we can make to other members of the ecological community, but why add care? Throughout our reflections on the ecological model, we have emphasized the mutual influence of human beings and nature—as José Ortega y Gasset graphically put it, "Tell me the landscape in which you live, and I will tell you who you are."[11] We live in a relationship of mutual influence with the other subjects in the earth community: we do influence them and they do influence us. This interrelationship is so profound, so thorough, and so pervasive that we usually do not see it. Could fishes answer the question, what is the ocean? We are, literally, bone of the bone, flesh of the flesh of nature. We come from it and will return to it; and our every waking moment is dependent on the air we breathe, the water we drink, the grain we eat. This influence can be seen in telescopic and in microscopic ways—in the ashes from the stars that compose the atoms in our bodies. It is, however, easier to see and feel our mutual interaction with nature in more daily, ordinary ways— for instance, in how the weather affects us and we it. We feel a lift in our spirits on the first springlike day after a harsh winter, but we also feel a nagging sense that our global warming may change spring itself. Do we doubt that the influence is mutual and that if we do indeed live in a community, then care for it becomes critical?

The model of community, then, implies an ethic of care: care for the whole, for a sustainable planet, and also care for the parts, for the local, particular bit of the planet that is our own neighborhood. This big caring and the small caring are related: if we learn to care for our local communities, the whole planet might have a better chance. What are some of the characteristics of an ethic of care? On the face of it, caring sounds simple. Anyone can take care of another, can't they? Doesn't it mean just attending to basic needs, like food and shelter? What often comes to mind when we hear the word "care" is a stereotype of what women do: they care for others.[12] An ethic of caring for different, real subjects is, however, anything but simple. As we have seen, knowing others very different from ourselves involves apprenticeship and world-traveling. Real caring depends on this sort of knowledge: on local, detailed knowledge. As Lorraine Code says, genuine caring means trying to discover what is best for the beneficiaries "from their point of view."[13] Such caring does not come "naturally"—to women or to anyone else. It is not enough to consult one's own needs or desires, because caring for real, different others is an outer-directed activity. To care for another (person, animal, forest, river), appropriately one must learn what *they* need to flourish. Care means "planning with care," giving serious attention and thought; it means "handling with care," avoiding damage and loss; it means "leaving in the care of," protecting and guarding; it means "feeling care for," being concerned about. All of these meanings of care involve local, detailed knowledge of the life and circumstances of the other. This does not mean that each of us must have a naturalist's knowledge with regard to every public environmental issue. But it does mean that when we join with others to make decisions that affect the natural world, we remember not to think solely about what we want. We need to be informed about what the natural world needs to survive and flourish. We certainly need to be minimally educated on the big issues and more deeply knowledgeable on the local ones—perhaps even on just one. If we learn how to think locally as ecological subjects, we may be able to act in appropriate ways globally. Just as someone or something that has not been cared for deteriorates gradually, one piece at a time, so caring for our planet to restore it to health will be a gradual, piece-meal affair. The ethic of care is one that must take place in this city, that village, our neighborhood, as people weave together the fabric of social justice and ecological integrity in particular places.

The kind of caring that the community model suggests is more like the care given by a friend than a parent.[14] It is the care that respects the others, becomes acquainted with their differences, learns their needs. It is not, like parental caring, focused on the survival of one's own offspring, nor is it self-sacrificing as parental love often is. Neither, however, is it instrumental, seeing others as simply means to one's own ends. An ecological ethic of caring does not deny the self in subservience to the other nor use others for self-aggrandizement.[15] An ecological ethic of care is like friendship, which is built on both respect for the other and fulfillment of the self. Since the model is an interactive one—a model of multiple subjects—friendship, in which the parties influence each other, is a better fit than either instrumentalism or altruism. Friends want the best for each other, but they also benefit from the others' responses. There is both closeness and distance—what Annette Kuhn calls "passionate detachment" or "compassion without passion," "knowing . . . at once involved and appropriately distanced."[16] We do what we can for our friends—and let it go. While we hope for gratitude from the friends we care for, we do not usually care for them *because* of it. The community-based ethic of care rests on the assumption that once we acknowledge ourselves to be part of the community, we want it and its members to prosper. People who join organizations like Friends of the Botanical Gardens befriend the garden out of "passionate detachment," a desire to see it flourish as well as pleasure from being able to benefit from its welcome shade trees and flowering bushes. On a much larger scale, people who see themselves as Friends of the Earth have the same sensibility: one of respect, care, and gratitude.

We have suggested that global concern—care for the earth—often arises from local encounters—such as care for a garden. It is hard to care for the earth if one has never cared for a piece of it. The particular is the basis for the universal. Teaching a child to care for a goldfish—learning about its needs, respecting its otherness, delighting in its shimmering colors and swimming skills—is a better education in caring than is a lecture on global warming.

Care and Justice

The Greeks, who had an ethics based on the community model, also valued friendship as an ethical virtue. Over the centuries, however, as societies have exchanged the communal base for an adversarial, contractual one, friendship has been privatized, as has care. The public realm is where rights and justice reign, while care and friendship have been relegated to the private domain. The masculine/feminine stereotypes here are too obvious to bear mentioning. As we return, however, to an ecological model of being—knowing now that we human beings and everything else are knit together in intricate, deep webs of inter-relationship and interdependence—we can see that the contractual/rights model is a poor fit with reality as currently understood. We are not atomistic, separate individuals who choose to get into relations with particular others, whether human or otherwise. Nor are we at the top of the pecking order, the species that "grants rights" to this or that group of others, depending on their similarity to us, the quintessential Subject. The Enlightenment rights tradition reveals its bias in Immanuel Kant's words: "Animals are not self-conscious and are there merely as a means to an end. That end is man."[17] People were also graded on the same scale: white, Western, educated men were considered the most self-conscious, the most rational, with other human beings (women, children, people of other races, the old, the poor, homosexuals, the mad, the mentally retarded, etc.) pegged in at different points. According to one's place on the scale, one deserved more or fewer rights.

It is obvious that most species, other than the higher mammals, will fare very badly with this ethic; nonetheless, it is important to include it within an ethic of care. The rights tradition is deeply ingrained in North American culture. One sees its darker side in the right of the individual to carry a gun. It can be grounds for libertarianism, the radical freedom of the roving, cowboy, do-what-you-want ethic. On the brighter side, however, the rights tradition is also the foundation of egalitarian justice: the assumption that *all* persons in a society deserve equal treatment. As the circle has grown larger of *who* is considered inside (almost all the groups named above in one way or another), the importance of the rights tradition becomes obvious. It is often the basis for whatever justice exists in the legal, economic, educational, medical, cultural, and familial aspects of American life. It is not care for different kinds of people in a diverse community of need that fuels most American programs of social justice, but a sense of fairness—an attempt to "level the playing field" in order to give everyone a chance to compete as individuals in a free society.

The merits of the justice tradition are evident, but its limitations are clear as well. Its greatest fault is that it is based on a false view of reality: we are not separate individuals who choose relationships. With a faulty foundation, it creates a society that does not work well: a society of haves and have-nots, of violence between the victors and the losers, of a deteriorating natural world that has minimal rights and hence is mainly a resource for humans, of hopelessness and despair among those who cannot make it in a world of radical individualism. It does not create healthy, sustainable communities of human beings and other species, living together with relative success. Hence, the rights model should not be the basic one, but it ought to be included within the community model. (When the reverse occurs and the community model is included within the rights model, care becomes merely palliative, band-aid treatment to patch up its failures—for instance, care for the homeless.) When we care about and for others, we imply that they have rights, that they deserve fair treatment, that justice demands attention to their needs and desires. There is nothing intrinsically alien about care and justice language; in fact, they belong together. "I care about your being treated right" makes perfect sense. The rights/justice tradition is necessary to the community model: it keeps it from being soft, from becoming private or personal, from depending merely on good feeling. It locks in good feeling toward others, taking it out of the range of changing minds and hearts. A stunning example is evident in the history of women's suffrage in the United States: half of the population was denied their right to vote, while being assured that their well-being would be cared for by the male voters. Fighting for the rights of others less fortunate (as, for instance, the right of rainforests or grizzly bears to survive) is an extension of the respect that is endemic to genuine caring. It is an extension of the detachment, the disinterestedness of genuine caring and friendship. It is pinning down and making permanent our wishes for the well-being of others. Contracts, laws, rights, justice have a major place within a community ethic of care: they make it tough-minded, dispassionate, and properly impersonal.

But whatever merits (or limitations) the rights/justice model has when applied to human beings, it is severely limited if it is the main or only ethical model used for our responsibilities to nature. To recall an earlier discussion, does the wolf have the right to eat the lamb for dinner, or does the lamb have the right to survive? How far do we take the notion of rights? It seems to make sense with songbirds, attractive mammals, and forests, but what of the AIDS virus? Does it have the right to survive? An individualistic, adversarial model is not helpful when thinking about the natural world (unless, of course, one is a strict DNA post-Darwinian who believes that spreading one's genes is the sole object of all forms of life, including human life). If one believes, however, that the next step in evolution is a cultural one of solidarity, rather than a genetic one of survival— or, more precisely, that we *will* survive only if we develop a social, sustainable planet—then the rights model cannot be the basic one.[18] A community model, a care model, a model that has the disinterested concern of the friendly eye, can manage better (remember, we are always working from within relative, inadequate models, none of which will be perfect). The community model says that the well-being of the whole is the final goal, but that this is reached through attending to the needs and desires of the many subjects that make up the community. Utopias, harmonious societies that people imagine and sometimes try to create, give us clues to what such communities might be like. They are almost always ones in which the lion and the lamb, the child and the snake, lie down together; where there is food for all; where neither people nor animals are destroying one another. The kingdom of God and the eucharistic banquet are such clues for Christians. We do not have utopias on earth, but we do have some towns and cities, and even some countries, here and there, that are closer to the dream than others. It is our responsibility to work for as close a match to the dream as we can in the places where we live.

Case Studies in Care: Wilderness or Garden?

A care model takes the good of the whole, not just the good of favored individuals, as its primary goal. Unlike the subject-object model that sets the rights of certain individuals, primarily human ones, against each other, the care model desires a community where different kinds of subjects can live together with relative satisfaction. It looks toward communities that *work*, not perfectly and not optimally for any particular subjects, but relatively well for most. The care ethic is pragmatic, local, and political, realizing that what works in one place may not in another and that when communities do work—both for different kinds of people and for the natural world—they involve a lot of hard political decisions, with active citizen participation.

We take heart when we hear of some success stories—some places in the world where communities of people and nature, living together, *are* working. Telling stories of recovery, such as the reforestation of New England, one of the most populated areas of the United States, is heartening.[19] In 1850 only 35 percent of Vermont was forested, the rest lumbered and cleared for farms; today 80 percent of the state has reforested. In New England today there are 40,000 black bears, along with the return of moose, deer, and beavers. While much of this has occurred through accident and circumstance rather than planning, it is heartening, nonetheless, to know that land and endangered species *can* recover. New England is not Eden, a pristine wilderness, but it is now a "second-chance" place.[20]

Nor should we want Eden—*we* can't live there. One of the greatest impediments to a workable care ethic for nature has been the

American dualistic sensibility that sets culture and nature over against each other. Nature equals wilderness while the city equals culture. We have had an ethic for the wilderness, beginning with John Muir and epitomized in the national parks movement, but we do not have an ethic for the rest of nature—the nature in our cities, the nature we use for resources, the nature we farm. We have, as Michael Pollan succinctly states, divided the country in two, "between the kingdom of the wilderness, which rules about 8 percent of America's land, and the kingdom of the market, which rules the rest."[21] As he elaborates:

> "All or nothing," says the wilderness ethic, and in fact we've ended up with a landscape in America that conforms to that injunction remarkably well. Thanks to exactly this kind of either/or thinking, Americans have done an admirable job of drawing lines around certain sacred areas (we did invent the wilderness area) and a terrible job of managing the rest of our land. The reason is not hard to find: the only environmental ethic we have has nothing useful to say about those areas outside the line. Once a landscape is no longer "virgin" it is typically written off as fallen, lost to nature, irredeemable. We hand it over to the jurisdiction of that other sacrosanct American ethic: laissez-faire economics. "You might as well put up condos." And so we do.[22]

A care ethic, however, refuses this dualism between sacred, untouchable wilderness and the profane, marketable rest. The real test of an ethic for nature is how it deals with the 92 percent—the big part that is more like a garden than a wilderness. While we should certainly preserve true wilderness areas of ancient forests for grizzly bears, wolves, tigers, and apes as well as for billions of smaller animals, insects, and plants, most of nature on our planet is garden—that is, it is land that we share with other lifeforms, that we inhabit, work, change, and enjoy. A garden, says Pollan, is "second nature," nature as interpreted, landscaped, cultivated, built upon, and transformed in innumerable ways. It is *our place*, where we build our homes, raise our children, grow our food, as well as stretch our muscles, delight our eyes, and rest our souls. Pollan says that the ethic of care that emerges from trying to take care of the garden is different from the wilderness ethic. The gardener looks for local solutions, proposing different ones in different places and times. She is frankly anthropocentric, in the sense that this garden *is* home. The gardener knows that one's own self-interest must be broad and enlightened, dependent as we are on the garden's health. He is not romantic about nature and often quarrels with it—nature is dangerous and capricious, as droughts, floods, and tornadoes illustrate. The gardener does not assume that our impact on nature is always negative—"second nature" is sometimes an improvement on first nature. Finally, she believes in making distinctions between good and bad interventions in nature.The difference between creating a small inner-city park and covering over a wooded area with a shopping mall shows that the issue is not all or nothing.

Pollan is right. We need to look for examples of towns and cities, communities, that are relatively good places for people and nature to co-inhabit. The ethic we need is not only one for the wilderness but also one for the garden, for the second nature that we share with the first nature. As we head into the twenty-first century, well aware of the devastation we have wreaked on our planet, of our burgeoning population, and especially of the excessive lifestyle of first-world people, despair is often our main emotion.[23] But among some environmentalists, there has been a change of heart from the apocalyptic, "death of nature" sensibility of earlier days.[24] That may well be the final outcome; but in the meantime there are pockets of hope, fueled by the assumption that "the world, conceivably, will meet us half-way; the alternative to Eden is not damnation."[25] But these are sobering scenarios—at least for those who believe the only good life is an affluent, high-energy, one-car-per-person one. The hopeful pockets portray a simpler, more limited lifestyle, in which a sense of community, a high literacy rate, low-energy technology, carefree childhood, the emancipation of women, preventive medicine, and ample green space are considered the good life.

All of us probably know of places—neighborhoods, towns, cities, and even a country or two—that, with such a sense of the "common good," are relative success stories. For instance, for several years Canada has been named by the United Nations as the country with the best quality of life—not just for the wealthy but for all its citizens. Bill McKibben in his book, *Hope, Human and Wild: True Stories of Living Lightly on the Earth*, tells the stories of two places, Curitiba, Brazil, and Kerala, India, that are "models of . . . post-utopia, places that resemble neither our pleasant daydream of a society nor the various nightmares so obvious in the world around us."[26] Curitiba is a city of a couple million people, not blessed with beautiful beaches or mountains, but measured by its "livability," 99 percent of its citizens like it. Curitiba was fortunate to have as its mayor a city planner named Jaime Lerner whose vision and great energy helped to spark widespread citizen concern for the city. That concern, over several decades, has resulted in a place to live where an excellent bus system rather than the car transports people; where a series of parks, cheaply built around small lakes from flood-control dams, has changed the amount of green space from two square feet per resident to one hundred fifty square feet; where education is available to all on an equal basis; and where people use the city safely at night and children play in its streets. It is a high density, workable, interesting city where ordinary people with limited incomes live along with nature. As McKibben remarks, "From every single window in Curitiba, I could see as much green as I could concrete."[27]

His second example is Kerala in southern India, a very poor area with one-seventieth the income per person compared to the United States, but which has 100 percent literacy, where men live only two years less on the average than in the United States, and where the birthrate is eighteen per thousand versus sixteen per thousand in the States. There is no air conditioning, no shopping malls, and few cars, but it is not a depressing place, giving lie to the assumption that only endless economic growth can provide a decent life. Early Marxist influences in Kerala created an atmosphere of sharing; moreover, an anti-caste reformer named Sri Narayana Guru undercut the worst instances of caste discrimination. The high literacy rate has meant that women have felt in charge of their lives, thus lowering the birthrate as well as the incidence of female infanticide. These various influences give Kerala a distinctive flavor of possibility and hope, though none of the factors operative in this place are utopian, impractical, or even especially unusual. Although it is a low-level economy, Kerala produces a decent life for people, where health, education, and a sense of community are priorities. It is also an environmentally light economy, with low levels of energy consumption.

As we think about the future of our planet—of how to care for it—it is clear that we cannot continue to grow, both in population and energy use. Other scenarios must be imagined, other ways of living within the limits of our garden.[28] The wilderness Eden—the land of unlimited possibilities—is not where we now live (or ever did, for that matter). We need an ethic that focuses on cultivating our gardens, living wisely and prudently, on the land, with the land. The American dream should no longer be city versus country, culture versus nature, shopping mall verses wilderness, but a garden, a second nature, where we make do with what we have. Second nature need not be second best—it all depends on how well we nurture, care for, our garden.

Care and the Social Self

Finally, it is important to recall that the ecological model is a *social* model: it claims that the self is constituted by relationships and exists only in relationships. This understanding of the self and others arises from the sense of touch and never loses that base. Throughout our lives we touch others and are touched by them. The model, however, does not fuse all subjects into one: each subject has its own individuality, its own distinctiveness, its own goals and ends. The model underscores the most radical unity possible (everything at some level is interrelated and interdependent with everything else) and the most radical individuality (everything is different from every other thing—including each of those six million leaves on the elm tree). The community model, therefore, is a type of organic model—not one built on the human body but on ecological systems. If we human beings understand ourselves within this model, we will *feel* like social beings. We will realize that what happens to us and what happens to others in a sense happens to all. It makes us *want* to work for the well-being of others, including the others in nature, as it adds to our own well-being. The social self means that ethics—doing good for others—is not just altruism or self-sacrifice (as an ethic of care might suggest), for "their" good is also "my" good and vice-versa.

But what about when bad things happen? How does the social self, the ecological model, handle that? Bad things happen not in general, but in concrete ways—to individual people and special groups of people (children, the poor, homosexuals, the old), as well as to particular animals, trees, bodies of water, ecosystems. Death and disaster are neither universal nor fair; they are specific, seemingly random, and often unjust. It is not the *social* subject that feels the pain of hunger, abuse, rape, discrimination, oppression, or murder—or the shock and loss of so-called natural disasters—but *particular* subjects. Nonetheless, the sense of solidarity in the ecological model—that "I" am "I" only in relationship with other people and other species—creates a different sensibility for dealing with failure, accidents, injustices, losses, and death than is possible within the standard model of the self. Whereas the subject-object, individualistic model implies that whatever happens, good or bad, is mainly due to the merits or fault of the individual, the ecological model realizes things are not that simple. On an unimaginably complex planet with a myriad of interlocking systems, both physical and cultural, as well as millions of species and billions of individuals with different desires and goals (both human and nonhuman), *things happen*, both good and bad, that do not have any one, simple cause. This does not remove responsibility from us self-conscious subjects for doing the best we can to accentuate the good, but it does create a context in which to view both the good and the bad things that happen.

To put it simply: it enlarges the sense of self. The borders of the self do not stop with my own body: I am, I exist, only as I am in touch with the others, the other subjects who influence me and whom I influence. This enlarged sense of self makes it possible to rejoice when others prosper, to mourn when they are diminished. It also makes it possible to feel comfort from others in one's own sorrow and to feel support from them in good times. The organic, interdependent, interrelational model is, then, a necessary part of the community model. An ecological self pushes back the boundaries, enlarging the sense of who and what one cares for. This is what the saints do: they identify with, connect with, others, often the most oppressed, despised others, as part of themselves. The joys and sorrows of others become their joys and sorrows. One of the most striking insights I have gained from reading religious autobiographies is how love gradually grows outward to include more and more others. St. Francis is a prime example: his love for others did not stop at the human line, but extended into the natural world. Dorothy Day, Black Elk, and Martin Luther King, Jr. show the same tendency: what often begins with a particular cause—*my* people—grows into care for all oppressed people and sometimes into a concern for environmental destruction. The place where this love starts is important—it begins with the nearby, the particular, the known, and grows gradually outward as the interlocking connections between different forms of need, discrimination, and oppression become evident. It is not a generalized, sentimental love for all beings, but the realization that one's own self and all other subjects are connected by networks that support both flourishing and diminishment. "We are all one lesson," as Alice Walker says—indeed, we are.

We have been looking at various dimensions of the ethic that emerges from the ecological model: at respect as its first note, at care for the community as the central characteristic of this ethic, of the relationship between care and justice, at some examples of communities built by the care ethic, of the social (organic) sense of self endemic to this ethic that allows us to identify with the joys and sorrows of others. All of this is from the side of the ecological model, but what is its special relevance to Christianity and what does Christianity offer to the model?

The Ecological Model and Christian Spirituality

Extending Christian Love to Nature

A Christian nature spirituality is Christian praxis extended to nature. It is treating the natural world in the same way we treat, or should treat, God and other people—as subjects, not objects. But, we have to admit, we seldom act this way. Only the saints seem able to do it: recall Francis of Assisi who let things be what they are— wind is wind, death is death—and *as they were* he both loved them and saw them as signs of God. Francis's way was "to commune with all things, respecting and reverencing their differences and distinctions."[29] What is often shocking to contemporary Christians about Francis is that he treated *nature* this way, as subject. Christians have always tried to treat other people as subjects; the subject-subjects model has been *the* model of how we ought to relate to God and to other people. God is the ultimate Subject whom we are to love with our whole heart, mind, and soul simply because God *is* God. We should not fuse with God (the Christian suspicion of mysticism) nor objectify God (the Christian insistence that God is to be loved for God's sake alone, and not out of self-interest). Likewise, we are to love our (human) neighbors "as we love ourselves," in other words, as subjects who have interests, wishes, and needs that are their own. We are to love them disinterestedly, for their own sakes, not for ours.

One of the main contributions of the ecological model to Christianity is the extension of its own subject-subjects thinking to nature. For most contemporary Christians, the line stops with human beings. Post-Enlightenment Christians have bought into the subject-object arrogant eye when it comes to nature. What the ecological model offers to Christianity is a way of extending its *own most basic affirmation* on how others should be treated—as subjects—to nature. If Christians were to embrace the ecological model, they would not be doing something radical or discontinuous with their historical faith. On the contrary, they would simply be extending that faith to include nature. If we are to love God with our whole heart, mind, and soul, and our neighbor as ourselves, how, in continuity with that model, should we love nature? The answer is: with the loving eye, with the eye that realizes that even a wood tick or a Douglas fir is a subject—that each has a world, goals, intentions (though not conscious), and modes of flourishing that make them good in themselves and not simply good for us. Surely, this is what the Genesis verse means: "God saw everything that God had made, and indeed, it was very good"(1:31a). This is an amazing statement. God does not say that creation is good for human beings or even, more surprising, good for me, God, but just good, in fact, very good. God is saying that nature is good in itself—not good for something or someone but just plain good. It is like a parent saying to a child, "I love you just the way you are," or lovers saying to each other, "I love you because you are you." God's pronouncement here is an aesthetic one: appreciation of something outside of oneself, in itself, for itself. Even God can recognize that something exists outside of the divine self—and that, as such, it is good!

Because the Genesis material is often accused of being a foundational anti-nature text, we need to substantiate this reading. The writer of the first chapter of Genesis leaves no doubt but that the goodness of creation is its message: it is repeated seven times in the space of thirty-one verses. After the very first act of creation—of day and night—the text reads: "And God saw that the light was good." After making the earth and sea, we read again, "And God saw that it was good" and when finishing the sun and moon, we hear the same refrain. In fact, after every creation God pronounces its goodness—after creating the birds and sea monsters as well as "the cattle and creeping things and wild animals." Finally, after we human beings are made, God surveys the entire panorama and with what appears to be great pleasure and delight, exclaims, "indeed, it was very good."

How have we missed this? Seven times it is repeated like a teacher drumming into a lazy student's head a bit of basic learning. We have not heard, "It is very good." What we have heard are two other motifs concerning nature that are also in Genesis 1: domination and stewardship. We have heard, "Fill the earth and subdue it; and have dominion . . . ," which is not mentioned seven times but only once. We have also heard, "I have given you every plant . . . you shall have them for food," suggesting that human beings ought to be good stewards of nature (but note that other creatures are also given the plants—"to . . . everything that has the breath of life, I have given every green plant for food").

Certainly, a conservation ethic of sustainability—an ethic of preserving and sharing the earth's bounty for all its creatures—is implicit in Genesis. And the domination theme is there also. But these three attitudes toward nature—appreciation, stewardship, and domination—are graded, with appreciation ("it is good") being the primary one. It is repeated over and over, literally pounded into our heads. Stewardship is also important in the text: it is the necessary daily practice so that the basics of life, such as food, can be shared by all. But domination, which has been the primary attitude of the West toward nature, takes up less than one verse of the thirty-one verses in the chapter. This is scant justification for treating the oceans as burial grounds for toxic waste, the forests as so many board feet, domestic animals as simply food to be eaten or material for medical experiments, and wild animals as expendable if human beings need the land.

We simply didn't get the point. The message of Genesis is not domination but appreciation. We who the text says are made in God's image ought to reflect God's attitude toward nature: appreciation. This attitude is in line with how we are supposed to relate to God and neighbor. God is the ultimate Subject: we love God (or should) because God is God and deserves our adoration. We love our neighbor (or should) because we see human beings as ends in themselves, as valuable just because they *are*. A human being is good, period. Genesis 1 is saying that we should extend the way we relate to God and neighbor *to nature:* nature is good, period. So, for Christians to relate to nature as subject is merely to extend its own relational model—loving God and neighbor—to all of creation.

This extension, however, has not been our practice; we do need help here. Throughout this volume we have been concerned with how we might develop such a sensibility within ourselves toward nature. How can we apply the ecological model to nature, and how can we develop the loving eye that respects nature as subject? There are many stories in the Bible on how to practice the loving eye toward God and other people; in fact, that is what much of both the Hebrew Scriptures and the New Testament are about. But apart from some sections in the Hebrew Scriptures (with a smattering in the New Testament), there are few biblical guides for Christians on how to practice love toward nature. Nor does traditional Christian theology or ethics help much; Francis stands out in part due to his singular concern with nature. Hence, we have turned to the ecological model and its loving eye to help educate the Christian's eye in order to develop what Christians, especially Protestants, have not had since the Middle Ages—a *nature* spirituality, sensitivity toward the natural world.

For most of its history, Christianity has preached the Good News to people, often forgetting that the redeemer of human beings is also the creator of *everything* that is. The health and well-being of the natural world have usually been a minor concern in Christian teaching and preaching.[30] We have suggested that it is an oversight, a lack, a fault in Christian faith and that Christianity should extend its own version of the subject-subjects model—loving God for God's sake and loving other people as oneself—to nature. By doing so it would be true to its own innermost dynamic, which is not subject-object, but subject-subjects. By doing so it would also intersect with the ecological model that is emerging in postmodern understandings of reality. In sum, our thesis and main question are very simple: What justification is there for limiting the subject-subjects model to human beings, drawing a line in the sand at our own species, with all other species and the rest of nature outside the circle? On the basis of Christianity's own most basic model, seeing God and others as subjects— as valuable in themselves, for themselves, and not just as for me or against me—should we not *also* love nature this way? Since we always think in terms of models (which are always relative and inadequate), is it not better (not perfect) to think of the rest of nature more or less *like ourselves,* rather than as utterly unlike us? Is it not only better for the health of our planet, but also more *Christian?*

If we were to think this way, allow this sensibility to grow deep inside ourselves, we would develop a way of thinking about God, human beings, and nature similar to the medieval view. That is, it would be an outer-directed, functional cosmology in which we and all other natural beings and entities would have a place. It would, however, be a worldview closer to that of Francis of Assisi than to most of his contemporaries: he saw all things in God, but not as signs pointing to God or as symbols transparent to God, but each and every thing telling of the glory of God *in its own distinctiveness.* Hence, the ecological model is a prime candidate to do for twenty-first-century Christians what the Great Chain of Being, the hierarchical model of interrelated signs and symbols, did for medieval people—to relate all things to one another. Christianity is always and rightly looking for ways to remythologize its understanding of the relationship between God and the world in new thought forms. There is such an obvious and close match between the ecological model and basic Christian spirituality—understanding God and other people as subjects to whom one relates in profound and disinterested ways—that Christians would be foolish not to embrace this rich paradigm as a contemporary way to construe their faith.

Deepening the Subject-Subjects Model

But Christianity is not only the learner, the receiver, in this conversation. What does Christian faith have to offer that goes beyond the ecological model? Christianity makes several very significant contributions. First, we recall how difficult if not impossible it is for most of us to treat others as subjects, whether these others be God, other people, or nature. We use these others in both explicit and subtle ways. Using God is so common we are often not even aware of it, but from tribalism (the assumption that God fights on the side of our nation or ethnic group) to fox-hole religion (the mentality that sees God as personal rescuer in times of disaster), religious functionalism is widespread. We often do not worship God because God is God and deserves our total adoration, but because we *need* God to save our country, win a basketball game, rescue our loved ones, or help someone recover from substance abuse. Likewise, we often find it very difficult if not impossible to love other people as we do ourselves. We do not treat them as subjects, as others, as having their own goals and desires; more often, they are means to *our* ends. If we do not, seemingly cannot, treat God and other people as subjects, how will we be able to treat nature this way—that part of creation that we have not even allowed inside the subjects circle?

It is at this point that Christian faith makes one of its major contributions to the ecological model. We have noted how fragile the subject-subjects model is, how anxiety pushes us either to objectify and control others or to flip over into fusion with others in the search for self-affirmation. Being a self and relating to others as selves is difficult. In fact, one definition of sin is precisely the objectification of others, using others as a means to an end—one's self-fulfillment. The classic doctrines of justification and sanctification speak to this dilemma. Justification acknowledges that we do not and cannot live as subjects relating to other subjects, whether these be the divine Subject or other persons, but that God forgives us for our failure. It says that we are accepted as we are, that we do not have to merit or win God's acceptance; we are given it as a gift. It says that we do not have to dominate others or fuse with them in fear lest we lose ourselves, because God loves us as we are (as the subjects we are). Justification grounds us as subjects, as beings valuable *as such*. As we accept our acceptance, we are directed and encouraged, through the doctrine of sanctification, to go and do likewise: to accept others as they are, in their own subjecthood. These two doctrines together set out a tough-minded agenda: justification acknowledges the depths of human sin, while sanctification insists that once free of it we have a task to do. While Christianity is certainly not the only remedy for the anxiety of human self-awareness, it is a classic and profound one. It is realistic in its analysis of the problem and persuasive in its solution, as hundreds of years of Christian history have shown.

A second major contribution of Christian faith to the ecological model is its community of care ethic. This ethic, as we have seen, is very close to Christian spirituality—the development of sensitivity toward God, other people, and nature. It fits well with the relational, subject-subjects character of Christianity: both the community-care ethic and Christian faith focus on the well-being of the entire community rather than on the rights of privileged members of it. Hence, super, natural Christians will be on the frontlines in caring for the communities of which they are a part: in working for diverse, sustainable communities where social justice and environmental integrity come together. They will join forces with others from different religious faiths and who for different reasons also want this common good. But Christianity goes further than the community-care ethic in at least one important respect. It gives preference to certain subjects: the needy. Here is another way in which Christians ought to be super, natural. The Christian eye is not just a loving eye, but that eye has a particular slant—it slants toward the oppressed, the poor, the despised, the forgotten. Christians will focus, on the basis of the logic of their own faith, on healing the wounds of nature and feeding its starving creatures, even as they also focus on healing and feeding needy human beings. This will mean that Christians will center on certain kinds of environmental issues, where, for instance, the neediest human beings and the neediest parts of nature meet. The phrase "environmental racism" brings these needs together—oppressed human beings and polluted nature. Christianity insists that the ecological model give priority to the neediest among both people and nature. For example, the kind of environmental issues that Christians should be concerned with, working out of the model suggested here, will be justice toward African Americans who complain that landfills are usually placed in their neighborhoods; creation and maintenance of wilderness areas to preserve forests and promote biodiversity; access by city people, especially poor ones, to small, close-by parks; opportunities for direct contact with nature by children, especially under-privileged ones; aid to third-world communities where both people and the environment are being exploited by multinational corporations. Christians will work toward creating more communities like Curitiba and Kerala, where mostly poor people and "second-chance" nature exist together in a sustainable, shared, modest lifestyle. Christianity gives a particular slant to the loving eye, a slant that confers preference to needy people in their negative and positive dealings with nature as well as to needy nature itself. Christianity says that "nature is the new poor" or the "also poor," which, in unity with poor people, commands our special attention.

A local example of a project that might command the special attention of Christians is the maintenance and health of urban parks. Such parks bring together poor people and the new poor, nature. In 1995 several bills were introduced into the U.S. Congress to close some urban parks and turn others over to local governments or private entrepreneurs in order to save money.[31] The Director of the National Park Service fought back, claiming that urban parks offer an inexpensive recreation alternative for people who cannot afford "to drive the Lexus to Glacier" for a vacation.[32] Targeting urban parks while shielding the national parks from threat is implicitly classist and racist, for national parks are used largely by the white middle and upper classes while urban parks offer minorities and poor people rare opportunities. A warden at Golden Gate Park in San Francisco said that for some kids a trip to the park means "going for a walk on the beach for the first time."[33] White, European-descended Americans follow an old tradition for their vacations of traveling to remote wilderness areas to fish, camp, and hike. More recent immigrants from Africa, Asia, and Latin America have a different idea of how to spend their leisure time, preferring family or clan gatherings in a village square, an orchard, or a city park. A policy that supports wilderness areas but not city greenspace discriminates against poor people and certain ethnic groups. While Christians certainly need to support wilderness areas for biodiversity, another priority might be city parks, which bring nature and poor people together.

Working at the local level to integrate needy nature and needy people will form a sensibility in Christians so that we might become a force supporting sustainable communities at all levels, with special attention to the poor, both human and natural. It is very difficult to imagine what sustainable regional, national, or global communities might be. That they are necessary is self-evident, if we accept the ecological model as the one in which we live, think, and act.[34] But we can educate ourselves in the global implications of this model as we practice it in our communities and cities. The basic pattern, whether small or large, is the same: it is a model of sustainability in which respect and care for others are primary, especially care of the neediest.

A global example of Christian care can be seen in the impending crisis of climate change. There is now consensus among weather experts that global warming has begun and that by 2050 c.e. we can expect a 2.5° C. increase in the worldwide temperature.[35] Since the earth's temperature during the last Ice Age was only 5° to 6° C. *cooler* than now, one can see that a 2.5° C. *increase* is substantial. The results will be devastating (desertification, scarcity of fresh water, loss of tree cover, flooding of coastal areas and islands, shortages of food, etc.). The effects will also be spread unevenly, with the southern, third-world countries experiencing the worst consequences, even though global warming is caused mainly by emissions from the burning of fossil fuels by northern, industrialized countries. What is the specific Christian response to this situation?[36] It is, I think, twofold: a word to the oppressor and a word to the oppressed.

A Christian ethic of care condemns the arrogant eye of the oppressor. A word of repentance should be spoken to the elites of both the first and third worlds as well as a call for a radical change in their consumer lifestyle. These people are not loving the earth; rather, they are casting an arrogant eye on it, perceiving it to be theirs for the taking. They do not accept the intrinsic value either of other people or other lifeforms: these others are simply "for" or "against" the one Subject, which is me and my kind. Christian witness, which demands that all God's creatures must have their basic needs met, condemns such outrageous greed.

A Christian ethic of care sides with the oppressed, in this case those creatures and aspects of earth that are experiencing the greatest deterioration. A symbol of this deterioration is a poor third-world woman of color, for she is a barometer of the health of both humanity and nature. Living as she does at the juncture of the poorest human beings and the most devastated nature, she tells us how both are faring. While the world's elites have the power to direct earth's diminishing resources to their own uses, this woman does not. In her increasing poverty, we see also the increasing poverty of nature.

Christian radicalism—love for the neediest humans and devastated nature—helps to push more moderate forms of the care ethic toward greater justice for the forgotten and the voiceless. Its particular role in issues of public policy is to move the powers in control beyond "business as usual" compromises on critical issues toward decisions that show concern for the most vulnerable.

Horizontal Christian Sacramentalism

Finally, Christianity also believes nature gives us intimations of the divine. As stated early on, the sacramental use of nature is the oldest and in many ways the noblest of Christian understandings of nature. We have avoided it, however, because of its utilitarianism: nature is seen as a way to reach God. Nonetheless, as we noted with Francis of Assisi, it is possible both to appreciate things in themselves, for themselves, *and* to see them as signs of God. Most of Francis's medieval brothers and sisters saw nature as a sign of God, but they failed to acknowledge it as having intrinsic value. The main project of this book has been to take us on a journey that would help us see nature this way—as subject. But now as we consider what Christianity might offer to the model, we must add a new sacramentalism. This sacramentalism would, while "holding on hard to the huckleberries," see all things in God. However, the focus of this Christian loving eye is not vertical but horizontal; not on "God in this tree," but "*this tree* in God." The focus of this eye is not on seeing God, but on seeing the tree (this particular tree) which, in its own way, as itself, is *also* in God. The Christian eye does not need training to see God but to see other things, especially earth others—and *then* to see them in God. The ecological model with its stress on the embodied, concrete, particularity of all things, each in its own subjectivity, helps us to do this. When the Christian eye has been so educated, it can and should then see them also as intimations of the divine.

Moreover, this new sacramentalism will give Christians a new, rich vocabulary with which to speak of God. The Christian tradition has limited God-language largely to metaphors taken from human beings: since we alone, among created beings, are made in the image of God, only we, in turn, can image God. God-talk has been mainly human talk writ large: God is imagined to be a super-person, doing things people do but on an infinite, eternal scale. Thus, God loves (as we do) but infinitely and eternally; God wills, judges, acts, sees, hears, knows, but always to the nth degree and in a perfect fashion. Language about God in the Western, Christian tradition has been accused of being anthropomorphic and anthropocentric. It is these things, but there is some justification. The reply to these accusations is: "Of course. Since all talk of God is necessarily metaphorical, shouldn't we use ourselves as metaphors with which to speak of God?" The counter-reply, however, goes like this: "Why limit talk of God to metaphors based on humanity? Does not the whole creation mirror God's being and glory? Are not other lifeforms and the earth itself subjects whom God loves and cares about?" Just as feminists, early and late, from Mary Daly to Elizabeth Johnson, have pointed out the error of limiting God-talk to male imagery, so also, as we now move the line beyond ourselves to include nature, ought we not to move our God-talk as well? As Daly said over twenty years ago, "If God is male, then the male is God" and as Johnson wrote recently, "The glory of God is . . . the human being, the whole human race, every individual person, fully alive."[37] If we now accept that language about God can result in "She who is" as well as "He who is," ought it not also, on the basis of the same reasoning, include "Nature which is"? Just as the psalmists and medieval women and men did not shrink from using the natural world to speak of God, neither should we.

But we do so now taking into full account the diversity, particularity, and thickness of natural forms. They are not transparent to the divine; they are first of all themselves, and as such, in the intricacy and uniqueness of who, what, they are, they speak elliptically of God. Just as feminists have insisted that there is no universal woman who can image the divine, that God must be spoken of in images from the actual, concrete, diverse circumstances of women's lives, so also "Nature" is not a metaphor for God. The natural world is not a single entity but a marvelously rich, multidimensional, diverse, and intricate collection of lifeforms and things. It is precisely this character of the natural world that presents itself to us as a new and exciting way to speak of God. (Actually, it is not new at all, but appears so to post-Enlightenment Christians, especially Protestants, who narrowed the world to themselves and God.) As Augustine noted many hundred years ago, we do not know how to speak of God, what words to use, and the words we do use are not much better than a baby's babble. One might say that in desperation we have turned to what we know best—ourselves—for material to talk about God. That tactic is understandable and it has been rewarding: we have a rich reservoir of personalistic words, concepts, and images for talking about God. But we have neglected another rich reservoir—

nature—both to the detriment of God and nature. We need to speak of God in metaphors drawn from nature for at least two reasons: the richness of the divine being demands it and nature deserves it. The fullness of God cannot possibly be reflected only through human reality, and nature should be honored, as we are, by being a source for metaphors for God.

Hence, the movement of the subjects line beyond us to include nature can and should restore nature as a divine sacrament. It will, however, be closer to Francis's kind of sacramentalism than to the typical medieval view. It will be a kind of sacramentalism that focuses on the things themselves rather than on their divine message. It will be a kind of sacramentalism that is radically incarnational: God is with us here and now in and on our earth. The things of the earth do not point away from the earth to God; rather, they are themselves the "body" of God—one of the major metaphors that Christians might now use from nature to speak of God. God's body in this metaphor is not one body, but all the bodies, from subatomic to galactic ones, and all the ones in between, from robins and tigers to mountains and oceans, from mites and microbes to trees and plants, as well as, of course, ourselves. All of these millions, billions of creatures and entities, are, like us, made for the glory of God, and they deserve, as all human beings do, to be part of the language we use to speak of God.

The color purple in its purpleness and a horse named Blue in his horseness are traces of God, even as each human being in his or her uniqueness is a witness to God's creative genius. Thomas Aquinas once said that the whole creation, every tiny scrap of it (and for us this would include every galaxy and every microbe) is necessary to even begin to mirror the glory of God. But he also suggested, and the ecological model affirms it, that each bit of creation, whether in interstellar space, Tinker Creek, or Kerala, gives glory to God by *being itself*, fully and wonderfully. God is glorified not by the denial of difference, but by its flourishing and fulfillment. The incarnation of God in Christ Jesus further claims that the glory of God is revealed in the least, the most despised, the most oppressed of God's creatures. Surely, in our time, the natural world is joined in its oppression with Christ: it too is being crucified. Just as in the face of a suffering child, woman, or man, Christians see the face of Christ, so also there is a trace of that face in a clear-cut forest, an inner-city landfill, or a polluted river.

To sum up: the conversation between the ecological model and

Christianity is a rich one, with important offerings from both sides. The ecological model offers Christianity a way to construe its own basic understanding of relationality between God and human beings, but extends it as well to nature; it also offers education in how to relate to other subjects with a loving eye. Christianity with its doctrines of justification and sanctification offers the ecological model a remedy for the anxious self, poised between objectification and fusion, while seeking genuine acceptance of its own and others' subjecthood. It also offers the ecological model a direction to the loving eye: toward the oppressed, both among people and nature. Finally, Christianity suggests that nature is not "just nature," but as one sees the face of Christ in the needy sister or brother, so also nature, in its own way, is a vision of God.

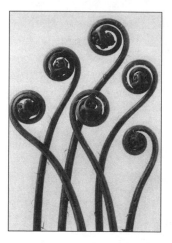

Epilogue

W HEN I WAS A YOUNG CHILD, I lived in the present, as most children do, and now that I am over sixty, I find myself living there once again. But during the middle years, from the teen ones up until I was fifty, I lived elsewhere—mostly toward the future but often in the past. Our progress-driven, workaholic Western culture supports this sensibility, but so does traditional Christianity. Christ came to earth to save humankind 2,000 years ago and will come again to usher the redeemed into heaven. Christian time has been about the past and the future, but usually not about the present.

Liberation theologies, however, insist that this is a perversion, because the Gospel is concerned with the liberation of the oppressed here and now. A Christian nature spirituality is also about the present; in fact, it rests on waking up to what is right before our eyes. It begins as a conversion, an awakening to what we often sensed as children but forgot as we grew older: that we are surrounded by wonder. A daffodil, cockroaches behind the kitchen sink, a goldfish named Ellery, the stars from a city roof, a horse named Blue, a butterfly on the nose, the splash of a frog in a pond, the color purple, and turtles basking in the sun: these awakenings return us to the present from our burial in the past or dreams of the future. Suddenly, we feel as if a veil has been lifted from our eyes and we see for the first time the specialness, intricacy, and beauty of something. This "something" need not be a bit of nature, but it should include bits of nature. Christian spirituality has limited its sense of wonder to God (and other human beings), but a Christian nature spirituality would extend it to nature.

If spirituality means growing in sensitivity toward others—God, neighbor, and nature—then it means being present, being awake, to them. This is the first step. While we can't stay there or live there, we should return there. Direct, immediate encounters with others fuel our respect for them and inform how we should relate to them. Just as prayer opens us to encounter God, and close association with other human beings teaches us how to love them, so also being present to some fragment of nature reminds us of the basis of a Christian nature spirituality: growing in sensitivity toward it. This growth will hopefully issue in all sorts of actions: the energy we put into fighting city hall for a neighborhood park, the time we give to elect city officials who will make our city one of the success stories, the money we contribute to preserve wilderness areas for wild animals, the protest march we join to help disempower multinational environmental destruction in third-world countries, and even the birdbath that we remember to fill every day.

The love of God and neighbor is based in prayer, as the saints who lasted over the long haul illustrate: praxis must be based in piety. So also a Christian nature praxis rests on the attitude toward nature that emerges from paying attention to it. It rests on respect for its otherness and concern for its vulnerability. This sensibility does not develop or endure unless it is cultivated day by day. As we must be open to, present to, God and neighbor, so also we must be to nature. We must be if we are to work, one day at a time over many years, for nature's health and well-being.

But will a change in sensibility cause us to act more wisely and caringly toward nature? We cannot be certain about this. As Paul said a long time ago, knowing the good does not necessarily mean that we will do the good. Nor is there any assurance that if we do act on the basis of a conversion to the earth our planet will be saved. We can certainly hope that our actions will have an effect, but Christians do not love the earth in order to save the planet. We should love nature for the same reason we should love God and our neighbor: because it is valuable in itself and deserves our love. The end of things is not in our hands and focusing on global outcomes can lead to despair. What we can do is act locally—loving nature in present, possible, available, concrete ways—leaving global apocalypticism to the ideologues and naysayers. (This does not mean, of course, that we hide our heads in the sand on planetary environmental issues, but hand-wringing over possible disasters is often an excuse for inaction.) We are energized by what we can touch, see, hear, and know—nearby nature. As we open ourselves to the bits and pieces of nature in the damaged lands of our cities, waking up for at least a few minutes each day to the presence of some particular earth other, we renew our acquaintance with and commitment to our oppressed Brother Earth and Sister Water.

At sixty, I am once again six. I am filled with wonder at ordinary things—a child's smile, a dog's loping run, sticky new buds on a tree. But there is a difference between being sixty and six. The six-year-old does not flinch at the sight of a forest clear-cut or the eyes of a starving child. A Christian nature spirituality is not nature romanticism. Nor is it very optimistic about the future (the planet may well deteriorate). It is, however, determinedly realistic: it begins and ends with a hymn to the things themselves. A Christian nature spirituality praises God for the wonder of the ordinary and promises to work on behalf of the sick and outcast wonderful, ordinary creatures. A Christian nature spirituality is also determinedly hopeful because it believes that the creator of these wonderful, ordinary creatures is working in, through, and on behalf of us all.

Notes

Chapter 1

1. Ludwig Feuerbach, *Essence of Christianity*, trans. Marian Evans (New York: C. Blanchard, 1855), 361.

2. For a discussion of nature as the "new poor," see my book, *The Body of God: An Ecological Theology* (Minneapolis, Minn.: Fortress Press, 1993), 165, 200-201.

3. For a discussion of the "planetary agenda," see *The Body of God*, 8-13.

4. For discussions of metaphors and models, see my books *Metaphorical Theology: Models of God in Religious Language* (Philadelphia: Fortress Press, 1983); also *Models of God: Theology for an Ecological, Nuclear Age* (Philadelphia: Fortress Press, 1987), ch. 2; and *The Body of God*, consult index.

5. For a description of this picture, see *The Body of God*, 38-47, 103-12.

6. In agreement with deconstruction's critique of the humanist, individualistic self, the ecological model insists that the self only exists within discourses or texts. Thus, the human self in this model exists in relation to nature not in a direct, unmediated, romantic way, but within the ecological narrative, which understands all selves (centers of existence) as radically interrelational. In disagreement with deconstruction, the ecological model insists that the natural world is not only "there" (apart from our interpretations) but also has its own rules and laws, which we must obey if we and the rest of nature are to survive. In other words, while all portrayals of the self-world correlation are narratives or models rather than descriptions, not all interpretations are equal because, I would argue, the results of some models (discourses) are healthier than others for the entities involved. The subject-object model is, in practice, not as good for the planet and its creatures as is the subject-subjects model. But *both* are interpretations, both are discourses.

7. "Working Party Report on 'Spirituality'" (Dunblane: Scottish Churches House, 1977), 3.

179

8. Leonardo Boff, "Spirituality and Politics," in *Liberation Theology: An Introductory Reader*, ed. Curt Cadorette *et al.* (Maryknoll, N.Y.: Orbis Books, 1992), 237.

9. Ibid., 238.

10. Jon Sobrino, "Christian Prayer and New Testament Theology: A Basis for Social Justice and Spirituality," in *Western Spirituality: Historical Roots, Ecumenical Routes*, ed. Matthew Fox (Notre Dame, Ind.: Fides/Claretian, 1979), 87.

11. The Gospel material on this point, especially on the status of women, is complex. For a classic and comprehensive treatment on women and the Jesus movement, see Elisabeth Schüssler Fiorenza, *In Memory of Her: A Feminist Theological Reconstruction of Christian Origins* (New York: Crossroad, 1983).

12. The sort of Christian nature spirituality I am suggesting is different from the creation theology of Matthew Fox or the nature spirituality of deep ecology. I have respect for both of these positions and have learned much from them, but what I am suggesting is distinctively different from either. For further discussion, see *The Body of God*, 69-73 (creation spirituality); 124-28 (deep ecology).

13. "Social ecology studies human historico-social systems in interaction with environmental systems. Human history is inseparable from that of the environment, and from the type of relationships that we have interwoven with it, in a dynamic interplay of mutual involvement" (Leonardo Boff, *Ecology and Liberation: A New Paradigm* [Maryknoll, N.Y.: Orbis, 1995], 88).

14. "Voluntary belt-tightening will not go far toward responding to the problem" (John B. Cobb, Jr., *Sustainability: Economics, Ecology, and Justice* [Maryknoll, N.Y.: Orbis, 1992], 35).

15. When statements insisting on profound changes among the elites of the world are made, someone invariably adds, "But what about the population issue?" (with the subtext that it is the developing, poor countries that are producing too many children). Since this book is addressed to the elites and since there is no evidence that we are making the changes *we* need to, I think we are scarcely in a position to call others to account. If and when we do make such changes, we will be in a position to do so. The major effect we can have on the population issue from *our side* is to support national and international efforts toward the redistribution of wealth between nations of the North and the South, as well as the education and status of women throughout the world.

16. John B. Cobb, Jr., "Economism or Planetism: The Coming Choice," *Earth Ethics* 3 (Fall, 1991).

17. "Through the economics of growth, nature is degraded to the level of mere 'natural resources,' or 'raw materials,' at the disposal of humankind. Workers are seen as 'human resources' and as a mere function of production. Everything is governed by an instrumental and mechanistic vision: persons, animals, plants, minerals. All creatures, in short, lose their relative autonomy and their intrinsic value" (Boff, *Ecology and Liberation*, 24).

18. For a fuller elaboration of the following analysis, see chs. 5 and 6 in *The Body of God*.

19. Gordon D. Kaufman, *The Theological Imagination: Constructing the Concept of God* (Philadelphia: Westminster Press, 1981), 213.

20. Ibid.

21. Ronald Rees, "The Taste for Scenery," *History Today* 25 (1975), 306.

22. Marjorie Nicholson, *Mountain Gloom and Mountain Glory: The Development of the Aesthetics of the Infinite* (Ithaca, N.Y.: Cornell University Press, 1959), 1.

23. Jorge Luis Borges, *Other Inquisitions*, 1952, as quoted in Londa Schiebinger, *Nature's Body: Gender in the Making of Modern Science* (Boston: Beacon Press, 1993), 40.

24. The following discussion is from Jakob von Uexküll, "A Stroll through the Worlds of Animals and Men" in *Instinctive Behavior*, ed. Claire Schiller (New York: International Universities Press, 1957).

25. Barry Lopez, *Arctic Dreams: Imagination and Desire in a Northern Landscape* (New York: Charles Scribner's Sons, 1986), 239.

26. "Essentialism . . . refers to the existence of fixed characteristics, given attributes, and ahistorical functions which limit the possibilities of change and thus of social reorganization" (Elizabeth Grosz, "Conclusion: A Note on Essentialism and Difference," in *Feminist Knowledge: Critique and Construct*, ed. Sneja Gunew [New York: Routledge, 1992], 334).

27. Simon Shama, *Landscape and Memory* (New York: Knopf, 1995), 119. I cannot resist adding another quote from this marvelous book. "Tacitus's observation that their isolated habitat made the Germans the least mixed of all European peoples would of course become the lethal obsession of the Nazi tyranny. *Germantentum*—the idea of a biologically pure and inviolate race, as 'natural' to its terrain as indigenous species of trees and flowers—featured in much of the archaeological and prehistorical literature both before and after the First World War. . . . Whenever possible, Hitler, the Reichforstmeister Göring, and Himmler were photographed in sylvan settings" (118).

28. Schiebinger, *Nature's Body*, 1-2.

29. Ibid., 39.

30. Karen J. Warren, "The Power and the Promise of Ecological Feminism," *Environmental Ethics* 12 (Summer, 1990), 133.

31. See Ian G. Barbour, *Religion in an Age of Science*, vol. 1 (New York: Harper & Row, 1990), 219.

32. See ibid. for a helpful table of the three worldviews.

33. Pertinent here is a definition of "naturalism" by Erazim V. Kohak as "any philosophy which recognizes the being of humans as integrally linked to the being of nature, however conceived, treating humans as distinctive only in as much as any distinct species is that, but as fundamentally *at home* in the cosmos. . . ." (*The Embers and the Stars: A Philosophical Inquiry into the Moral Sense of Nature* [Chicago: University of Chicago Press, 1984], 8).

34. Martin Buber, *I and Thou* (New York: Scribner's, 1970), 18.

35. As quoted in James A. Gustafson, *A Sense of the Divine: The Natural Environment from a Theocentric Perspective* (Cleveland, Ohio: Pilgrim Press, 1994), 19.

36. Annie Dillard, *Pilgrim at Tinker Creek: A Mystical Excursion into the Natural World* (New York: Bantam Books, 1975), 126.

37. For two excellent books elaborating this point, see Gary Paul Nabhan and Stephen Trimble, *The Geography of Childhood: Why Children Need Wild Places* (Boston: Beacon Press, 1994); and Robert Michael Pyle, *The Thunder Tree: Lessons from an Urban Wildland* (Boston: Houghton Mifflin, 1993).

38. E. O. Wilson, *Biophilia: The Human Bond with Other Species* (Cambridge, Mass.: Harvard University Press, 1984).

39. Pyle, *The Thunder Tree*, ch. 9.

40. As quoted in Nabhan and Trimble, *The Geography of Childhood*, xxi-xxii.

41. Martin Buber, *Between Man and Man* (London: Routledge and Kegan Paul, 1947), 20.

Chapter 2

1. *The Confessions of St. Augustine*, bks. 1-10, trans. F. J. Sheed (New York: Sheed and Ward, 1942), 10.6.

2. Letter to Mrs. Joseph Sweetser, 1884, *Letters of Emily Dickinson,* ed. Mabel Loomis Todd (New York: World Publishing Co., 1951), 349.

3. Iris Murdoch, *The Sovereignty of the Good* (London: Routledge and Kegan Paul, 1970), 91, 52.

4. Ibid., 84.

5. Ibid., 85.

6. *Lift Every Voice: Constructing Christian Theologies from the Underside*, ed. Susan Brooks Thistlethwaite and Mary Potter Engel (San Francisco: Harper & Row, 1990), 51.

7. Frederick Buechner, *Listening to Your Life* (San Francisco: Harper & Row, 1992), 53.

8. As quoted in Douglas Burton-Christie, "'A Feeling for the Natural World': Spirituality and Contemporary Nature Writing," *Continuum* 2 (2 & 3, n.d.): 176.

9. May Sarton, *Endgame: A Journal of the Seventy-ninth Year* (New York: W. W. Norton, 1992), 336-37.

10. Alice Walker, *The Color Purple* (New York: Washington Square Press, 1978), 178.

11. The reverse, however, is also true: loving another motivates knowing. As we will see later (ch. 6), the love of particular places (Georgia O'Keefe's Southwest, Annie Dillard's Tinker Creek) is the basis for wanting to know the place more deeply and intimately.

12. As quoted by Burton-Christie, "'A Feeling for the Natural World,'" 175-76.

13. Iris Murdoch, "The Sublime and the Good," *Chicago Review* 13 (Autumn, 1959), 52.

14. Annie Dillard, *Pilgrim at Tinker Creek: A Mystical Excursion into the Natural World* (New York: Bantam Books, 1975), 126.

15. Yaakov Jerome Garb, "Perspective or Escape? Ecofeminist Musings on Contemporary Earth Imagery," in *Reweaving the World: The Emergence of Ecofeminism*, ed. Irene Diamond and Gloria Feman Orenstein (San Francisco: Sierra Club Books, 1990), 267-68. I am indebted to Garb for the analysis in the following paragraph.

16. Yaakov Jerome Garb, "The Use and Misuse of the Whole Earth Image," *Whole Earth Review* 45 (March 1985), 20.

17. Marilyn Frye, "In and Out of Harm's Way: Arrogance and Love," *The Politics of Reality: Essays in Feminist Theory* (Trumansburg, N.Y.: Crossing Press, 1983), 53-83.

18. Ibid., 67

19. Ibid., 75, 76.

20. Lorraine Code, *What Can She Know? Feminist Theory and the Construction of Knowledge* (Ithaca: Cornell University Press, 1991), 165.

21. The following analysis is indebted to Evelyn Fox Keller and Christine R. Grontkowski, "The Mind's Eye," in *Discovering Reality: Feminist Perspectives on Epistemology, Metaphysics, Methodology, and Philosophy of Science*, ed. Sandra Harding and Merrill B. Hintikka (Dordrecht, Holland: D. Reidel Publishing Co., 1983), 207-24.

22. Garb, "Perspective or Escape," 276.

23. Murdoch, "The Sublime and the Good," 51.

24. As quoted in Keller and Grontkowski, "The Mind's Eye," 219.

25. For one such analysis, see Ruth Berman, "From Aristotle's Dualism to Materialist Dialectics: Feminist Transformation of Science and Society" in *Gender/Body/Knowledge: Feminist Reconstruction of Being and Knowing* (New Brunswick, N.J.: Rutgers University Press, 1989), 244-55.

26. Jim Cheney, "Eco-Feminism and Deep Ecology," *Environmental Ethics* 9 (Summer, 1987), 124.

27. Code, *What Can She Know?*, 273.

28. See, for instance, Maria Lugones, "Playfulness, 'World-Travelling,' and Loving Perception," *Hypatia* 2 (Summer, 1987), 3-19; and Maria C. Lugones and Elizabeth V. Spelman, "Have We Got a Theory for You! Feminist Theory, Cultural Imperialism, and the Demand for 'The Woman's Voice,'" *Women's Studies International Forum* 6 (1983), 573-81; Elizabeth V. Spelman, *The Inessential Woman: Problems of Exclusion in Feminist Thought* (Boston: Beacon Press, 1988), 181-82.

29. Anne Sellar, "Should the Feminist Philosopher Stay at Home?" in *Knowing the Difference: Feminist Perspectives in Epistemology*, ed. Kathleen Lennon and Margaret Whitford (New York: Routledge, 1994).

30. This phrase is used by Evelyn Fox Keller, *Reflections on Gender and Science* (New Haven: Yale University Press, 1985), 165.

31. Dillard, *Pilgrim at Tinker Creek*, 269.

32. Walker, *The Temple of My Familiar* (New York: Pocket Books, 1989), 289.

33. Quoted in *Earth Prayers from around the World*, ed. Elizabeth Roberts and Elias Amidon (San Francisco: Harper, 1991), 267.

34. Ibid., 365.

Chapter 3

1. One such intermediary position, treating both people and the land more like subjects than objects, is Leonard Weber's suggestion of a communitarian ethic, which lies somewhere between the present capitalist and a utopian ecological ethic. See his essay, "Land Use Ethics: The Social Responsibility of Ownership," *Theology of the Land*, ed. Bernard F. Evans and Gregory D. Cusack (Collegeville, Minn.: Liturgical Press, 1987), 13-39.

2. See the analysis of the Cartesian separation of mind and body in R. G. Collingwood, *The Idea of Nature* (Oxford: Clarendon Press, 1945). The problem, as Collingwood summarizes it, is "how can the mind have any connection with something utterly alien to itself, something essentially mechanical and non-mental, namely nature?" (7).

3. For a further discussion of "functional cosmology," see my book, *The Body of God: An Ecological Theology* (Minneapolis: Fortress Press, 1993), ch. 4.

4. There are many excellent studies dealing with various aspects of the medieval world-picture. A few I have found especially helpful are as follows: John Hedley Brooke, *Science and Religion: Some Historical Perspectives* (Cambridge: Cambridge University Press, 1991); E. A. Burtt, *The Metaphysical Foundations of Modern Science* (Atlantic Highlands, N. J.: Humanities Press, 1980); James A. Carpenter, *Nature and Grace: Man and Society in the Twelfth Century* (Chicago: University of Chicago Press, 1968); Michel Foucault, *The Order of Things: An Archaeology of the Human Sciences* (New York: Vintage Books, 1973), chs. 2, 3; Arthur O. Lovejoy, *The Great Chain of Being: A Study of the History of an Idea* (Cambridge: Harvard University Press, 1933); Carolyn Merchant, *The Death of Nature: Women, Ecology and the Scientific Revolution* (New York: Harper & Row, 1980); Keith Thomas, *Man and the Natural World: A History of the Modern Sensibility* (New York: Pantheon, 1983); Yi-Fu Tuan, *Topophilia* (Englewood Cliffs, N.J.: Prentice-Hall, 1974); N. Max Wildiers, *The Theologian and His Universe: Theology and Cosmology from the Middle Ages to the Present* (New York: Seabury, 1982).

5. Foucault, *The Order of Things,* 22.

6. John Donne, "The First Anniversary," from "An Anatomy of the World," ll.213-14; pp. 191-92 in *Major Poets of the Earlier Seventeenth Century,* ed. Barbara K. Lewalski and Andrew J. Sabol (New York: Odyssey Press, 1973).

7. See my book *Metaphorical Theology: Models of God in Religious Language* (Philadelphia: Fortress Press, 1982), 10-14.

8. See David Tracy, *The Analogical Imagination: Christian Theology and the Culture of Pluralism* (New York: Crossroad, 1981).

9. See the excellent discussion of this point in Neil Evernden, *The Social Creation of Nature* (Baltimore: Johns Hopkins University Press, 1992), ch. 4.

10. This is the interpretation of Hildegard by Barbara J. Newman. Newman sees Hildegard not as a mystic interested in her own spirituality but as a prophetic visionary making correlations between creation, incarnation, and human reality. "Reverent meditation on the cosmos and its proportions, which all have their analogues in the microcosm of the human body, leads to the same eternal center as meditation on history in its divinely ordained stages" (Introduction, Hildegard of Bingen, *Scivias,* trans. Mother Columba Hart and Jane Bishop [New York: Paulist Press, 1990], 16).

11. Ibid., 94.

12. Ibid., 98.

13. Evernden, *The Social Creation of Nature,* 43.

14. George Hendry suggests that natural theology is to a theology of nature as moonlight is to sunlight: natural theology reflects theology of nature and is only possible in a time when nature is understood in the context of divine creation and redemption—in other words, in a time like the Middle Ages when nature was "naturally" seen as divinely ordained and governed. "I want to suggest that the demise of natural theology is the inevitable consequence if not, in fact, the obverse of the demise of a theology of nature. For if it is not possible to establish a knowledge of nature in the light of God (and this may be taken as a rough definition of a theology of nature), it is hardly to be expected that it will

be possible to establish a knowledge of God in the light of nature" (*Theology of Nature* [Philadelphia: Westminster Press, 1980], 13-14).

15. Foucault's description captures this close and intricate relationship: "The universe was folded in upon itself; the earth echoing the sky, faces seeing themselves reflected in the stars, and plants holding within their stems the secrets that were of use to man" (*The Order of Things*, 17). "In the vast syntax of the world, the different beings adjust themselves to one another; the plant communicates with the animal, the earth with the sea, man with everything around him. Resemblance imposes adjacencies that in their turn further resemblances. Place and similitude become entangled: we see mosses growing on the outside of shells, plants on the antlers of stags, and a sort of grass on the faces of men; and the strange zoophyte, by mingling together the properties that make it similar to the plants as well as to the animals, also justaposes them" (ibid., 18).

16. Thomas, *Man and the Natural World*, 64. I am indebted to this book for my treatment of emblemism.

17. See Thomas, *Man and the Natural World*, 85ff.

18. See the analysis of Francis along these lines by Max Scheler in *The Nature of Sympathy*, trans. Peter Heath (Hamden, Conn.: Shoestring Press, 1973).

19. Thomas of Celano, "Second Life of St. Francis," *St. Francis of Assisi: Writings and Early Biographies,* ed. Marian A. Habig (Chicago: Franciscan Herald Press, 1973), 165; Bonaventure, "Major Life of St. Francis," ibid., 8.6.

20. Leonardo Boff, *Saint Francis: A Model for Human Liberation*, trans. John W. Diercksmeier (New York: Crossroad, 1982), 38.

21. *Francis and Clare: The Complete Works*, trans. and introduced by Regis J. Armstrong and Ignatius C. Brady (New York: Paulist Press, 1982), 39.

22. Ibid., 38.

23. Boff, *Saint Francis*, 39.

24. See, for instance, the analysis by Alexander Murray, "Nature and Man in the Middle Ages," *The Concept of Nature*, ed. John Torrance (Oxford: Clarendon Press, 1992). The "vertical" and "horizontal" as well as introverted and extroverted influences on the medieval picture are so complex and numerous that I cannot begin to name them all, but certainly the Hebraic tradition would contribute to the horizontal and extroverted, while the early Gnostic to the vertical and introverted.

25. See Arthur O. Lovejoy's classic study in the plenitude and continuity of the Great Chain of Being, an ontology in which every niche in the universe is filled, fully and with no gaps, by entities reflecting the divine glory by being who and what they are (*The Great Chain of Being*).Thomas Aquinas illustrates this sensibility very well: "But creatures cannot attain to any perfect likeness of God so long as they are confined to one species of creature; because, since the cause exceeds the effect in a composite and manifold way. . . . Multiplicity, therefore, and variety, was needful in the creation, to the end that the perfect likeness of God might be found in things *according to their measure*"(emphasis added), as quoted in Lovejoy, 76.

26. Carpenter, *Nature and Grace*, 33.

27. "Its [the Counter-Reformation church] preoccupation with the distinction between nature and supernature, and its location of salvific divine action in the sphere of supernature tended to restrict the reference of 'nature' to an

abstract foil for grace. This preoccupation, however, did as much to 'disenchant' nature as the Protestant turn to history was doing" (Gabriel Daly, "Foundations in Systematics for Ecological Theology," *Preserving the Creation: Environmental Theology and Ethics*, ed. Kevin W. Irwin and Edmund D. Pellegrino [Washington, D.C.: Georgetown University Press, 1994], 40).

28. *Poems of Gerard Manley Hopkins*, 4th ed., ed. W. H. Gardner and N. H. MacKenzie (New York: Oxford University Press, 1967), poem #57.

29. Ibid., poem #37.

30. *The Sermons and Devotional Writings of Gerard Manley Hopkins*, ed. Christopher Devlin (New York: Oxford University Press, 1959), 7.8.82 (129).

31. Burtt, *The Metaphysical Foundations of Modern Science*, 238-39.

32. Neil Evernden, an ecological philosopher, puts it harshly: "In deciding to annex subjectivity to ourselves alone, we left nothing to relate to, no one else in the world to reciprocate. . . . And what the environmental movement appears to protest—the extermination of other forms of life—is simply the physical manifestation of a global genocide that is long since accomplished in the minds of us all. The subjects are first destroyed, and later their bodies crumble" (*The Natural Alien: Humankind and Environment* [Toronto: University of Toronto Press, 1985], 136).

33. *Topophilia*, 21.

34. For two highly interesting treatments of the body/nature/culture metaphorical correlation, see Mary Douglas, "Just as it is true that everything symbolizes the body, so it is equally true (and all the more so for that reason) that the body symbolizes everything else" (*Purity and Danger* [New York: Praeger, 1966], 122; Anthony Synnott, *The Body Social: Symbolism, Self and Society* (New York: Routledge, 1993).

35. Thomas Berry, *The Dream of the Earth* (San Francisco: Sierra Club, 1988), 11.

36. Barry Lopez, *Crossing Open Ground* (New York: Vintage Books, 1989), 65.

37. Ibid., 64.

38. Ibid., 67.

39. Ibid.

40. A recent book on emotions in animals illustrates how far we have removed ourselves from other animals: Jeffrey M. Masson and Susan McCarthy, *When Elephants Weep: The Emotional Lives of Animals* (New York: Delacorte Press, 1995). Its central thesis is the scientific community's absolute dualism between human beings and other animals, as illustrated by the fear of being accused of anthropomorphism—of attributing emotions similar to ours to other animals. "A monkey cannot be angry; it exhibits aggression. A crane does not feel affection; it displays courtship or parental behavior. A cheetah is not frightened by a lion; it shows flight behavior" (34). The authors' wry comment is a telling one: "In science, the sin against hierarchy is to assign human characteristics to animals. Just as humans could not be like God, now animals cannot be like humans (note who has taken God's place)"(32).

41. The following analysis is indebted to John Berger's essay, "Why Look at Animals?" in his *About Looking* (New York: Vintage Books, 1980).

42. Annie Dillard, *Teaching a Stone to Talk: Expeditions and Encounters* (New York: Harper & Row, 1982), 114.

43. "Men attributed to animals the natural impulses they most feared in themselves—ferocity, gluttony, sexuality—even though it was men, not beasts, who made war on their own species, ate more than was good for them, and were sexually active all year round. It was as a comment on *human* nature that the concept of 'animality' was devised" (Thomas, *Man and the Natural World*, 40-41).

44. "It is hard to believe that the system would ever have been tolerated if negroes had been credited with full human attributes. Their dehumanization was a necessary precondition of their maltreatment" (Thomas, *Man and the Natural World*, 44-45).

45. Our ambivalence toward animals is a complex subject, epitomized in the statement by Oliver Goldsmith in the eighteenth century that we pity and eat the objects of our compassion. Keith Thomas says, "The same might be said of the children of today who, nourished by a meat diet and protected by medicine developed by animal experiments, nevertheless take toy animals to bed and lavish affection on lambs and ponies. For adults, nature parks and conservation areas serve a function not unlike that which toy animals have for children; they are fantasies which enshrine the values by which society as a whole cannot afford to live" (*Man and the Natural World*, 301).

46 Barbara Novak, *Nature and Culture: American Landscape Painting 1825–1875* (New York: Oxford University Press, 1980); Simon Schama, *Landscape and Memory* (New York: Alfred A. Knopf, 1995).

47. Schama, *Landscape and Memory*, 191.

Chapter 4

1. In the article on "Perspective" in *The New Encyclopaedia Britannica*, we find the following helpful comment, contrasting pre- and post-Renaissance methods of painting. "Perceptual methods of representing space and volume, which render them as seen at a particular time and from a fixed position . . . are in contrast to conceptual methods. The pictures of young children and primitives (untrained artists), many of the paintings of cultures such as ancient Egypt and Crete, India, Islam, and pre-Renaissance Europe, as well as the paintings of many modern artists, depict objects and surroundings independently of one another, as they are known to be, and from the views that best present their most characteristic features; in many Egyptian and Cretan paintings, for example, the head and legs of a figure are shown in profile, while the eyes and torso are shown frontally" (Vol. 19, 15th ed. [Chicago: University of Chicago], 1989, 313). For our concerns, the interesting point here is that nonperspectival painting renders things in terms of what they are in themselves ("their most characteristic features") rather than how they appear to a viewer; the point of view of so-called primitive (as well as much contemporary art) is, therefore, more "realistic" or "objective" in its concern to render the thing characteristically than is the perspectival rendering, where the main concern is how things appear from one privileged point of view, that of the spectator.

2. Hans Jonas, *The Phenomenon of Life* (Chicago: University of Chicago Press, 1982), 147.

3. Annie Dillard, *Pilgrim at Tinker Creek: A Mystical Excursion into the Natural World* (New York: Bantam Books, 1975), 19.

4. Dillard, *Pilgrim at Tinker Creek*, 31.

5. Penelope Lively, *Oleander, Jacaranda: A Childhood Perceived* (New York: HarperCollins, 1994), 22.

6. Oliver Sacks, *An Anthropologist on Mars: Seven Paradoxical Tales* (New York: Knopf, 1995), 206. Even Wiltshire, however, interprets or at least perceives differently at different times. For instance, he copied a Matisse painting several times, but each time there were changes.

7. Sacks, *An Anthropologist on Mars*, 114.

8. Lorraine Code, *What Can She Know? Feminist Theory and the Construction of Knowledge* (Ithaca, N.Y.: Cornell University Press, 1991), 141.

9. Numerous feminist and other postmodern critiques make this point; see, for instance, Evelyn Fox Keller and Christine R. Grontkowski, "The Mind's Eye" in *Discovering Reality: Feminist Perspectives in Epistemology, Metaphysics, Methodology, and Philosophy of Science*, ed. Sandra Harding and Merrill B. Hintikka (Dordrecht, Holland: D. Reidel Publishing Co., 1983), 207-24; Jonas, *The Phenomenon of Life*; Code, *What Can She Know?*; Susan Bordo, *The Flight to Objectivity: Essays on Cartesianism and Culture* (Albany, N.Y.: SUNY Press, 1987); Luce Irigaray, *This Sex Which Is Not One*, trans. C. Porter and C. Burke (Ithaca, N.Y.: Cornell University Press, 1985).

10. "For each knower, the Cartesian route to knowledge is through private, abstract thought, through the efforts of reason unaided either by the senses or by consultation with other knowers. It is this individualistic, self-reliant private aspect of Descartes's philosophy that has been influential in shaping subsequent epistemological ideals" (Code, *What Can She Know?*, 5).

11. In regard to nature as machine, Morris Berman writes: "In line with its Cartesian and positivist principles, it considers the whole to be composed of individual separable units, which can be taken apart and put together again, the entire machine operating in a repeatable, predictable fashion. Natural processes are abstracted, distanced from nature, made perfect, and converted into immutable laws. The *particular* characteristics and dynamics of each individual situation are blurred, lost in statistical summations. This freezes living systems into static models of themselves, denying the uniqueness of their development in time and space. Phenomena lose their specific, idiosyncratic responses and interactions and they are seen as better or worse approximations of some ideal system" (*Coming to Our Senses: Body and Spirit in the Hidden History of the West* [New York: Bantam New Age, 1989], 240).

12. See, for instance, Carolyn Merchant's classic, *The Death of Nature: Women, Ecology and the Scientific Revolution* (New York: Harper & Row, 1980). Susan Bordo describes the condition in which nature is left: "By Descartes's brilliant stroke, nature became *defined* by its lack of affiliation with divinity, with spirit. All that which is God-like or spiritual—freedom, will, and sentience—belongs entirely and exclusively to *res cogitans*. All else—the earth, the heavens, animals, the human body—is merely mechanically interacting matter" (*The Flight to Objectivity*, 102).

13. Evelyn Fox Keller, *Reflections on Gender and Science* (New Haven, Conn.: Yale University Press, 1985), 116.

14. Lorraine Code notes that the positivist scientific paradigm "appears to have gained ascendancy, in part, because of the justification it provides for human exploitation of nature: because of its efficacy in serving the *interests* of

the powerful. Hence, for all its self-proclaimed objectivity, there is evidence that its hegemony is sustained by *subjective* forces: by interests and self-interest" (*What Can She Know?*, 48).

15. See Keller, *Reflections on Gender and Science*, 134ff.

16. The term "ecological model of knowledge" is from Lorraine Code, who means something different by it than I do. I wish to use it to suggest the reciprocal, maze-like character of our knowledge of the natural world; that we know our world by participating in and paying attention to nature, rather than imagining we are separate from it and can view it from afar. Code uses the term to underscore the importance of other people in all knowledge (in contrast to the individualistic Cartesian model): "Ecologically rather than individually positioned, human beings are interdependent creatures, 'second persons' who rely on one another as much in knowledge as they do for other means of survival" (*What Can She Know?*, 269).

17.John Berger, *Ways of Seeing* (London: Penguin and BBC, 1972), 16.

18. Yi-Fu Tuan, *Topophilia* (Englewood Cliffs, N.J.: Prentice-Hall, 1974), 19.

19. Berger, *Ways of Seeing*, 54.

20. Ibid., 63. As Berger shrewdly notes, there is a significant difference between nudity and nakedness: the former objectifies the other, while nakedness is a shared vulnerability, possible only when both parties are without clothes (54).

21. "The visual is particularly important in the definition of feminity, both because of the significance attached to images in modern culture and because a woman's character and status are frequently judged by appearance" (Rosemary Betterton, "Introduction: Feminism, Femininity, and Representation," *Looking On: Images of Femininity in the Visual Arts and Media*, ed. Rosemary Betterton (New York: Pandora Press, 1987), 7.

22. Berger, *Ways of Seeing*, 47. Psychoanalytic theories, such as that of Jacques Lacan, support classical visual theories of knowledge: Lacan's mirror stage perpetuates the logocentric gaze. Luce Irigaray, former pupil and critic of Lacan, says that for Lacan woman symbolizes the mirror stage: she is the flat surface that reflects the male subject. Her bodily surface, which lacks the male penis—where there is nothing to see—becomes a mere mirror reflecting the male back to himself. This "specular economy," however, reveals itself as homosexual, unable to deal with genuine otherness. "Woman's desire does not speak the same language as man's desire. In this logic, the prevalence of the gaze . . . is particularly foreign to female eroticism. Women find pleasure more in touch than in sight. . . ."("This Sex Which Is Not One," *The New French Feminisms: An Anthology*, ed. Elaine Marks and Isabelle de Courtivan [New York: Schoken Books, 1981], 101).

23. Lisa Tickner in Betterton, ed., *Looking On*, 204.

24. Svetlana Alpers as quoted in Betterton, "Introduction," *Looking On*, 12.

25. John Ciardi, the American poet, as quoted in Berman, *Coming to Our Senses*, 66.

26. Berman, *Coming to Our Senses*, 66, 85.

27. Mary Midgeley, *Animals and Why They Matter* (Athens, Ga.: University of Georgia Press, 1983), 118-19.

28. See Berger, "Uses of Photography," in *About Looking*, 52–57.

29. Susan Sontag, *On Photography* (New York: Farrar, Straus and Giroux, 1973), 154.

30. Ibid., 154.

31. "The extinction of experience" is from Robert Michael Pyle, *The Thunder Tree: Lessons from an Urban Wildland* (Boston: Houghton Mifflin, 1993).

32. Sontag, *On Photography*, 14.

33. Sue Sutton, "Sometimes Cameras Really Do Steal Souls," *Toronto Globe and Mail,* (October 12, 1995), A22.

34. Ibid.

35. E. Ann Kaplan, *Women and Film: Both Sides of the Camera* (London: Methuen, 1983); Laura Mulvey, "Visual Pleasure and Narrative Cinema," *Film Theory and Criticism: Introductory Readings*, 3rd ed., ed. Gerald Mast and Marshall Cohen (Oxford: Oxford University Press, 1985), 803-16.

36. More frequently now, as women directors emerge and some male directors become aware of scopophilia, we see occasional films that do not share that gaze, such as *Fried Green Tomatoes, Sense and Sensibility, The Piano*, and most remarkably, *Dead Man Walking*, where an extreme form of scopophilia undergoes a conversion in the confession of a condemned death-row murderer.

37. "Scopophilia, or sexual pleasure in looking, is activated by the very situation of the cinema: the darkened room, the way the gaze of the spectator is controlled by the aperture of first, the camera and second, the projector, the fact that the spectator is watching moving images rather than either static ones (painting) or live actors (theatre), all help to make the cinematic experience closer to the dream state than is possible in the other arts" (Kaplan, *Women and Film*, 14).

38. Ibid.

39. Dietrich Bonhoeffer, *Letters and Papers from Prison* (New York: Collins, 1953), 51.

40. Catherine A. Lutz and Jane L. Collins, *Reading National Geographic* (Chicago: University of Chicago Press, 1993), 8.

41. Ibid., 262.

42. Stephen Greenblatt, "Kindly Visions," *The New Yorker* (October 11, 1993), 114.

43. Ibid., 118.

44. This is true of other issues dealt with as well. "Hunger, poverty, and inequality, to the extent that they are depicted, have been presented as problems that right-thinking people can band together and solve, not as conflicts of interest. Like mainstream news organizations, the *Geographic* adheres to a notion of balance between the two sides of a conflict . . . Soldiers have been portrayed in acts of kindness; deposed dictators mark 'the passing of an era.' The cameras of the *Geographic* are trained on the vibrant, ebullient, sometimes long-suffering, but always noble human spirit" (Lutz and Collins, *Reading National Geographic*, 271).

45. Ibid., 279.

46. John Perry Barlow, Sven Birkerts, Kevin Kelly, Mark Slouka, "What Are We Doing On-Line?" *Harpers Magazine* (August, 1995), 35-46.

47. Slouka, "What Are We Doing On-Line?," 42.

48. Birkerts, "What Are We Doing On-Line?," 43-44.

49. Tom Cavanagh, "Nature has no 'virtual' equal," *Toronto Globe and Mail* (January 5, 1996), A20.

50. For elaboration on this point as well as the argument that follows in my text, see various works by Val Plumwood: "The Ecopolitics Debate in the Politics of Nature," *Ecological Feminism*, ed. Karen J. Warren (New York: Routledge, 1994); *Feminism and the Mastery of Nature* (New York: Routledge, 1994); "Feminism and Ecofeminism: Beyond the Dualistic Assumptions of Women, Men and Nature," *The Ecologist* 22 (1992), 3-27; "Nature, Self and Gender: Feminism, Environmental Philosophy, and the Critique of Rationalism," *Hypatia* 6 (1991), 3-27.

51. "As 'nature,' oppressed groups have been located outside the sphere of reason, the sphere Western elites have particularly seen themselves as representing. The story of the control of the chaotic and deficient realm of 'nature' by mastering and ordering 'reason' has been the master story of Western culture. An examination of this story reveals that this ideology of the domination of nature plays a key role in structuring all the major forms of oppression in the West, which are thus linked through the politics of nature" (Plumwood, "The Ecopolitics Debate and the Politics of Nature," 74).

52. Ibid., 77.

53. "A dualism is an intense, established and developed cultural expression of a . . . hierarchical relationship, constructing central cultural concepts and identities so as to make equality and mutuality literally unthinkable. Dualism is a relation of separation and domination inscribed and naturalised in culture and characterised by radical exclusion, distancing and opposition between orders constructed as systematically higher and lower. . ."(Plumwood, *Feminism and the Mastery of Nature*, 47-48).

54. I am indebted to Plumwood, *Feminism and the Mastery of Nature*, ch. 2 for the following analysis.

55. Mary Midgley, *Beast and Man: The Roots of Human Nature* (Ithaca, N.Y.: Cornell University Press, 1978), 358.

56. Michel Foucault, "The Eye of Power," in *Power/Knowledge: Selected Interviews and Other Writings, 1972–77*, ed. Colin Gordon, trans. Colin Gordon, Leo Marshall, John Mepham, Kate Soper (New York: Pantheon, 1980), 155.

Chapter 5

1. A. N.Whitehead's comment on sight as the most disembodied of the senses is relevant to my point: "In the case of sight, the irrelevance of the body is at its maximum. We look at the scenery, at a picture, or at an approaching car on the road, as an external presentation given for our mental entertainment or mental anxiety. There it is, exposed to view. . . . The bodily reference is recessive, the visible presentation is dominant" (*Modes of Thought* [Cambridge: Cambridge University Press, 1938], 209).

2. It is very surprising that there are so few sources on touch and its importance. One of the best, however, is Conrad Bonifazi, *A Theology of Things: A Study of Man in His Physical Environment* (Philadelphia: Lippincott, 1967). Other related materials are from feminism and phenomenology, especially various writings by the French deconstructionist Luce Irigaray; Maurice Merleau-

192 Super, Natural Christians

Ponty, *The Phenomenology of Perception*, trans. Colin Smith (London: Routledge and Kegan Paul, 1962); works by the later Martin Heidegger; of special interest are two recent books that relate Heidegger's work (as well as that of Emmanuel Levinas) to ecological concerns: Bruce V. Foltz, *Inhabiting the Earth: Heidegger, Environmental Ethics, and the Metaphysics of Nature* (Atlantic Highlands, N.J.: Humanities Press, 1995); and John Llewelyn, *The Middle Voice of Ecological Conscience: A Chiasmic Reading of Responsibility in the Neighborhood of Levinas, Heidegger and Others* (New York: St. Martin's Press, 1991).

3. See Bonifazi, *A Theology of Things*, 57ff.

4. Gemma Corradi Fiumara, *The Other Side of Language: A Philosophy of Listening* (New York: Routledge, 1990), 3

5. Ibid., 7. The historical background to logocentricism covers not only the Word epistemology of Christianity and the Greeks, but also the present focus of deconstruction on textuality—a focus, by the way, that ipso facto excludes the natural world, which has no "voice." Martin Heidegger's critique of Western culture as technological leads up to his accusation of our refusal to dwell appropriately in nature (see Llewelyn, *The Middle Voice of Ecological Conscience* and Foltz, *Inhabiting the Earth*). Ecofeminists also accuse deconstruction of limiting reality to text and hence of eliding nature (see, for example, Val Plumwood, *Feminism and the Mastery of Nature* [New York: Routledge, 1994]; and Sue Ellen Campbell, "The Land of Language and Desire: Where Deep Ecology and Post-Structuralism Meet," *Western American Literature* 24 [1989], 199-211).

6. As a side note, it is curious that Christians, especially Protestants, who place enormous emphasis on hearing the Word of God (the sermon is the centerpiece of Protestant worship) appear to shy away from touch, from embodied, relational contact with the world and its many others. Rather, it is the sacramental tradition, the tradition of the eye, that has been more open to embodiment. This openness is, however, as I have suggested, more dependent on seeing things as *in God*, rather than as related to touch: neither Protestants nor Catholics have taken their incarnational roots as a reason to embrace the body. See the writings of Margaret Miles on this point, e.g., *Practicing Christianity: Critical Perspectives for an Embodied Christianity* (New York: Crossroad, 1990); and *Carnal Knowledge: Female Nakedness and Religious Meaning in Christian West* (New York: Random House, 1991).

7. Evelyn Fox Keller, *Reflections on Gender and Science* (New Haven, Conn.: Yale University Press, 1985), 164.

8. Annie Dillard, *Pilgrim at Tinker Creek: A Mystical Excursion into the Natural World* (New York: Bantam Books, 1975), 2.

9. Ibid., 12.

10. Lorraine Code, *What Can She Know? Feminist Theory and the Construction of Knowledge* (Ithaca, N.Y.: Cornell University Press, 1991), 165.

11. See ch. 2 of my book *The Body of God: An Ecological Theology* (Minneapolis: Fortress Press, 1993) for a brief description of the postmodern sense of reality.

12. Penelope Lively speaks of this tempting wish as "an ability to fuse with the physical world which we love in adult life. . . . Does this then mean that animistic belief is childlike or that children have an insight into some primal state of unity with the natural world?" (*Oleander, Jacaranda: A Childhood Perceived* [New York: HarperCollins, 1994], 35). Perhaps so, but the wish must be resisted.

13. Keller, *Reflections on Gender and Science*, 164.

14. For instance, here are some excerpts to illustrate the point from Max Oelschlaeger, *The Idea of Wilderness: From Prehistory to the Age of Ecology* (New Haven, Conn.: Yale University Press, 1991): "We have been weaned early from her breast, and we are not as wise as the day we were born. But our Mother will speak to us, if we will listen. Her words yet have earth clinging to their roots; her statements are grounded in granitic truth. . . . Humankind must learn to kiss and feel the earth again, to let life run down to the roots and become calm and full of ocean. . . . We are . . . stardust, and we've got to get ourselves back to the Garden" (351-52).

15. As quoted in Campbell, "The Land of Language and Desire," 207.

16. There is reason not to reject deep ecology too quickly, for in spite of its excesses as well as its dismissal of subjectivity and otherness, it knows some important truths. For instance, in the following description of a deer, one can imagine writing a similar paragraph about a human being and the network of interrelations that supports it: "A deer . . . has no being apart from things like the presence or absence of wolves, the kind of forage in its environment, the temperature and snowfall of any given winter, the other animals competing for the available food, the number of hunters with licenses, the bacteria in its intestines that either keep it healthy or make it sick. Theory [feminism] and ecology agree that there's no such thing as a self-enclosed, private piece of property, neither a deer nor a person nor a text nor a piece of land" (Campbell, "The Land and Language of Desire," 208).

17. Martin Buber, *I and Thou* (New York: Scribner's, 1970), 18.

18. Whitehead, *Modes of Thought*, 188.; Merleau-Ponty, *Phenomenology of Perception*, xvi; Thich Nhat Hanh, "Love in Action," *The Soul in Nature: Visions of a Living Earth*, ed. Michael Tobias and Georgianne Cowan (New York: Continuum, 1994), 132; Bruce Foltz, "Dwelling Poetically Upon the Earth: Toward a New Environmental Ethic," *Inhabiting the Earth*, 15; Buber, *I and Thou*, 11; Thomas Moore, *Care of the Soul: A Guide for Cultivating Depth and Sacredness in Everyday Life* (New York: HarperCollins, 1992), 271; Caroline Whitbeck, "A Different Reality: Feminist Ontology," *Women, Knowledge and Reality*, ed. Ann Garry and Marilyn Pearsall (Boston: Unwin Hyman, 1989), 64; Donna Haraway, "The Actors Are Cyborg, Nature Is Coyote, and the Geography Is Elsewhere: Postscript to 'Cyborgs at Large,'" *Technoculture*, eds. Constance Penley and Andrew Ross (Minneapolis: University of Minnesota Press, 1991), 21-26.

19. Leonardo Boff, *Ecology and Liberation: A New Paradigm* (New York: Orbis, 1995), 78.

20. Buber, *I and Thou*, 8.

21. Ibid., 75.

22. The whole passage of the last quotation is as follows: "Every particular *Thou* is a glimpse through to the eternal *Thou*; by means of every particular *Thou* the primary word addresses the eternal *Thou* . . . the inborn *Thou* is realised in each relation and consummated in none. It is consummated only in the direct relation with the *Thou* that by nature cannot become *It*" (Ibid.).

23. Ibid., 7.

24. Ibid., 79.

25. Ibid.

26. Ibid., 62-63.

27. The expression is from a book by that title by literary critic R.W.B. Lewis.

28. Jessica Benjamin, *The Bonds of Love: Psychoanalysis, Feminism and the Problem of Domination* (London: Virago, 1988), 53.

29. Catherine Keller, *From a Broken Web: Separation, Sexism, and Self* (Boston: Beacon Press, 1986), 4-5.

30. Plumwood, *Feminism and the Mastery of Nature*, 154.

31. Keller, *Reflections on Gender and Science*, 99.

32. Ibid., 117-18.

33. Whitbeck, "A Different Reality," 62, 68.

34. See "A Cyborg Manifesto: Science, Technology, and Socialist-Feminism in the Late Twentieth Century," *Simians, Cyborgs, and Women: The Reinvention of Women* (New York: Routledge, 1991).

35. On the issue of incorporation, see various writings by Nancy Chodorow, e.g. *Feminities, Masculinities, Sexualities: Freud and Beyond* (Lexington: University Press of Kentucky, 1994); and Luce Irigaray, *The Sex Which Is Not One*, trans. Catherine Porter and Carolyn Burke (Ithaca, N.Y.: Cornell University Press, 1985).

36. John Woolman, *The Journal of John Woolman* (New York: Corinth Books, 1961).

37. Donna Haraway, "The Actors Are Cyborg," 22.

38. There are some similarities here with Emmanuel Levinas's proto-ethical responsibility to the other in the face-to-face encounter—and there are differences. John Llewelyn, expanding Levinas's "face-to-face" to nature (with the help of Heidegger), claims that respect for the other at this level is not anthropomorphism but simply acknowledgment of the *existence* of another—stone, tree, mountain, or whatever. Such respect is not a matter of rights or value, but due simply because something *is* (see his *The Middle Voice of Ecological Conscience*). But another reading of Levinas, one by Roger Gottlieb, claims that Levinas's ethic of primordial acknowledgment of the other stems from his acceptance of "a masculine theoretical culture," where "human identities are formed in rigid isolation and opposition to one another" ("Ethics and Trauma: Levinas, Feminism, and Deep Ecology," *Cross Currents* 44 [Summer, 1994], 228). "In patriarchal thought we never start in connection with others. We are not seen as beginning, as we in fact do, as babies at our mother's breast, after having come out of her body. Or if the beginning is there, that image of connection is not carried into the heart of the theoretical representation of adult ethical life" (229).

39. Iris Murdoch, "The Sublime and the Good," *Chicago Review* 13 (Autumn, 1959), 51.

40. See Keller, *Reflections on Gender and Science*, 117-18.

41. Ibid., 99-101.

42. As we investigate extending subjectivity to the nonhuman realm, it is interesting to note that poststructuralism joins ecology in criticizing humanism, the hegemony of the individual self. Both movements insist that human beings are embedded in networks—for poststructuralism, it is a network of textuality while for ecology, it is a natural network (which, although we participate in its construction, is also *there*). Hence, while the two movements are similar in questioning humanism, poststructuralism is still anthropocentric in its denial of the reality of the natural world, folding it into textuality. For further elaboration of

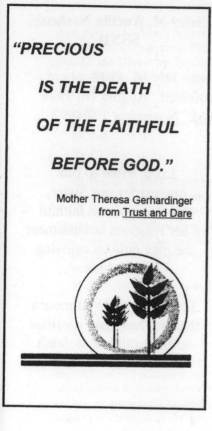

"PRECIOUS

IS THE DEATH

OF THE FAITHFUL

BEFORE GOD."

Mother Theresa Gerhardinger
from <u>Trust and Dare</u>

ssing the Postmodern Divide (Chicago:
Campbell, "The Land of Language and
he Mastery of Nature.
Harm's Way: Arrogance and Love," in
eminist Theology (Trumansburg, N.Y.:

istery of Nature, 159.

Aldo Leopold, especially A Sand County
(New York: Oxford University Press,
ms; and the writings of James Lovelock,
ng Earth (New York: W. W. Norton and
ie earth as a whole.
and Science, 99-101.

astery of Nature, 124.
re Cyborg . . . ," 21.

as a potential intentional subject, as one
hus we can begin to conceive a potential
e with nature. Earth others can be seen
'other nations of roots or wings or legs,'
erms as well as ours. These terms must
h that earth others are exhausted by our
ze in their limitless heterogeneity beings
w or want. Thus the intentional stance
elationships to earth others in ethical and
fined as the domain of response to the
other's needs, ends, directions, or meaning" (Plumwood, *Feminism and the Mastery of Nature*, 137-38).

56. "Once nature is reconceived as capable of agency and intentionality, and human identity is reconceived in less polarised and disembodied ways, the great gulf which Cartesian thought established between the conscious, mindful human sphere and the mindless, clockwork natural one disappears" (Plumwood, *Feminism and the Mastery of Nature*, 5).

57. The critique of objects (substances) as the basic units of reality is practically universal among epistemologies and theologies influenced by the postmodern scientific paradigm of reality. While this critique can result in the pansychism of Whitehead's process philosophy or the somewhat questionable "drift" toward complexification of Teilhard de Chardin's evolutionary theology, it takes many other forms, all of which see the human subject as the prime analogate for the entities that constitute nature, from the atom through living forms. For instance, Edward Farley, in his recent work *Divine Empathy: A Theology of God*, sketches a theory of entities based on human beings, applicable to all living creatures and even speculatively to nonliving things (Minneapolis: Fortress Press, 1996). The distinctive features of entities are similar to the char-

acteristics of subjects in this essay. Entities are composites or ecosystems in miniature; they have a natural ecocentricism, autonomy, or self-determination; they exist interdependently with other entities; they also exist in a mode of desire, need, and struggle (291–92, 301–3). Farley claims that entities are "teleonomic" or responsive, in the sense of attempting to find solutions to problems the environment presents to what is (consciously or unconsciously) valuable or important to their own well-being (202–3). These characteristics, I would suggest, are more appropriately expressed by the metaphor of subject than of object.

58. "Knowledge of other people is possible only in a persistent interplay between opacity and transparency, between attitudes and postures that elude a knower's grasp, and traits that seem to be clear and relatively constant. Hence knowers are kept on their cognitive toes; the 'more-or-lessness' of this knowledge constantly affirms the need to reserve and revise judgment" (Code, *What Can She Know?*, 38).

59. From Code's treatment of Rachel Carson, in ibid., 154.

60. Code's epistemology, for instance, is built on "second-person" knowledge—that everything we know is from others—with friendship as the key illustration.

61. Moore, *Care of the Soul*, 268.

62. Ibid., 270.

63. Ibid.

64. Ernest Schachtel, in his book *Metamorphosis: On the Development of Affect, Perception, Attention, and Memory* (New York: Basic Books, 1959), uses this concept for a child's native interest in the world. It is one aspect of what is needed for a mature relationship with others: "The pursuit of objectivity, in this view, has a twofold requirement: first, the survival of the child's native interest in the world, and second, the development of the capacity for focusing on objects as separate and distinct from one's own needs, desires, and individual perspective" (119).

65. Elizabeth Spelman, *Inessential Woman: Problems of Exclusion in Feminist Thought* (Boston: Beacon Press, 1988), 181.

66. As quoted in Schachtel, *Metamorphosis*, 225.

67. Iris Murdoch makes this point repeatedly and effectively. "It is important too that great art teaches us how real things can be looked at and loved without being seized and used, without being appropriated into the greedy organism of the self. This exercise in *detachment* is difficult and valuable whether the thing contemplated is a human being or the root of a tree or the vibration of a colour or a sound. Unsentimental contemplation of nature exhibits the same quality of detachment: selfish concerns vanish, nothing exists except the things which are seen. Beauty is that which attracts this particular sort of unselfish attention. It is obvious here what is the role, for the artist or spectator, of exactness and good vision: unsentimental, detached, unselfish, objective attention" (*The Sovereignty of Good* [London: Routledge and Kegan Paul, 1970], 65-66).

68. Murdoch, *The Sovereignty of Good*, 65.

69. Murdoch, "The Sublime and the Good," 51.

70. Murdoch defines fantasy as "the tissue of self-aggrandizing and consoling wishes and dreams which prevents one from seeing what there is outside one" (*The Sovereignty of Good*, 78).

71. As quoted in Spelman, *Inessential Woman*, 189.

72. See Maria Lugones, "Playfulness, 'World-Travelling,' and Loving Perception," *Hypatia* 2 (Summer, 1987), 3-19.

73. See Maria C. Lugones with Pat Alake Rosezelle, "Sisterhood and Friendship as Feminist Models," in *The Explosion of Knowledge: Generations of Feminist Scholarship*, ed. Cheris Kramarae and Dale Spender (New York: Teachers College Press, 1992), 406-12; and Maria C. Lugones and Elizabeth V. Spelman, "Have We Got a Theory for You! Feminist Theory, Cultural Imperialism and the Demand for 'The Woman's Voice,'" *Women's Studies International Forum* 6 (1983), 573-81.

74. For one treatment of friendship, see my book, *Models of God* (Philadelphia: Fortress Press, 1987), ch. 3.

75. "Friendship is a kind of practical love that commits one to perceptual changes in the knowledge of other persons. The commitment is there because understanding the other is central to the possibility of loving the other person practically. Practical love is an emotion that involves a commitment to make decisions or act in ways that take the well-being of the other person into account" (Lugones, "Sisterhood and Friendship in Feminist Models," 410).

76. Richard Austin, *Baptized into Wilderness: A Christian Perspective on John Muir* (Atlanta, Ga.: John Knox Press, 1987), 17.

77. As quoted in ibid., 29.

78. There are two other highly interesting attempts to deal with trees as subjects that I would recommend. One is Brian J. Walsh, Marianne B. Karsh, and Nik Ansell, "Trees, Forestry, and the Responsiveness of Creation," *Cross Currents* 44 (Summer, 1994), 149–62. The authors speak of what they call the "new forestry" movement: "Neither a naive preservationism nor a distanced objective management, it will be a stewardship of care that attends to trees in all their rich and nuanced diversity, variability, and individuality. Instead of reducing trees to economic objects that can be explained from a distance through quantifying measurements, the new forestry, rooted in 'kindred subjectivity,' will attempt to understand trees as eloquent others who have wisdom to impart" (157). The other is a rare, beautiful set of essays by Stephanie Kaza, *The Attentive Heart: Conversations with Trees* (New York: Fawcett Columbine, 1993). Very few people could subtitle a book this way and avoid romanticism, but naturalist Kaza succeeds in interacting with trees as subjects.

Chapter 6

1. Robert Michael Pyle, *The Thunder Tree: Lessons from an Urban Wildland* (Boston: Houghton Mifflin, 1993), 145.

2. Ibid., 147.

3. E.O. Wilson, *Biophilia: The Human Bond with Other Species* (Cambridge: Harvard University Press, 1984).

4. Gary Paul Nabhan and Stephen Trimble, *The Geography of Childhood: Why Children Need Wild Places* (Boston: Beacon Press, 1994), 37.

5. Pyle, *The Thunder Tree*, 146.

6. Annie Dillard, *An American Childhood* (New York: Harper Perennial, 1988), 11.

7. Ibid., 157.

8. Ibid., 159, 160,

9. Ibid., 249.

10. Ibid., 250.

11. As quoted in a review by Heather Pringle in *Toronto Globe and Mail* (January 28, 1996) of *Dinosaur in a Haystack: Reflections in Natural History*, by Stephen Jay Gould (New York: Harmony Books, 1996).

12. As a female growing up in the forties, my kind of freedom was unusual and very important to my sense of self and self-esteem: I can recall feeling more competent when at the Cape than at home because of the freedom I had to roam on my own. Nabhan and Trimble note that comparatively few women became naturalists in the late 19th and early 20th centuries not only because of the strictures of marriage and children but also because girls were not allowed to wander in the woods as boys were. See their interesting discussion of these issues on pp. 56-63 of *The Geography of Childhood*.

13. Gary Nabhan mentions the value of becoming acquainted with a species very different from one's own—such as a reptile—in contrast to the comfort one finds with similar species, such as apes or dogs. "All I am sure is that sooner or later, someone must simply take us by the hand, and show us another world. They must initiate us into the delight of encountering *the other* in the form of lizard, hawkmoth, or bat. They must move us out of our comfort zone and into the unknown terrain where lives somewhat different from our own still dwell" (Nabhan and Trimble, *The Geography of Childhood*, 150).

14. These statistics are from ibid., 11.

15. The quotation is from Paul Shephard and cited in Nabhan and Trimble, *The Geography of Childhood*, 28.

16. Ibid., xv.

17. Both Pyle, *The Thunder Tree*, and Nabhan and Trimble, *The Geography of Childhood*, speak at length about the difference between wildness and wilderness, but this distinction is discussed widely by others as well. See, for instance, Neil Evernden's fine discussion of the difference, in which wildness stands for nature's otherness, whereas wilderness can be seen as a thing (as simply a tract of land): "To encounter the wild other, to greet another 'I am,' is to accept the other's existence in one's life world" (*The Social Creation of Nature* [Baltimore: Johns Hopkins University Press, 1992], 112).

18. Pyle, *The Thunder Tree*, xviii, 148.

19. Cathy Johnson, *The Naturalist's Path: Beginning the Study of Nature* (New York: Walker and Co., 1991), xviii.

20. Ibid., 54.

21. "The pastoral ideal has been used to define the meaning of America ever since the age of discovery, and it has not yet lost its hold upon the native imagination" (Leo Marx, *The Machine in the Garden: Technology and the Pastoral Ideal in America* [New York: Oxford University Press, 1964], 3).

22. The second United Nations conference on human settlements (Habitat II), which met in Istanbul in the spring of 1996, claimed that by 2015, 4.1 billion people will be living in cities, three quarters of them in the poorer countries.

23. "Our society's token nature-lovers are treated as overgrown but harmless juveniles, dilly dallying away their time and money on matters undeserving of serious attention by mature adults" (Nabhan and Trimble, *The Geography of Childhood*, 40).

24. "Park Prospects," *New Yorker* (February 14, 1994), 8.

25. Richard M. Stapleton, "Wild Times in the City: Urban Preserves Meet the Needs of People and Nature," *Nature Conservancy* (September/October, 1995), 13.

26. Stapleton, "Wild Times in the City," 15.

27. Ibid.

28. Jules Pretty and Michel Pimbert, "Trouble in the Garden of Eden," *Toronto Globe and Mail* (May 13, 1995), D8. Pretty and Pimbert co-authored "Parks, People and Professionals," a discussion paper written for the United Nations Research Institute for Social Development.

29. Ibid.

30. There is at least one significant difference that I need to emphasize between the "I" of classic Western religious autobiography and the self in the ecological model: the former epitomizes the humanist essentialist self that deconstruction has so roundly criticized, while the latter is, *by definition,* social. As I have emphasized throughout, the ecological self is a construction by other human selves as well as a myriad of natural contexts and influences. Thus, the private/public split or the individual/social dualism of the humanist essentialist split does not apply to the ecological self.

31. Douglas Burton-Christie, "'A Feeling for the Natural World': Spirituality and Contemporary Nature Writing," *Continuum* 2 (2&3, n.d.), 161, 162.

32. Nabhan and Trimble, *The Geography of Childhood,* 56.

33. For this treatment of Krutch, I am indebted to Burton-Christie, "'A Feeling for the Natural World,'" 168-70.

34. Joseph Wood Krutch, *The Desert Year* (Tucson: University of Arizona Press, 1985), 5.

35. I am indebted to Burton-Christie, "'A Feeling for the Natural World,'" for the following discussion.

36. Gretel Ehrlich, *The Solace of Open Spaces* (New York: Viking Penguin, 1985), 63.

37. Ehrlich, *The Solace of Open Spaces,* 64.

38. Wilson, *Biophilia,* 18.

39. Ibid., 18-19.

40. Ibid., 10.

41. Joyce Carol Oates, "Against Nature," *On Nature: Nature, Landscape, and Natural History,* ed. Daniel Halpern (San Francisco: North Point Press, 1987), 136.

42. Annie Dillard, *Pilgrim at Tinker Creek: A Mystical Excursion into the Natural World* (New York: Bantam Books, 1975), 134, 135.

43. As quoted by Frederick Buechner, *Listening to Your Life* (San Francisco: Harper, 1992), 53.

44. I am indebted to Burton-Christie, "'A Feeling for the Natural World,'" for the following analysis.

45. John McPhee, *Basin and Range* (New York: Farrar, Straus, Giroux, 1981), 24.

46. Ibid., 25.

47. Neil Evernden expresses the aesthetic stand well when he says that it is "a way of being, a stand towards the world; an aesthetic experience requires a relationship between a seeking subject and a responsive world" (*The Natural*

Alien: Humankind and Environment (Toronto: University of Toronto Press, 1985), 54.

48. My students do it and some do it very well. Annie Dillard mentions in the autobiography of her childhood that drawing animals and plants helped to train her eye to see them better in nature; the same can be said of nature writing—even the attempt to do it, even if it is done awkwardly and with difficulty, is helpful for training a person to pay attention to some particular aspect of nature carefully and in detail. Most students find it illuminating in surprising ways—both in terms of what they learn about the piece of nature they are dealing with and their own response to it.

49. Sharon Butala, *The Perfection of the Morning: An Apprenticeship in Nature* (Toronto: HarperCollins, 1994); Sue Hubbell, *A Country Year: Living the Questions* (New York: Harper & Row, 1987); Dillard, *Pilgrim at Tinker Creek.*

50. Butala, *The Perfection of the Morning,* 110, 106.

51. Ibid., 106.

52. Ibid., 141.

53. Ibid., 142, 145.

54. Ibid., 146.

55. Ibid., 147-48.

56. Ibid., 105.

57. Ibid., 207.

58. Her theme of living the questions comes from the following passage by Rainer Maria Rilke, which she quotes on the frontispiece. "Be patient toward all that is unsolved in your heart and try to love the questions themselves. . . . Do not . . . seek the answers, which cannot be given you because you would not be able to live them. And the point is to live everything. Live the questions now. Perhaps you will . . . gradually, without noticing it, live along some distant day into the answer" (*Letters to a Young Poet,* Letter No. 4, trans. M. D. Herter [New York: Norton, 1934], 35).

59. Hubbell, *A Country Year,* 83.

60. Ibid., 57-58.

61. Ibid., 77.

62. Ibid., 137-38.

63. Ibid., 186.

64. Ibid., 192.

65. Ibid., 221.

66. Dillard, *Pilgrim at Tinker Creek,* 178.

67. Ibid., 179, 271.

68. Ibid., 8.

69. Ibid., 184.

70. Ibid., 136.

71. John Donne, *The Divine Poems,* ed. Helen Gardner (Oxford: Clarendon Press, 1978), 11.

72. Dillard, *Pilgrim at Tinker Creek,* 269.

73. Ibid., 180.

74. Ibid., 147.

75. Ibid., 7-8.

76. Ibid., 275.

77. Annie Dillard, *Teaching a Stone to Talk: Expeditions and Encounters* (New York: Harper & Row, 1982), 97.

78. Dillard, *Pilgrim at Tinker Creek*, 273.

79. Ibid., 278.

80. Pyle, *The Thunder Tree*, xvii.

81. The Backyard Wildlife Habitat Program maintains a National Register of Backyard Wildlife Habitats. To learn more about it and to obtain "A Gardening with Wildlife Kit," contact National Wildlife Federation, Backyard Habitat Program, 1400 Sixteenth Street, N.W., Washington, D.C. 20036. One of the most advanced programs in North America for constructing a backyard wildlife habitat is Naturescape British Columbia, which for $15 will send you all the information you need to create one (Naturescape British Columbia, 300-1005 Broad Street, Victoria, BC, V8W 2A1). Another resource is a handsome, coffee-table book with superb photographs by Ken Druse with Margaret Roach, *The Natural Habitat Garden* (New York: Clarkson Potter, 1994).

82. One such project is the Cameron Middle School's Environmental Education Program (1034 First Avenue South, Nashville, TN 37210). This ambitious program involves 1000 students in grades 5-8, from both a federal housing project and adjoining suburbs as well as parents, teachers, and several businesses and agencies. The activities are wide-ranging: several different kinds of gardens (herb, vegetable, hydroponic, bamboo), a weather instrument house, bird and butterfly feeders, a nature trail, a soil erosion test site, a tracking station to identify wildlife, a mini-greenhouse, and much more. A brochure on the project states: "Five years ago the school plant was covered with litter and had very little vegetation. To date, students have landscaped our barren campus, planting a total of 154 trees and 209 shrubs, old-fashioned roses, and hundreds of bulbs and plants. *We have reclaimed our land!* We have expanded the environmental horizons for our students; we have begun to develop a history of environmental consciousness."

83. "Farm Plots Sprout Up in Major Cities," Toronto *Globe and Mail* (April 20, 1996).

84. Ibid.

85. Pyle, *The Thunder Tree*, 147.

Chapter 7

1. Alice Walker, *Living by the Word: Selected Writings, 1973-87* (New York: Harcourt, Brace, Jovanovich, 1988), 6.

2. Ibid., 7.

3. Ibid., 147.

4. Ibid., xx.

5. James Gustafson has written long and eloquently on this important point. "If God saw that the diversity God created was good, it was not *necessarily* good for humans and for all aspects of nature" (*A Sense of the Divine: The Natural Environment from a Theocentric Perspective* [Cleveland: Pilgrim Press, 1994], 44).

6. Val Plumwood, for instance, says in our attitude toward nature "we may often have to settle for that of respectful but wondering strangers. . . . The earth other is a being whose company may be fearful or enticing, fruitful or bitter, intimate or indifferent, but whose presence is always more than the nullity and closure of the world presented by mechanism" (*Feminism and the Mastery of Nature* [New York: Routledge, 1994], 139-40).

7. No one has written more thoughtfully on this subject than James

Gustafson. "Humans are to seek to discover what God is enabling and requiring them to be and to do as participants in the patterns and processes of interdependence of life in the world. The divine ordering is perceived, insofar as it is humanly possible, in and through the ordering of nature, culture, history, and personal living. It has no equilibrium which guarantees the realization of all justifiable ends, and our ends as developers of technology and culture infinitely complicate the achievement of even a dynamic one. We are to relate all things to each other in ways that concur with their relations to God, again, insofar as this can be discerned. But God will be God. As intentional participants we have responsibility, and the destiny of the natural environment and our parts in it is heavily in our hands, but the ultimate destiny of all that exists is beyond our human control" (*A Sense of the Divine*, 148-49).

8. Whereas I use a version of the organic model extensively in my book, *The Body of God*, it is derived from an understanding of ecological unity and individuality, and hence open to and supportive of diversity, difference, and subjecthood. Two other versions of the organic model (the medieval and deep ecology) are not. The medieval version is not, because it is based on the human being and privileges the mind over other parts of the body. The deep ecology version is not, because in it all parts are fused. In both cases, there is only one subject: the human being, especially its mind, in the one case and in the other, all of life as one subject. See *The Body of God: An Ecological Theology* (Minneapolis: Fortress Press, 1993), 30-38, 124-29.

9. See, for instance, Bill Devall and George Sessions, *Deep Ecology: Living as if Nature Mattered* (Salt Lake City: Peregrine Smith Books, 1985).

10. See, for instance, Roderick Nash, *The Rights of Nature: A History of Environmental Ethics* (Madison: University of Wisconsin Press, 1989).

11. As quoted in Kathleen Norris, *Dakota: A Spiritual Geography* (New York: Ticknor and Fields, 1993), frontispiece.

12. Joan Tronto claims that in our culture women "care for" people and concrete objects, whereas men "care about" ideas and projects—the one is in the private and the other in the public sphere. See her essay, "Women and Caring: What Can Feminists Learn About Morality from Caring?" in *Gender/Body/Knowledge: Feminist Reconstruction of Being and Knowing*, ed. Alison Jaggar and Susan R. Bordo (New Brunswick, N.J.: Rutgers University Press, 1989), 172-87. The classic study on a care vs. rights ethic is, of course, Carol Gilligan's *In a Different Voice: Psychological Theory and Women's Development* (Cambridge: Harvard University Press, 1982).

13. Lorraine Code, *What Can She Know? Feminist Theory and the Construction of Knowledge* (Ithaca, N.Y.: Cornell University Press, 1991), 182.

14. I am indebted to the fine studies of ethics and friendship in the writings of Lorraine Code, especially *What Can She Know?* and Val Plumwood, *Feminism and the Mastery of Nature*.

15. See Plumwood, *Feminism and the Mastery of Nature*, chs. 6 & 7.

16. As quoted by Code, *What Can She Know?*, 108.

17. Immanuel Kant, "Duties to Animals and Spirits," *Letters on Ethics*, trans. Louis Infield (New York: Harper and Row, 1963), 239.

18. For a fuller discussion of this point, see my book, *The Body of God*, 171ff.

19. The following material is from Bill McKibben, *Hope, Human and Wild:*

True Stories of Living Lightly on the Earth (Boston: Little, Brown, and Co., 1995).
20. Ibid., 35.
21. Michael Pollan, *Second Nature: A Gardener's Education* (New York: Dell Publishers, 1991), 224.
22. Pollan, *Second Nature*, 223.
23. A sobering lesson to first-world consumers is one by McKibben on the relationship between wealth and pollution: for every dollar spent, one-half a litre of petroleum is used (and hence also sent as pollution into the atmosphere). For instance, for a $20 book (adding together the energy used in logging, pulping, printing, shipping, and advertising), a 10 lb. cloud of carbon dioxide, the greenhouse gas, is emitted. "Simply by living according the customs of such places [first-world countries], each of us powers the planet's decline. We don't need to own strip mines or chop down ancient forests—our daily life is sufficient" (*Hope, Human and Wild*, 51).
24. Larry L. Rasmussen's fine study of sustainable communities (vs. sustainable development) is one persuasive witness to this turn. "Hope is real. There are grounds for it. Something is clearly afoot, though it is often 'off camera.' Local citizens' movements and alternative institutions are emerging and are trying to create greater economic self-sufficiency, internalize costs to earth in the price of goods, sustain livelihoods, work out agricultures appropriate to regions, preserve traditions and cultures, revive religious life, maintain human dignity, repair the moral fiber, resist the commodification of all things, be technologically innovative with renewable and nonrenewable resources, revise urban designs and architecture, preserve biological species and protect ecosystems, and cultivate a sense of earth as a sacred good held in trust and in common.

"This inspiring melange has no one configuration. By definition it probably ought not to, given the pluralism of place and peoples and their insistent and varied participation. But it is real and it shares community-focused alternatives to the destructive homogenization of globalization and its monocultures. Barnet and Cavanagh, who judge this disparate movement as presently 'the only force we see that can break the global gridlock,' close their study with a judgment about the stakes: 'The great question of our age is whether people, acting with the spirit, energy, and urgency our collective crisis requires, can develop a democratic global consciousness rooted in authentic local communities.'

"Such authentic communities are not *only* local, we have argued. But community from the local to the cosmic is the focus and frame for meeting the great adventure hard upon us. That adventure is sustainability as the capacity of earth's communities to survive and thrive together indefinitely" (*EarthCommunity/EarthEthic* [Maryknoll, N.Y.: Orbis Books, 1996], 330-31).
25. McKibben, *Hope, Human and Wild*, 36.
26. Ibid., 55.
27. Ibid., 72.
28. The focus of Habitat II, the 1996 UN conference in Istanbul on housing, is both sobering and hopeful. Its projection that by early in the next century the majority of the world's inhabitants will live in cities illustrates how crucial the garden mentality will be. While some cities, such as Chongqing in China and Los Angeles are close to being dysfunctional, other ones such as Santos in Brazil and New York are relative success stories. Through attention to the

basics of transportation, housing, and drainage as well as education and green space, they are places that people find interesting and liberating. Even cities that do not work well are often an improvement over rural areas in terms of jobs, education, medical care, and opportunities for women. The fate of the city, Habitat II suggests, is not predetermined; what it will be rests in large part on human decisions.

29. Leonardo Boff, *Saint Francis: A Model for Human Liberation*, trans. John W. Diercksmeier (New York: Crossroad, 1982), 39.

30. Just how minor Christianity's concern for creation has been until recently is evident in statements from the World Council of Churches as late as the 1960s. From the 1961 New Dehli assembly we read: "The Christian should welcome scientific discoveries as new steps in man's domination of nature." And from the world conference on Church and Society, Geneva 1966, we find a statement that depicts nature as merely the setting for human history. "The biblical story . . . secularizes nature. It places creation—the physical world—in the context of covenant relation and does not try to understand it apart from that relation. The history of God with his people has a setting, and this setting is called nature. But the movement of history, not the structure of the setting, is central to reality. Physical creation even participates in this history; its timeless and cyclical character, as far as it exists, is unimportant. *The physical world, in other words, does not have its meaning in itself.*" Both of these statements are quoted by Wesley Granberg-Michaelson, "Creation in Ecumenical Theology," *Ecotheology: Voices from South and North*, ed. David G. Hallman (Geneva: WCC Publications and Maryknoll, N.Y.: Orbis Books, 1994), 97, 96.

31. See Jim Woolf, "Metropolitan Mosaic," *National Parks* (January/February, 1996), 41-44.

32. Ibid., 42.

33. Ibid., 44.

34. For a recent, detailed analysis of sustainable communities at various levels, from local to global—and one oriented to Christians—see Rasmussen, *EarthCommunity/EarthEthics.*

35. See the *Intergovernmental Panel on Climate Change: Second Assessment—Climate Change 1995,* published by the World Meteorological Organization and the United Nations Environmental Programme.

36. The World Council of Churches has published materials relevant to answering this question. See, e.g., *Accelerated Climate Change: Sign of Peril, Test of Faith*, 2nd ed. (Geneva: W.C.C., 1994).

37. Elizabeth A. Johnson, *She Who Is: The Mystery of God in Feminist Theological Discourse* (New York: Crossroad, 1992), 14.

Index